PUBLIC AFFAIRS AND POLICY ADMINISTRATION SERIES

Social Insurance

Other titles in the PUBLIC AFFAIRS AND POLICY ADMINISTRATION SERIES edited by Donald F. Kettl

PUBLIC AFFAIRS AND POLICY ADMINISTRATION SERIES

Social Insurance

AMERICA'S NEGLECTED HERITAGE AND CONTESTED FUTURE

THEODORE R. MARMOR

JERRY L. MASHAW

JOHN PAKUTKA

Los Angeles | London | New Delhi
Singapore | Washington DC

Los Angeles | London | New Delhi
Singapore | Washington DC

FOR INFORMATION:

CQ Press

An Imprint of SAGE Publications, Inc.

2455 Teller Road

Thousand Oaks, California 91320

E-mail: order@sagepub.com

SAGE Publications Ltd.

1 Oliver's Yard

55 City Road

London EC1Y 1SP

United Kingdom

SAGE Publications India Pvt. Ltd.

B 1/I 1 Mohan Cooperative Industrial Area

Mathura Road, New Delhi 110 044

India

SAGE Publications Asia-Pacific Pte. Ltd.

3 Church Street

#10-04 Samsung Hub

Singapore 049483

Publisher: Charisse Kiino

Editorial Assistant: Davia Grant

Production Editor: Olivia Weber-Stenis

Copy Editor: Judy Selhorst

Typesetter: C&M Digitals (P) Ltd.

Proofreader: Jennifer Grubba

Indexer: Julie Grayson

Cover Designer: Cristina Kubota

Marketing Manager: Erica DeLuca

Permissions Editor: Jennifer Barron

Printed in the United States of America

Library of Congress Cataloging-in-Publication Data

Marmor, Theodore R. Social insurance : America's Neglected Heritage and Contested Future / Theodore R. Marmor, Yale University, Jerry L. Mashaw, Yale University, John Pakutka.

pages cm. — (Public affairs and policy administration series) Includes bibliographical references and index.

ISBN 978-1-4522-4000-8 (alk. paper)

1. Social security—United States. I. Mashaw, Jerry L. II. Title.

HD7125.M324 2014
361.973—dc23   2013018040

This book is printed on acid-free paper.

Certified Chain of Custody
SUSTAINABLE FORESTRY INITIATIVE
Promoting Sustainable Forestry
www.sfiprogram.org
SFI-01268
SFI label applies to text stock

13 14 15 16 17 10 9 8 7 6 5 4 3 2 1

Contents

Figures and Tables

Figures

Tables

Series Foreword

So much of politics is about individual threads. Public policy is about how the threads weave a fabric. Across the vast landscape of American politics, there is an enormous amount of writing about the individual threads of social welfare policy. It is impossible to scratch the surface of public debate and not have an avalanche of books and articles on programs such as Social Security, Medicare, and Medicaid come tumbling out. Until this lively and insightful book by an exceptionally insightful team of writers, however, there has been almost nothing on how these threads knit the fabric of America's broad policy on social insurance—what role society, and its government, ought to play in supporting citizens who encounter risks and threats in their personal lives. If there ever was an area where the whole is more than the sum of its parts, it is this hugely important, but remarkably unexplored, puzzle: How does this collection of individual programs work as a whole? And just as important but even less explored: What does this intricate fabric tell us about ourselves, as a country, and about our values?

This great book begins with two building blocks. It starts with stories that make the abstract notion of "social insurance" jump to life. From the heartbreaking accounts of nightclub patrons injured in a fire to the struggles of the unemployed to make ends meet, Marmor, Mashaw, and Pakutka frame the basic question sharply: Just what have we as a nation done to help those in need by creating programs through our government? They then frame the story by painting a rich tableau of history. Our public programs are not only reactions to the problems of individuals and the political pressures of those seeking to solve individual social problems. They are also reflections of the times and values that gave birth to them. Looking closely at each individual thread thus tells us a great deal about the underlying goals the programs' creators were seeking to accomplish.

But social insurance is about much more than creating a series of programs to protect citizens from troubles and to help them through difficult times. Woven together, the fabric of social insurance tells us about ourselves as a nation. We are, after all, a country of self-evident truths, including the right to "Life, Liberty and the pursuit of Happiness," as the Declaration of Independence puts it. "We the People," the Constitution says, seek "to form a more perfect Union" and "promote the general Welfare," all the better to "secure the Blessings of Liberty to ourselves and our Posterity." Here we sit, as the posterity, trying to understand how best to pursue happiness and achieve the general welfare. Part of the story is making possible limitless possibility, but that also raises the issue of the collective actions we take on behalf of individual citizens who are—or might be—in need.

The "Blessings of Liberty" play an especially strong role in this debate. We Americans have always cherished liberty—so much so, in fact, that a flag with the word emblazoned on it was a banner held high during the Revolutionary War. It is impossible to imagine the pursuit of happiness without liberty, and a huge part of America's remarkable economic growth and global success has come through the unleashed entrepreneurial energy of its citizens. Competitive markets are at the center of this national entrepreneurship, and perhaps only restraints on gun ownership rival restraints on markets in getting the national blood boiling. Competitive markets, though, can bring a high price. The risks that come with becoming a big winner in the market economy can also cause serious problems for those who lose, who become collateral damage along the way, or who suffer serious problems through no fault of their own. What about children whose providers suffer an early death? Wage earners who become ill and cannot work? Hard workers who are laid off because the economy stalls? Or earnest, careful individuals, blessed with good health and great health care, who outlive their savings? One answer is for private markets to provide for those who suffer these threats, but sometimes market competition *causes* these threats. At other times, private markets cannot or will not compensate, and voluntary contributions often fall short.

And that frames the question of social insurance as a national Rorschach test. To what degree are we, as a nation, willing to tolerate hunger, poverty, and suffering in our midst? To what degree do we want to pool our resources to help those in need? At what point do we— indeed, must we—say that we cannot afford to solve *every* social problem, because costs mount to crippling levels? How we frame and answer these questions tells us a great deal about who we are, what we value, and how the individual threads of the fabric of social insurance shape the fabric of our national politics. One of this book's great contributions is the way it lays that fabric out, describes how it works, and explains how it came to be. In typical American fashion, we never set out to design and build a sophisticated social insurance system. We cobbled it together one program at a time, in response to the needs of different times and varying motivations. But build it we did, and the authors do us a great service by holding a mirror up to our national selves.

Lying underneath that fabric, however, is a tough set of questions. Fierce debate is now rocking the social insurance system that we once took for granted. It has become very expensive, and some reformers contend we can no longer afford the benefits the government provides—or that the effort to provide them risks undermining the security of our children and grandchildren. Our social insurance system has also created a strong and interlocking set of incentives and disincentives, and other reformers argue that the growth of this system risks eroding the very entrepreneurial spirit that made the country great. Critics advancing both lines of argument point to a single solution: turn much of the system back to the private sector and use market-based reforms to enhance America's protection against big social threats.

At its core, of course, that is as fundamental a question about the role of government as we can ask. It shapes the debate over the balance between public authority and market forces, between individual choice and collective responsibility, between freedom and the pursuit of happiness. This book is an important one because it helps us understand all the levels of the puzzle: what social insurance is, how its pieces fit together, how the fabric came into being and what it now looks like, what role it plays in shaping the general welfare, and what the role of government ought to look like in the twenty-first century. The authors, not surprisingly, have a very strong point of view about the answers to these questions. Many readers are sure to disagree with them. But they will soon discover that Marmor, Mashaw, and Pakutka have led them to considering the *right* questions, and they will find themselves vastly better informed in trying to answer those questions. And perhaps the authors will even change some readers' minds.

Regardless of where the reader comes down in the debate, the authors have done We the People an enormous service. With this book's rich and unique framing of the not-so-self-evident truths that weave the fabric of social policy debate today, they help us understand the individual threads that make that fabric so rich and the questions so enduring.

Donald F. Kettl
Annapolis, Maryland

Preface

This book's title—*Social Insurance: America's Neglected Heritage and Contested Future*—accurately describes its subject. Social insurance programs—from Medicare to Social Security pensions, from disability coverage to unemployment insurance—are central to the economic life of the United States. But, while broadly supported by Americans of all stripes, these programs are not well understood. The purposes, processes, and predictable effects of protecting American families against economic risks are no longer common subjects of either American higher education or public policy commentary. Indeed, the term *social insurance* itself has almost disappeared from discussions of American social policy.

This faded understanding is what we refer to as our neglected heritage. To address that, our book first portrays the financial threats that social insurance programs were historically meant to cushion: birth into a poor family, early death of a family breadwinner, ill health, involuntary unemployment, disability, and outliving one's retirement savings. Chapters 2 through 4 then discuss the history, politics, economics, and conceptual bases of social insurance.

The middle chapters of the book turn to describing the size and character of each of America's social insurance and related programs. The chapters present the expenditures and beneficiaries of the programs and evaluate the programs' performance in providing a decent level of economic security from the predictable threats to family economic security in modern economies.

The economic risks that social insurance programs address, their conceptual, economic, and political underpinnings, and their programmatic expression together anticipate the third part of the book. The chapters in Part III focus on evaluating contemporary debate about these programs, their benefits, their affordability, and their durability. Much of that debate features the view that modernizing American social insurance should take the form of making it more like commercial insurance, and that using market forces and market incentives is the key to improvement. This book challenges that view.

Indeed, we were motivated to write the book by our belief that American social insurance is little understood and that contemporary discussions of discrete programs suffer from persistent myths and serious misunderstandings. The antidote we suggest here has three parts, the first of which is to see social insurance whole. That means understanding social insurance as a set of interventions designed to reduce the impacts of common threats across each person's life cycle, threats that simply cannot be countered effectively by individual prudence and private markets. Second is to understand in detail exactly what various programs of social insurance have and have not done, and third is to bring that understanding to bear on contemporary debates that often portray a mythical, threatened world of social insurance.

This approach is to be found nowhere else in the literature on American social provision. Books and articles abound on Social Security, Medicare, workers' compensation, public assistance, and unemployment insurance. There is no lack of scholarly attention to the history of the American "welfare state" or dearth of broadsides popularizing the idea of a looming "entitlements crisis." Problems of "moral hazard" and "adverse selection" in insurance markets have hardly escaped the notice of the economics profession—or the insurance industry. But nowhere else, to our knowledge, can a student or concerned citizen learn about the historical bases and unifying vision of American social insurance, along with the institutional details and successes and failures of discrete social insurance programs, and simultaneously be invited to deploy those understandings in analyzing contemporary political debates concerning social insurance. The closest analogues are perhaps Marmor, Mashaw, and Harvey's *America's Misunderstood Welfare State* and Graetz and Mashaw's *True Security*. This book is greatly indebted to both of those earlier efforts.

We are also indebted to a host of others. Donald F. Kettl, the editor of the series of which this book is a part, was an early and firm advocate, seeing the promise of a book in an article on social insurance two of us wrote for *Health Affairs* some years ago. His colleagues at CQ Press—especially Charisse Kiino and Olivia Weber-Stenis—supported the publishing process with admirable professionalism.

An effort of this sort requires a team. Ours has been a fine one. Corey Deixler, Eleesa Marnagh, Megan Cole, and Kimberly Kushner painstakingly supported the extensive data collection and analysis efforts. The Yale Law School provided the funds to hire two of its gifted students,

Kate Hadley and Travis Silva, to check the reliability of our factual claims and the plausibility of our inferences. Camille Costelli and Patti Page provided administrative and personal support with extraordinary devotion. All of these teammates' contributions have been very substantial and much appreciated. Any errors are the authors' own.

Others read the manuscript at various stages of the process and offered a range of encouragement, critical commentary, and suggestions that vastly improved the final product. They include Dan Meyer, Steven LaVoie, David Boyum, Sudhakar Kosaraju, Kieke Okma, Peter Gundy, Pete Spain, Carlos Cano, John Foggle, Lawrence Levenson, Mae and Ron Pakutka, Ruth Brinkley, Peter Bernard, Michael Spine, and Christine Pakutka. (John is especially thankful to Chris for her generous love and patient support for the project during its lengthy period of gestation.)

We also thank the reviewers CQ Press commissioned: Matthew Eshbaugh-Soha, University of North Texas; Melissa Bass, University of Mississippi; Krista Perreira, University of North Carolina; Susan Tolchin, George Mason University; Pavel Terpelets, University at Albany, SUNY; Leah J. Wilds, University of Nevada, Reno; Leslie Baker, Mississippi State University; Andrea Mayo, Arizona State University; Paul Quirk, University of British Columbia; and John Portz, Northeastern University.

There is a broader set of colleagues who, while they have not contributed directly by reading chapters, have nonetheless importantly stimulated our thinking about social insurance and American politics over many years. This group includes the late Brian Barry, Michael Graetz, Jacob Hacker, Philip Harvey, Rogan Kersh, Rudolf Klein, Jim Morone, Jon Oberlander, Virginia Reno, Carolyn Tuohy, Albert Weale, Robert Reich, Jim Wareck, Kevin Wheeler, Stefan Pryor, Andy Quinn, Congressman Bruce Morrison, Senator Tom Daschle, the late Senator Paul Wellstone, and Vice President Walter Mondale.

The book owes a great deal to the intellectual legacy of American social insurance's greatest figure in the decades after World War II, the late Robert Ball, to whose memory this book is dedicated. Bob Ball was commissioner of Social Security in both Democratic and Republican administrations, the organizing force behind the founding of the National Academy of Social Insurance, and a tireless advocate for the preservation and improvement of social insurance programs.

August 2013, New Haven, Connecticut

About the Authors

 **Theodore R. Marmor**, Professor Emeritus of Yale University, taught politics, management, and law there from 1979 to 2009. From 1992 to 2003 he directed the Robert Wood Johnson Foundation's postdoctoral program in health policy and social science. Professor Marmor's scholarship has concentrated on the modern welfare state. The author (or coauthor) of thirteen books, he has also published more than two hundred articles in a wide range of scholarly journals. His opinion essays have appeared in major U.S. newspapers. The second edition of *The Politics of Medicare* appeared in 2000; the first edition of this book became something of a political science classic and launched his career in health politics, policy, and law. His best-known other works include *Understanding Health Care Reform* (1994), *Why Are Some People Healthy and Others Not?* (1994), and *America's Misunderstood Welfare State* (1990), coauthored with Yale colleagues Jerry L. Mashaw and Philip Harvey. A collection of his recent articles appeared in 2007: *Fads, Fallacies and Foolishness in Medical Care Management and Policy.*

A member of President Carter's Commission on the 1980s Agenda and a senior social policy adviser to Walter Mondale in the presidential campaign of 1984, Professor Marmor has testified before Congress about medical care reform, social security, and welfare issues and has been a consultant to governmental and nonprofit agencies as well as private firms. He has served recently as an expert witness in cases involving asbestos liability, pharmaceutical pricing fraud, and health financing controversies. An emeritus fellow of the Canadian Institute for Advanced Research, he is a member of the Institute of Medicine of the National Academy of Sciences and the National Academy of Social Insurance, and since 2009 a corresponding fellow of the British Academy.

Jerry L. Mashaw is Sterling Professor of Law at Yale Law School, where he teaches courses in administrative law, social welfare policy, regulation, legislation, and the design of public institutions. His prizewinning books include *Bureaucratic Justice* (1983), awarded Harvard University's Gerard Henderson Memorial Prize in 1993; *The Struggle for Auto Safety* (with David Harfst, 1990), awarded the Sixth Annual Scholarship Prize of the American Bar Association's Section on Administrative Law and Regulatory Policy in 1992; and *Greed, Chaos, and Governance: Using Public Choice to Improve Public Law* (1997), awarded the Section's Twelfth Annual Scholarship Prize in 1998 and the Order of the Coif Triennial Book Award in 2002 for books published between 1997 and 1999. He is a frequent contributor to legal and public policy journals and to newspapers and newsmagazines. Professor Mashaw is a founding member and past president of the National Academy of Social Insurance. He is a fellow of the National Academy of Arts and Sciences and was founding coeditor (with O. E. Williamson) of the *Journal of Law, Economics, and Organization*. He has served as a consultant for a number of U.S. government agencies and private foundations and to the governments of Peru, Argentina, and the People's Republic of China.

Professor Mashaw and his wife, Anne MacClintock, are enthusiastic sailors and together contribute articles to sailing periodicals. Their book *Seasoned by Salt: A Voyage in Search of the Caribbean* (2003) received the 2007 John Southam Award for excellence in sailing journalism.

John Pakutka is managing director of The Crescent Group, an advisory services firm with expertise in health care management, policy, and litigation. Firm clients have included Fortune 500 companies, Global 100 law firms, health systems, investment banks, state governments, and the U.S. Department of Justice. Prior to founding The Crescent Group, he completed employment stints at Exxon/Reliance Electric, the U.S. Government Accountability Office, Yale University, and APM/Computer Sciences Corporation. He has served on numerous public and nonprofit boards and commissions, most recently the Connecticut State Legislature's Task Force on Small Business Health Costs and the Citizenship Fund of the Connecticut

Secretary of the State. He holds a B.S. in electrical engineering from Cornell and a master's in public and private management from Yale, where he lectures annually in the product planning class at the School of Management. He is a member of the Sorin Society of the University of Notre Dame and Fleur-de-Lis Society of Bon Secours. A native of Duryea, Pennsylvania, and longtime resident of Vestal, New York, he now lives on the Connecticut shoreline with his wife and partner, Christine, and three wild, wonderful children, Noah, Elaina, and Isabella. John blogs about social insurance protections at www.sixthreats.com and can be followed on twitter @sixthreats.

To the memory of Robert M. Ball

American Social Insurance

1

Economic Risks
and Social Insurance Realities

THREE STORIES

A Club Fire

At a concert in February 2003, pyrotechnics ignited sound insulation in the wallboards and ceilings of the crowded Station nightclub in West Warwick, Rhode Island. Within minutes, flames and smoke engulfed the club. Power failed, cloaking the club in darkness. Panicking customers fled to the small number of exits, but many found passage to the safety of the winter night blocked.

Exactly one hundred people perished. Sixty-five children lost one or both parents. Almost two hundred other victims suffered burns, lung damage due to smoke, or broken bones in the rush to escape. The financial troubles for the victims and their families were just beginning.

National media coverage helped swell a victims' fund set up by the United Way to almost $3 million. The coordinating committee for the fund developed assistance priorities: funeral expenses, victim rent, utility bills, and child-care bills. The fund chairman, the Reverend John Holt, explained the seemingly absurd decision not to pay any health care bills: "The entire fund," he claimed, "could be exhausted on two victims." Nor would compensation for lost wages be offered.[1]

The fire burned the hands of pianist Arthur Conway and killed his friend Shawn Sweet. Uninsured, Arthur spent a week in the hospital and ran up thousands of dollars in bills that he could not pay. Nor could he bear the expense of emotional counseling.[2] Instead, he spent time making pleas to hospital financial counselors for reductions in bills, affordable payment schedules, and outright charity care.

Linda Fisher endured five surgeries to treat burns on her hands and face. Smoke inhalation incapacitated her lungs; simple acts such as carrying laundry left her breathless. Going back to work was not an option for her. Todd King, chairman of the Station Family Fund, a grassroots organization that continued to raise money for the fire victims after the United Way fund was exhausted, noted the typical nature of such a case: "People that were making $30,000, $40,000 a year had to take jobs making eight bucks an hour because they are so physically challenged."[3] Eventually, Linda qualified for a Social Security disability payment of $1,000 per month.

Emergency room doctors stabilized the badly burned Joe Kinan and managed his trauma. Through dozens of surgeries, burn specialists painstakingly grafted skin onto Joe's face and arms. Months of recovery time in the hospital and rehabilitation followed. The bills Joe received from physicians, hospitals, and rehabilitation therapists amounted to more than $4 million.[4]

The United Way fund, its $3 million balance wiped out in two years, received donations of only $25,000 in 2006 and $84,000 in 2007. Arguing that the music industry "needed to take care of its own," Twisted Sister lead singer Dee Snider organized a benefit concert to mark the fifth anniversary of the fire in 2008. During an interview promoting the concert, radio "shock jock" Howard Stern told Station Family Fund chairman King, "I thought those people were taken care of." King replied, "No one was taken care of."[5]

A Half Million Autistic Children

The United States welcomes about four million babies annually. At some point in their young lives one in eighty-eight of them is diagnosed with a mysterious disorder known as autism.[6] The children become withdrawn, fail to respond to normal social cues, and sometimes lose language skills that seemed to be developing normally. Intellectual development slows.

Autism has grown rapidly since the 1970s. Then, a diagnosis of autism meant eventual institutionalization. Families and public schools were not well equipped to care for or educate autistic children as they matured. Researchers have not found an obvious biological cause, and they cannot agree on whether autism is a medical or developmental problem. The debates are surely not academic to the half million American families struggling to raise autistic children.[7]

By the mid-1980s, however, researchers had developed therapy-intense regimens called applied behavioral analysis (ABA) that appeared to improve the cognitive and behavioral development of autism-afflicted young children. One such study showed that more than half the children receiving such daily care developed sufficiently to live independently as adults. This was in contrast to the less than 5% of children in a control group that did not receive the intense care.

By 2005, the medical community had adopted ABA as the standard of care for autism. Unfortunately, its cost is generally more than $20,000 per child annually.[8] The typical American family, with a total annual income of about $60,000, cannot possibly finance such care. Among the impossible choices for parents determined to get the recommended care for an autistic child: load up the credit card, take a second mortgage, or forgo college savings for all the kids.

Beverly Chase thought she was lucky. She and her 4-year-old autistic son Jake lived in Indiana, one of a handful of U.S. states that required health insurance companies to pay for ABA care. Nonetheless, her requests for payment were met with silence and then resistance. She fought with her insurance carrier for six months before payment was approved. Even then, she faced $6,000 per year in co-payments.[9]

For the Robichaux family of Shreveport, Louisiana, the outcome was not as promising. Trenton, 8, received autism care paid for by the federal/ state government program Medicaid, until his father T.J.'s income rose to $39,000—above the threshold for qualification. Nor was private health insurance a viable option: T.J.'s company did not offer health insurance, and private insurance was prohibitively costly. Trenton receives three hours per month of therapy at school, well below the recommended regimen.[10] Whether he will be able to live independently as an adult remains in question.

A Business Collapse

At year-end 2000, Enron stock closed around $80 per share; the Houston, Texas–based energy company ranked seventh largest among America's companies.[11] The company skyscraper soared atop the city skyline; the Enron logo marked the stadium in which the Houston Astros played. George W. Bush, who took office as U.S. president in January 2001, counted Enron's president, Kenneth Lay, as a personal friend and adviser (not to mention a top fund-raiser).[12]

Financial analysts from Wall Street's most prestigious firms toasted Enron's success. A Merrill Lynch analyst claimed that "Enron is uniquely positioned to be the General Electric of the new economy."[13] A Paine Webber analyst agreed with the sentiment, noting that Enron had "one of the deepest and most innovative management teams in the world."[14] Mr. Lay and his senior team boasted to employees about the company's performance and prospects.[15]

On December 1, 2001, less than a year later, Enron stock traded for 50 cents per share. The board of directors declared bankruptcy. Prosecutors filed criminal and civil charges against not only Enron's senior managers but also its "Big Eight" accounting firm, Arthur Anderson. In time, investigations showed the firm had conspired with Enron to hide company losses in off-the-book partnerships that even the most seasoned Wall Street observers failed to understand. Nobody saw Enron's collapse coming.

Jan Fleetham worked at Enron for twenty years. A single mother, she raised four daughters, putting three through college. She saved diligently for her retirement through a 401(k) pension plan, which grew in value to almost $200,000. Enron matched her personal contributions with company stock.

When the company stock began in the fall of 2001, Jan decided to diversify her pension holdings, but she found a "lockdown" in place on employee sales of company shares, effectively preventing her from protecting her retirement savings. During the lockdown period, Enron stock lost 90% of its value. Jan's pension savings and retirement plans were dashed.[16] In her prepared testimony to a congressional investigative committee, Jan reported:

> Enron's collapse has wiped out my retirement savings. I don't know if anything can be done to help me or other Enron employees . . . [but] if anything can be done to prevent this from happening to other workers in the future, it is important that you take immediate and decisive action.[17]

Charlie Prestwood retired from Enron in 1996 after thirty-three years working as a power plant welder. His pension fund totaled $1.3 million, but it was heavily weighted in Enron stock. By 2002, he and his girlfriend were living on a Social Security check and an Enron pension of $100 per month. He told CNN, "I'm living 180 degrees of what I had planned on living . . . right now, I guarantee you I'd have to make a loan to go to the county line."[18]

RISKS AND SOCIAL INSURANCE

These three stories—of a fire, a childhood illness, and a business collapse—illustrate risks faced by all citizens. Four risks—early death of a breadwinner, partial or total disability, illness or injury, and involuntary unemployment—bring with their realization the *loss* of family income and *unexpected increases* in expenses. Two other risks—being born into a poor family and outliving (or losing) one's savings—make insufficient family income a certainty. The unlucky American family suffers not just from the primary event itself, but also from the secondary income loss.

Notice a further common element to these stories. Individual efforts at self-protection and private charity are weak defenses against the unexpected loss of family income. Charlie Prestwood, a welder by trade, had saved for retirement and amassed a pension fund that was gigantic by the standards of most Americans' retirement savings. He was invested heavily in a stock that was the darling of financial analysts, yet he ended up with only $100 a month from his Enron pension. Charlie's story is replicated tens of thousands of times when companies and private pension funds fail or when stock markets shed trillions of dollars of value, as they did in 2008 and have done countless times before.

The Enron employees who suddenly lost their jobs had no private insurance against job loss (such insurance doesn't exist), nor was it likely that any of those injured in the Station nightclub fire had private temporary or permanent disability insurance to provide a substitute for lost wages. Such policies are rare and almost never look like a sensible buy for younger workers, the people most likely to frequent places like the Station. Nor do young workers invest heavily in life insurance policies, which might have provided some protection for the sixty-five children left behind by those who died.

Many of those same nightclub patrons, like Arthur Conway and Joe Kinan, would have been among the 53 million Americans without health insurance. And while generous donors and artists tried to help, private charity was no match for the deprivations caused by a single untoward event in a small club in our smallest state. Similarly, the autism story barely scratches the surface of the material calamity of having a sick family member and no or inadequate health insurance. A 2007 study by researchers at Harvard University estimated that 62% of all personal bankruptcies were the result of incurring unavoidable, but unaffordable, health care expenses.[19]

Around the edges of these stories, however, we glimpse something else going on. Charlie Prestwood also gets a Social Security retirement pension. Linda Fisher eventually qualified for a Social Security disability stipend. The Robichaux family had Medicaid financing for their autistic son, Trenton, until his father's annual income reached $39,000, at which point all Medicaid payments ceased. Additionally, some of the people in these stories might have had other public protections—unemployment insurance, Social Security survivors insurance, or wage supplements through the Earned Income Tax Credit. Yet, despite this combination of private insurance, private charity, and public income protections, the financial consequences of the misfortunes these families suffered were devastating. And, as the next chapter details, these stories are not cherry-picked examples. The six risks we have identified are ubiquitous for American families.

Must it be this way? Is there nothing we, as concerned citizens or prudent consumers, can do to prevent the financial hardships that follow an initial tragedy? Why do our political and business leaders, our government and markets, seem to serve us so inadequately here? Are there programs that do or could shield us more effectively? If so, are they affordable, effective, and sustainable solutions? What might we do differently in the United States?

Before we turn to these questions, let us be explicit about our own perspective. While we will examine all sides of the issues, we believe there are better answers for Americans—answers that many developed nations have already adopted, answers that the United States has adopted, but only incompletely. That incompleteness has numerous explanations—some ideological, some a result of our political institutions and how American interest groups operate. But none of these explanations, in our view, provides a justification for the nation's failure to do better. Other developed countries shield their citizens more completely than we do through a set of public policies known collectively as *social insurance*. Americans, who live in the richest nation in all of human history, have fewer protections than most of the citizens of this country's democratic competitors and allies. An examination of national income data (see Table 1.1) makes it clear that the protections we might desire are well within our means.

To be sure, social insurance is hardly absent from American public policy. Social insurance expenditures for Medicare and Social Security pensions alone make up a substantial portion of the federal budget.[20] Nevertheless, unlucky Americans still suffer because our social insurance protections are incomplete (recall the health care bills of the autistic children and fire victims) and often meager (recall the disability payment level of the burn victim). Furthermore, for the past two decades, even those incomplete protections have been under sustained political attack. We do not believe, however, that these policy outcomes or the crisis rhetoric of social insurance skeptics reflect what Americans actually believe or desire. We believe Americans have forgotten or never understood why, when, and where social insurance makes sense. This book aims to awaken that understanding in some and introduce it to others.

Table 1.1 The World Economy, 2010

Country	Gross Domestic Product (in trillions of US$)	Share (%)	Per Capita Income (US$)
United States	14,658	23.3	47,284
China	5,878	9.3	4,382
Japan	5,459	8.7	42,820
Germany	3,316	5.3	40,631
France	2,583	4.1	41,019
United Kingdom	2,247	3.6	36,120
Brazil	2,090	3.3	10,816
Italy	2,055	3.3	34,059
Canada	1,574	2.5	46,215
India	1,538	2.4	1,265
Russia	1,465	2.3	10,437
Spain	1,410	2.2	30,639
Top 12	44,273	70.4	
Other 171	18,615	29.6	
All	62,888	100.0	

Source: International Monetary Fund, World Economic Outlook Database, April 2011.

SOCIAL INSURANCE VERSUS PRIVATE INSURANCE

What is social insurance, and how does it differ from private, commercially available insurance? There are similarities between the two, but also many crucial differences.

A Quasi Contract

Social insurance is the political equivalent of a contract among all American families and across generations. In their purest form, social insurance schemes cover the entire population. One of social insurance's core principles, universal availability, is simply that all those facing the same risks should be members of the same insurance pool.

Private insurance is a contract between an *individual* (or the individual's employer) and an insurance company. In its purest form, private insurance is a transaction between two willing parties. Many people will choose not to insure themselves; insurance companies will deem many people and many risks uninsurable. Government may have much to say about the rules under which insurance companies operate, but *regulation* of private transactions is not social insurance.

Why Is Social Insurance America's Neglected Heritage?

Note that the press coverage of the Station nightclub fire's aftermath focused on private contributions to special funds for the victims. Similar news coverage occurs in the wake of many other natural and human-made disasters. Social insurance's role in ameliorating the financial distress of victims is generally ignored. A major example involves the victims of the 9/11 attacks. At the time, much was made of the special compensation system Congress established to aid victims and their families. But there was also considerable controversy about the fairness of a scheme heavily weighted toward compensating higher-earning households, and the receipt of benefits was years in coming. Meanwhile, virtually no press attention was paid to the rapid response of the Social Security survivors insurance program, which sent its first checks to victims' families on October 3, 2011. Within a few months, 3,000 children and surviving spouses were receiving payments totaling $2.8 million each month. Given this lack of attention, it is hardly surprising that most Americans are unaware that Social Security provides more life insurance protection for American families than all private life insurers combined. (For further details on the Social Security survivors insurance program, see Chapter 7.)

Benefits

The main goal of social insurance is protection against the loss of income caused by the six risks we have outlined. The benefits are cash payments to the victims of misfortune or the economic equivalent of cash payments, such as coverage of medical bills that otherwise would have been borne by the patient or the patient's family.

Private insurance provides coverage for many types of losses—automobile accidents, home fires, floods and so on—but typically does not treat insufficient family income as an insurable event. Private insurance, if acquired, is available for only three of the six risks we have highlighted—premature death, disability, and ill health—and even where private coverage is available, it comes with many limitations. As we will explain in more detail, private insurers rightly fear that they might attract pools of only high-risk beneficiaries (adverse selection) or that the purchase of insurance coverage itself will lead some individuals to take risks that increase the probability of loss (moral hazard). Either would make coverage a losing proposition for insurance companies, and private companies lack the regulatory authority to protect themselves effectively from these well-known causes of insurance "market failure."

Mandates and Universality

Like private insurance companies, social insurance programs must guard against adverse selection and moral hazard. But because governments can require enrollment and premiums or levy taxes to fund programs, they can substantially lessen the adverse selection problem. Governmental regulatory policies can also provide some protection from moral hazard. This avoidance of insurance market maladies means that participation in social insurance schemes is typically mandatory, which in turn means that coverage is generally universal. We are all in this together—a politically and socially desirable feature even if it were not an economic necessity.

Contributions

In exchange for coverage, social insurance schemes require regular contributions, or payments, by citizens. The vehicle of payment is typically a payroll or income tax. In limited cases it might be called a *premium*, particularly when the program or some part of it is voluntary rather than mandated. *Premium*, the standard language of the private insurance contract, denotes the regular payment required to keep a policy in force. Both social and private insurance plans collect contributions in a *pool*. Ideally, that pool is managed prudently to ensure that funds are available when losses occur.

Redistribution

Both public and private insurance programs redistribute resources from the lucky to the unlucky, but social insurance often does this both within and across generations of citizens. This is the model of Social Security pensions: today's workers fund the pension benefits of yesterday's workforce, just as members of that workforce funded the pensions of the prior generation. And while contributions are a flat percentage of wage income, benefits replace a larger proportion of preretirement income for low-wage workers. Medicare, the social insurance program that covers a good share of elderly Americans' health care expenses, takes the same form: the contributions of current workers pay for the Medicare program's expenditures on behalf of former workers who have retired or become disabled.

In traditional American private health insurance, by contrast, current contributors receive benefits only as long as their insurance coverage continues. There is no guarantee that coverage will continue beyond the policy period, typically one year. Redistribution from the lucky healthy to the unlucky sick or disabled is limited to that contractual period.

PLAN OF THE BOOK

The remainder of Part I sets the stage for a more detailed analysis of America's social insurance arrangements. In Chapter 2, we assess the seriousness of our six threats to the economic security of American families. We move from stories to data, from poignant vignettes to the statistical probabilities, since it is the combination of risks common to all Americans and predictable in their rate of occurrence that makes social insurance an urgent topic for collective action.

In Chapter 3, we step back to consider the commitments underlying public social welfare programs. Americans have different views of our obligations to each other and to those who suffer from any of the six risks we all face. Few would have government do nothing, but the bases for our sense that collective action is justified vary greatly. From the rationales that underlie social welfare programs, we distill five clusters of commitments. These are social welfare philosophies that have been important historically, both in the United States and elsewhere, and help to explain current programs as well. We argue in Chapter 3 that the political debates about our social welfare programs are misleading as a guide to what the United States has actually done and what most Americans say they desire. While commentators typically speak of an American welfare state, we actually have, and support, what should be called an insurance-opportunity state.

Philosophical commitments and political beliefs do not realize themselves of their own force, however. Chapter 4, therefore, provides an overview of the history and politics of social insurance in the United States. If our social insurance provision is a large patchwork quilt that is thin in spots and ragged in others, we need to understand how it got stitched together and why some pieces are missing. If maintaining and improving American social insurance provokes contentious, even vitriolic, political debates (as it does) and yet prompts broad public support, we need to understand why that is the case.

In Part II, Chapters 5 through 10, we move to a ground-level view. We examine the arrangements in place in the United States to cope with the six risks identified—sickness, early death, disability, involuntary unemployment, outliving one's savings, and being born into a poor family. We review data on the incidence of the troubles against which social insurance protects and the extent and effectiveness of the current public and private solutions. We compare the American experience to the experiences of other rich democracies and present our own suggestions for improvement.

Part III returns to broader issues of critical commentary and reform. In Chapter 11, we look back at the programmatic details provided in Part II and weave them into a more coherent general picture of America's social insurance arrangements. Our aim is to explain how programmatic complexity and heterogeneity fit into American political institutions and culture.

But where do we go from here? Much popular discussion of social insurance portrays America's largest programs, Social Security and Medicare, as fiscally unaffordable and intergenerationally unfair. From this perspective, "reform" is not about patching holes in social insurance protections but about increasing individual and family responsibility for economic security and scaling back public programs in favor of private provision. Chapter 12 addresses the question of how to assess these criticisms. Do they provide a plausible future for American's largest social insurance programs? Or do they represent a misunderstanding of American political values and America's economic circumstances? The epilogue summarizes the argument of the book, emphasizing the importance of separating myths from facts in the political struggles over social insurance past, present, and future.

2

Assessment of the Six Threats to Family Income

WHAT LEVEL OF THREAT TO FAMILY INCOME DO AMERICANS FACE? Is there reason for great worry or only modest concern? How likely is it that each of the risks we have outlined will become a reality? We will review the available historical data and expert estimates in our attempt to answer this question, but first we need to establish a baseline for evaluation: To what extent could the average American family bear the financial burdens of the occurrence of one or more of these risks out of current income and assets?

FAMILY INCOME AND ASSETS

What do we know about American family income? In 2011, the *median* American family income (the amount at which half were above and half were below, not to be confused with an *average*) was $61,455.

Three-fifths of families earned $75,000 or less. Only a quarter made more than $100,000, but that quarter accounted for a majority of total family income. Indeed, in 2010, families in the top income quintile received 47.8% of aggregate income, and families in the top 5% received 20% of aggregate income.[1] (See Figure 2.1.)

In real terms (or so-called inflation-adjusted dollars, which take into account that most things cost less decades ago), median family income has grown from $52,963 in 1980, or by about 12%.[2] This occurred during a period when "real" per person, or *per capita,* income was in decline. How can this make sense? More family members work now than in 1980. Because per capita income was on the decline, the typical family required two incomes to keep pace. Women entered the workforce in large numbers. The dependence on two workers' incomes leads to the

Figure 2.1 Money Income of U.S. Families, Percentage Distribution by Income Level, 2010

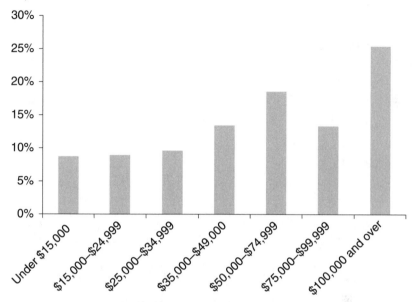

Source: U.S. Census Bureau, *Current Population Survey, Annual Social and Economic Supplements* (Washington, DC: Government Printing Office, 2010), Table F-23, as cited in U.S. Census Bureau, *Statistical Abstract of the United States: 2012* (Washington, DC: Government Printing Office, 2012), Table 696.

counterintuitive result that family financial well-being is less secure than when one income provided a family's livelihood.[3] Since it is more likely that one of two breadwinners will lose a job than one of one, family income has become less secure.

Some families make more money than they spend. They invest the difference in *assets* that are financial (bank deposits, investment accounts, stocks and bonds) and nonfinancial (first and second homes, family businesses). Financial assets are cash or "near cash," that is, easily convertible into cash, while nonfinancial assets often require months or even years for conversion into cash.

Almost all families hold some financial assets, but the median value of holdings is quite modest—$21,500 in 2010—and likely to be tied up in retirement accounts or life insurance.[4] In fact, the bottom 80% of American families, on average, have only $700–$5,300 available in their checking or savings accounts.[5] As these numbers suggest, family financial assets are much more unevenly distributed than family income. Earners in the top 10% have more financial assets than those in the bottom 90% combined (see Figure 2.2).

Figure 2.2 U.S. Family Holdings of Financial Assets by Percentile of Income, 2010

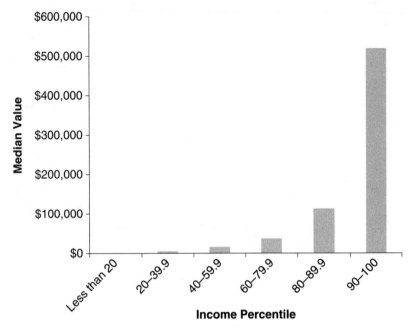

Source: "Changes in U.S. Family Finances from 2007 to 2010: Evidence from the Survey of Consumer Finances," *Federal Reserve Bulletin* 98 (June 2012): 30.

The vast majority of American families hold nonfinancial assets as well. Close to 90% own cars, just over two-thirds own the homes in which they live, and a smaller percentage own second properties or businesses. In 2010, the median value of such family holdings was $187,200, most of which was accounted for by the value of homes and cars.[6]

To say an American family "holds" an asset is not to say they own it free and clear. Most borrow to finance their purchases of homes and cars. Hence, three-quarters of American families hold some sort of debt. More than $100,000 is owed on the median home mortgage, and $12,600 is owed on the family cars or school loans.[7] A portrait of family debt by income class shows that as income grows, so does debt (see Figure 2.3).

The difference between the value of family assets and debt (also known as liabilities) is called *net worth*. While the average value for family net worth is $556,300, that number can be quite misleading. Median net worth—$120,000—is much lower.[8] Remember: when Bill Gates walks into a room of sixty people, they all become billionaires on average, but the group's median income and wealth have hardly changed.

Figure 2.3 U.S. Family Holdings of Nonfinancial Assets and Debt by Percentile of Income, 2010

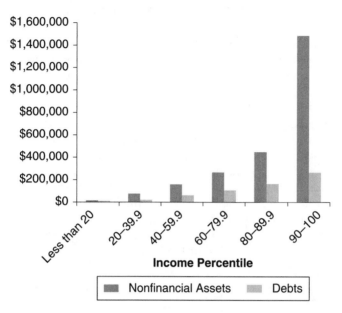

Source: "Changes in U.S. Family Finances from 2007 to 2010: Evidence from the Survey of Consumer Finances," *Federal Reserve Bulletin* 98 (June 2012): 63.

Because most of a typical American family's wealth is tied up in a home, retirement accounts, and life insurance, the family has quite limited financial assets available to deal with any financial shock, and there is little to cushion the resulting interruption of family income. Simply stated, four-fifths of American families are poorly positioned to shoulder large and unexpected costs brought about by any source. Even many families in the top fifth, as you will see, can easily lose much of what they have accumulated because of the realization of any one of the risks that we have identified.

THE NATURE OF THE THREATS

Threat 1: Being Born into a Poor Family

Consider newborn children. They might be the grandchildren of billionaires or descendants of those who have inhabited an impoverished inner-city neighborhood or rural mining town for multiple generations. These children did nothing to earn their status. Birth into a particular

---

Is Individual Family Economic Risk
the Only Rationale for Social Insurance?

This chapter emphasizes the economic risks that families run in a market economy—risks that can be alleviated only imperfectly by prudence and private insurance. But as Chapter 4 will demonstrate, policy makers have had other substantial reasons to initiate and continue social insurance programs. Politically, social insurance supports a market economy by making its inevitable risks more bearable. Socially, social insurance helps to mitigate class antagonisms that accompany disparities in income and wealth. And economically, social insurance benefits are strongly countercyclical—that is, they preserve significant consumer demand in economic downturns that might be significantly worse without income transfers. When the economy tanked in 2008, Social Security benefits kept flowing and unemployment benefits increased, as did eligibility for food stamps and the Earned Income Tax Credit.

---

family is a totally random event for the newborn, but one with major consequences.

Births are not evenly distributed across income groups. Richer families have more children than do poorer families, but most children are not born rich. In 2010, 3.7 million women gave birth in the United States. About a quarter of these babies were born lucky—that is, born into families with incomes greater than $75,000. Another one-third of these births were to families with incomes in the range of $35,000–$75,000. These are the families many call the American middle class. The other 40% of these babies went home to lower-income families, 27% to families officially defined as poor.[9] Depending on how strictly we define poverty (and the U.S. government's official definition is very strict), the risk of being born into a poor American family is at least 27%. Not great odds. (See Figure 2.4.)

What are the likely consequences of being born into a poor family? Studies of *economic mobility* are attempts to understand the extent to which an individual's initial position explains that person's position later in life. If research showed that someone born into a poor family is as likely to end up wealthy as someone born into a wealthy family, it would be strong evidence for high levels of economic mobility. Birth into a poor family would have little bearing on a person's lifetime prospects.

Figure 2.4 Numbers of Women Having Children by Family Income Range, 2010

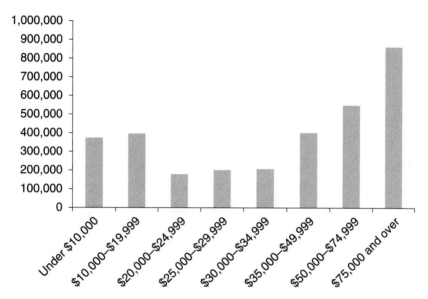

Source: U.S. Census Bureau, *Current Population Reports,* P20-555 and unpublished data, as cited in U.S. Census Bureau, *Statistical Abstract of the United States: 2012* (Washington, DC: Government Printing Office, 2012), 71, Table 92bi.

An analysis of available data suggests the opposite is true. Researchers from the U.S. Treasury Department examined changes in family income over the period 1995 to 2006. They found that 15% of families among the bottom fifth of income earners at the beginning were able to raise their income level into the top two quintiles by decade's end. This contrasted with the 87% of families that started in the top fifth and ended up in the top 40%, almost a sixfold difference.[10] This difference suggests that while economic mobility is not absent in the United States, an American's station at birth is highly predictive of that individual's future prospects. Studies over a longer time horizon show increased mobility, but the gap is still wide.[11]

Economic mobility is important, but it is not the end of the story. If members of poor families did as well as those from better-off ones along other dimensions of life—educational attainment, health status, and physical security, to name a few—we would be less alarmed by limited economic mobility.

Alas, starting off poor has negative consequences for all the standard markers of well-being. Teenagers in families in the poorest fifth drop out of high school at an 8% annual rate, twice that of the middle three-

Figure 2.5 15–24-Year-Olds Who Dropped Out of Grades 10–12, by Family Income, October 1972–2008

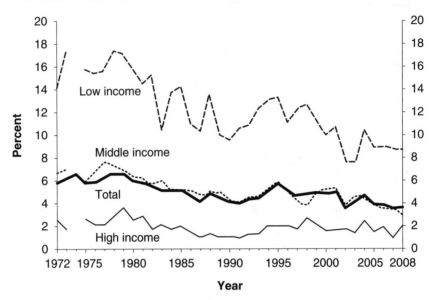

Source: Chris Chapman, Jennifer Laird, Nicole Ifill, and Angelina KewalRamani, *Trends in High School Dropout and Completion Rates in the United States: 1972–2009* (NCES 2012-006) (Washington, DC: National Center for Education Statistics, 2011), http://nces.ed.gov/pubs2012/2012006.pdf.

fifths and five times that of the highest-income fifth. Over four years, almost 30% of teens from the poorest fifth drop out of high school (see Figure 2.5). This, of course, helps explain the lack of income mobility. A high school graduate makes about 50% more than does a dropout. A college graduate with a bachelor's degree makes 77% more than someone with only a high school diploma, but one-fourth less than a person with an advanced degree.[12]

The data on health status paint a similarly bleak picture. Infant mortality rates are twice as high in the poorest U.S. states as in the richest.[13] In 2005, 31% of those with family incomes below the federal poverty level (FPL) reported "poor" or "fair" health. As family income rose, the percentage of such reports dwindled. At higher income levels, four times the poverty level and above, or about $80,000, only 6.6% made similar reports (see Figure 2.6).

Low income is associated with a host of other social ills. For example, being born into a poor family also means greatly heightened chances of early death, incarceration, and being the victim of violent crime. This is not to say that individuals cannot, with a lifetime of striving and hard

Figure 2.6 Percentages of Adults Reporting Fair or Poor Health by Family Income Level, 2005

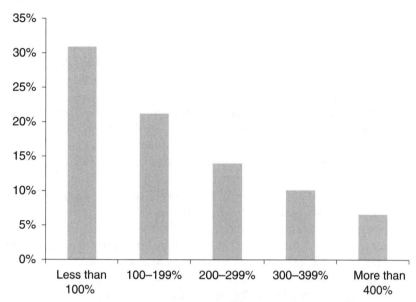

Income as percentage of federal poverty level

Source: National Health Interview Survey, 2001–2005, as cited in Robert Wood Johnson Foundation, Commission to Build a Healthier America, *Race and Socioeconomic Factors Affect Opportunities for Better Health,* Issue Brief 5 (Princeton, NJ: Robert Wood Johnson Foundation, April 2009), 4.

work, achieve the standard "American dream." It does mean that for children born into lower-income families the path to that dream's fulfillment is a much steeper climb. What American social insurance arrangements do to decrease the gradient is the topic of Chapter 5.

Threat 2: Early Death of a Family Breadwinner

Every year, approximately 2.5 million Americans die, about half as a result of heart disease or cancer.[14] More than 100,000 Americans die from injuries annually.[15] Motor vehicle accidents—the single largest cause—account for more than 30,000 of these deaths. Close to three-quarters of all deaths occur among people 65 or older. About 36,000 children die, as do 30,000 young adults ages 15–24. While devastating to friends and families, the deaths of the old and the young tend not to leave dependent families in a state of financial peril. Deaths among those ages 25–54 often do.

Just over 300,000 American adults of working age died in 2009.[16] Of these, 40% succumbed to either heart disease or cancer. Accidents of all kinds claimed 49,000 more, and 9,000 fell victim to violent crime. The rest died from one of a long list of diseases other than cancer or heart disease.

What is the likelihood of an early death? Of the approximately 120 million Americans ages 25–54, 300,000 died in 2009. That is about one-fourth of 1%, not a large fraction annually. But with those odds recurring every year, 1 of 13 Americans currently 25 years old will not reach 55; 1 out of 10 will not reach 65. The majority dying during that 30–40 year period will leave dependent families with greatly reduced finances.

American families come in many shapes and sizes, so, to assess the scale of financial losses associated with the death of a breadwinner, we must consider three major family types: (1) the two-breadwinner family; (2) the two-parent, one-breadwinner family; and (3) the one-parent, one-breadwinner family. Family income will fall by a significant percentage in the first case and disappear in the other two, at least temporarily. Child-care expenses are likely to rise in the second case, as the surviving parent begins or continues to work outside the home.

Summary data on the scale of income losses in these cases is unavailable, but a defensible way of examining the differences in income among family types is to estimate the scale of loss from the death of a breadwinning parent. In 2009, the median income of married-couple families with two breadwinners was $85,948; it fell by 45%, to $47,649, when one spouse was not in the workforce. In families led by a male householder (without a spouse present), that median drops to $41,501, or 50% less. In a female-led single-parent home, the median drops to $29,770, or 65% less.[17] And, obviously, in the case of the death of a single parent, family income would be reduced from those levels by 100%.

The early death of a parent is obviously both sad and stressful for the remaining family members. The surviving parent must raise children alone with a fraction of prior family income. Chapter 6 will discuss the social and private insurance arrangements in place to help surviving family members, but for now, keep in mind the odds of early death during the typical working life and the associated financial consequences: a 5% chance of loss of one breadwinner, and then a dramatic cut, 50–100%, in family income. While the entire loss may not be permanent, the adjustments necessary—workforce entry or remarriage of a surviving spouse—are likely to happen over a period of many years. And the data on single-person households suggest that much of the economic effect is persistent.

Threat 3: Ill Health

Serious illness or injury leaves its victim with diminished capacity to work in the short run, and, at times, in the long run. Either exposes a family to potentially ruinous medical expenses. How likely is a devastating health event for an American during the prime working years of life? How expensive are the direct medical costs of such an episode?

Neither of these questions has a ready answer. Diseases and injuries are broad categories with varied probabilities and a wide range of treatment costs within a single diagnosis. For illustrative purposes, we will look at cancer and cardiovascular disease, the two major classes of disease likely to strike a working-age adult.

Cancer

Cancer is not one disease but more than one hundred different diseases. Every year, doctors diagnose more than 1.5 million Americans with cancer, and more than half a million Americans die of these dreaded diseases (see Table 2.1).

What do we know about the odds of developing cancer? First, the odds vary greatly by site. The lifetime odds of a woman developing breast cancer are a staggering 1 in 8, but for uterine cancer, only 1 in 147. Second, as life progresses, one's odds of developing cancer increase from very low to very high. American Cancer Society research suggests that these odds for an American man go from 1 in 69 before the age of 40 to 1 in 3 after the age of 70. (For an American woman, the odds go from 1 in 46 to 1 in 4.) For our purposes, we can estimate that during the

Table 2.1 Estimated New Cancer Cases and Deaths, 2012

Site	New Cases	Deaths
Prostate	241,740	28,170
Breast	229,060	39,920
Lung	226,160	160,340
Colon/rectal	143,460	15,690
Skin	81,240	12,190
Lymphoma	79,190	20,130
Bladder	73,510	14,880
Kidney	64,770	13,570
Uterine	47,130	8,010
Thyroid	56,460	1,780
Pancreas	43,920	37,390
Oral	40,250	7,850
All other sites	312,020	217,270
Total	**1,638,910**	**577,190**

Source: American Cancer Society, *Cancer Facts and Figures—2012* (Atlanta: American Cancer Society, 2012), 4.

Figure 2.7 Probability of Developing Cancer over Selected Age Intervals, United States, 2006–2008

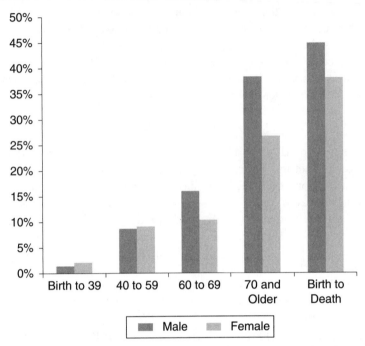

Source: American Cancer Society, *Cancer Facts and Figures—2012* (Atlanta: American Cancer Society, 2012), 14.

working years of ages 25–65, the probability of being diagnosed with cancer is approximately 10% (see Figure 2.7).

The onset of cancer leads to a dramatic increase in medical expenses, one that only a small percentage of families can bear with their own assets. The care required costs tens of thousands, even hundreds of thousands, of dollars.[18] Few will have the assets to pay for the cost of care directly. In addition, the disease and care will reduce the capacity of the individual to work for at least the period of acute illness and possibly for the rest of the person's life. For some cancer victims, their working lives will be cut short.

Cardiovascular Disease

Cardiovascular disease attacks the body's blood generation (heart) and distribution (arteries and veins) system. And, once again, this category refers to a set of diseases, including hypertension (high blood pressure), coronary heart disease, heart failure, and stroke. Death from heart disease can come suddenly in the form of an acute myocardial infarction, better known as a heart attack, but typically death comes slowly, as a damaged heart loses its pumping power or artery-clogging plaque builds up.

In 2008, Americans suffered 935,000 heart attacks and 795,000 strokes.[19] Broader cardiovascular diseases claimed more than 811,000 lives and afflicted more than 82 million more as a chronic condition.[20] About 10 million of the sick were working-age Americans, as were 150,000 of the dead. As with cancer, rates of cardiovascular disease increase with age (see Figure 2.8), and incidence and costs of care vary both with the type of disease involved and from patient to patient diagnosed with the same disease.

The risk of cardiovascular disease during an American's working life is in the range of 1 in 7 to 1 in 12. The associated expenses will be in the tens of thousands of dollars and likely much more. The median American family, with $6,000 in immediately available funds, is ill prepared to finance these

Figure 2.8 Incidence of Cardiovascular Disease by Age/Sex per 1,000 Person Years, 1980–2003

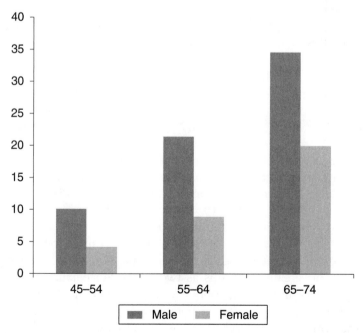

Source: American Heart Association, "Heart Disease and Stroke Statistics—2012 Update," *Circulation* 125 (2012): Chart 3-2.

Note: Data include congestive heart disease, heart failure, stroke, and intracerebral hemorrhage, but not hypertension.

costs alone. Most will have some form of health insurance. Whether they will have insurance and at what level of adequacy is the topic of Chapter 7.

We have here discussed the incidence and expenses for only two broad classes of diseases. Add to that picture the likely incidence of all other illnesses and injuries, and the chance of needing significant, and expensive, health care over a lifetime becomes almost a certainty.

Threat 4: Involuntary Unemployment

Most Americans count on current income to pay for current expenses. Other than a house and a car—both of which generate current liabilities in the forms of monthly mortgage and car payments—Americans hold few assets. Precious little extra cash is available to handle even a brief stint of unemployment.

How likely is a period of unemployment for the average American? One way of analyzing the possibility is to examine unemployment rate data. The U.S. Department of Labor collects data monthly and has reported unemployment rates since 1948. Rates have varied from as low as 2.9% in 1953 to as high as 9.7% in 1982.[21]

These data suggest that, over those six decades, between 3 and 10 of every 100 American workers were unemployed at any one time. But the official Labor Department definition of "unemployment" turns out to count only those actually looking for work. Not counted are "discouraged workers," who have given up searching for jobs, and the "underemployed"—part-time or part-year workers who wish to be working full-time. Economists estimate that the addition of these groups would bump up the official rate by up to 7%.[22] One such estimate placed the rate of actual unemployment at about 15% in mid-2012.[23]

Another factor to consider is the duration of unemployment. Labor Department data show that between 1948 and 2008, the seasonally adjusted average duration of unemployment ranged from 8 to 20 weeks.[24] In 2009 and 2010, the average durations were 30 and 35 weeks, respectively. The Labor Department data underestimated the duration of unemployment, however, since it did not allow workers to report unemployment longer than two years, counting all unemployment duration greater than this as two years. Since January 2011, the department has allowed respondents to report durations of up to five years.[25] The average duration of unemployment rose to 40.8 weeks in 2011 and remained at a similar level in 2012.[26] Of course, neither the old nor the new estimates include discouraged or underemployed workers.

For our purpose of estimating the incidence of unemployment, we will ignore the inadequacy of the definition. That will ensure that we end up with a conservative estimate, one that understates the incidence of the threat.

The annual rate tells us only how likely a spell of unemployment is over one year. To estimate the chances of unemployment across an American's working life, we would need to consider a period of forty to fifty years. Because we do not know whether future experience will be better or worse than that of the past, let's examine the working life of a fictitious person who graduated college in 1951 and retired from the workforce in 1997. During that period, Labor Department data indicate just over 329 million "first payments" were made to newly unemployed workers. We estimate that over those forty-six years approximately 120 million people were in the workforce. This translates into an average number of unemployment spells of almost three per worker. It might be that unemployment spells are highly concentrated among a small percentage of the population, and that the average is not a good measure of typical experience. Data are not available on the distribution of unemployment spells for 1951–1997, but they are available for the period 1978–2006. What we see is a somewhat worse average experience than for our fictitious 1951 college graduate: an average of five spells of unemployment across a shorter period (twenty-eight years). The risk of unemployment seems to be increasing (see Figure 2.9).

The bottom line is this: only 9% of Americans did not have a spell of unemployment between 1978 and 2006, and 80% had two or more such spells. Unemployment is difficult to avoid over the long run.

A skeptic might argue that a good work ethic or advanced education reduces the likelihood and number of spells of individual unemployment. There are data to test the latter, but not the former, proposition. And it turns out to be true that the higher the level of educational attainment, the lower the average number of unemployment episodes. Yet, surprisingly, the effect is rather small. Those with a bachelor's degree or higher still averaged close to four spells of unemployment over the period (see Figure 2.10).

Just as with the early death or disablement of a breadwinner, involuntary unemployment reduces family income by anywhere from 50% to 100%. The duration of the reduction is shorter, however, with three to six months the typical period. That said, the average duration was 39 weeks in late 2012, down from a record-setting 40 weeks in late 2011 and early 2012.[27] "Long-term unemployment" has become a topic of news stories. The period 2008–2013 may ultimately be remembered as a terrible, but temporary, time of high unemployment, but it will be years before anyone can reliably offer such a characterization.

Figure 2.9 Distribution of Unemployment Spells per U.S. Worker, 1978–2010

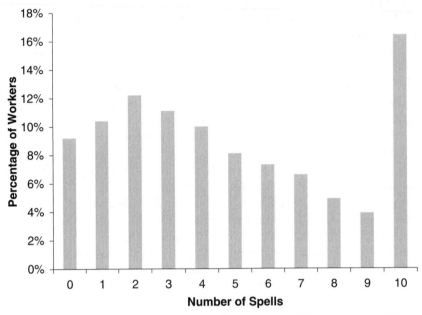

Source: U.S. Bureau of Labor Statistics, "National Longitudinal Surveys, 1978–2010," accessed October 10, 2012, http://www.bls.gov/nls.

This portrait reinforces the appeal of prudent family spending and saving, as well as diligence at the workplace. But bad things happen even to those who play by the rules and live frugally. Enron's thousands of employees did not bankrupt their company, and the financial meltdown of 2008 was a Wall Street collapse that created a Main Street disaster.

Threat 5: Disability

According to a 2012 report published by the Cornell University Center on Disability Demographics and Statistics, roughly 12% of Americans are disabled.[28] Disability may limit the type of work one can do, or it may prevent one from gaining any substantial paid employment. The latter is the standard criterion for an individual to receive disability benefits under both the Social Security Disability Insurance (SSDI) program and the Supplementary Security Income (SSI) program. Approximately 13.5 million working-age Americans receive benefits under these two programs.

Most disabled worker beneficiaries have little or no outside income. As in cases of early death of a breadwinner, family income falls anywhere

Figure 2.10 Average Number of Unemployment Spells per Worker by Educational Attainment Level, 1978–2010

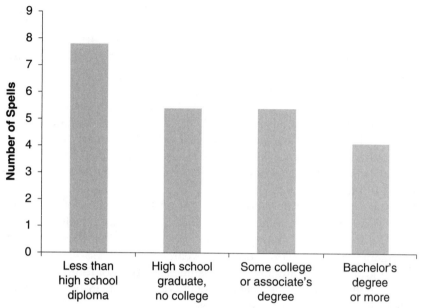

Source: U.S. Bureau of Labor Statistics, "National Longitudinal Surveys, 1979–2010," accessed October 10, 2012, http://www.bls.gov/nls.

from 50% to 100% when work stops. With total disability, the only question is the duration of disability. For SSI or SSDI recipients, the duration must be at least one year but is usually permanent. Vanishingly few workers meeting these programs' strict standards ever return to work. Moreover, the medical expenses of disabled persons are almost certain to increase, which means that disability is a double threat to family income.

In summary, the likely risk of total disability is 5–10% over an American's working life. Many others—approximately one in four Americans—will have a stint of disability in excess of ninety days at some point during their working lives.[29]

Threat 6: Outliving One's Savings

As we have seen, the risks of sickness and disability increase with age, as does the risk of medical expenses. Even absent these risks, one's capacity (and likely desire) to work decreases as one moves from one's 60s into one's 70s, 80s, and 90s. The reduced prospects for work income place a premium on the availability of savings and investment earnings on those savings—and we know there is little of either in America. Savings rates, as we have seen, are quite low. Many of those who saved diligently and invested broadly in the stock market saw the value of their portfolios cut in half during the financial turmoil of 2008. Diversification did not protect anyone from the damage.

Even if we make the optimistic assumption that Americans can or will save more, the chances that most would save enough for their retirements would still be small. For one thing, planning for retirement is full of uncertainties. How long will I live? What kind of return can I expect on my savings over time? What if I have large, unexpected expenses (of the sort already seen or others not yet imagined)? What rate of inflation should I figure into my calculations?

Actuarial analysis can shed some light on the question of how long one will live. The probability of a 65-year-old American female surviving to age 80 is over 71%; to age 90, 31%.[30] Is she saving for fifteen years of retirement? Probably. For twenty-five years? Probably not. But she just doesn't know. (And, of course, this assumes she did not forgo her career to raise children and thus was not totally dependent on her husband's ability to save and willingness to do so.)

Analysts have developed sophisticated models that attempt to answer the salient question: What percentage of Americans is at risk for having insufficient funds to cover the expenses of retirement? One such rigorous model, created by the Employee Benefit Research Institute (EBRI), considers the current state of various demographic groups' retirement savings and provisions (including the current Social Security program). In 2010 the model projected that 47% of early Baby Boomers, 44% of late Boomers, and 45% of Generation Xers will lack adequate retirement income for basic expenses and uninsured health care costs.[31] Adjusting the long-term expected rate of return on stocks and bonds downward increases the proportion at risk to just over 50%.[32] A reduction in Social Security benefits does as well. (The EBRI researchers did not attempt to test the case in which Social Security benefits did not exist at all, but extrapolation suggests that without those benefits three-quarters of Americans would have insufficient funds for basic expenses and uninsured health care costs.)[33] Other models predict similar ranges of Americans with inadequate means (see Figure 2.11).

Historically, outliving one's savings has meant dependence on one's own family or one's community. While community poorhouses no longer exist, America's nursing homes are full of senior citizens who have

Figure 2.11 Percentage of U.S. Population "at Risk" for Inadequate Retirement Income

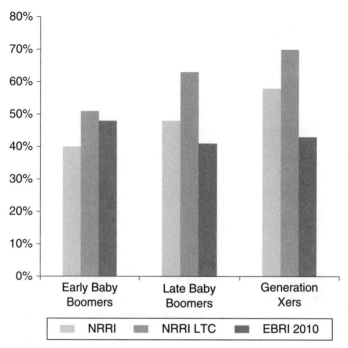

Source: Jack VanDerhei and Craig Copeland, *The EBRI Retirement Readiness Rating: Retirement Income Preparation and Future Prospects,* Issue Brief 344 (Washington, DC: Employee Benefit Research Institute, 2010), 7.

Note: NRRI = National Retirement Risk Index; NRRI LTC = National Retirement Risk Index with consideration of long-term care expense; EBRI = Employee Benefit Research Institute.

outlived (or spent down) their savings and are now totally reliant on government-financed health programs and Social Security pensions. Approximately three-quarters of America's 1.4 million nursing home residents rely on federal and state government support alone.[34]

The Six Threats Collectively

Table 2.2 summarizes the likelihood and consequences of the six threats being realized over the life of an individual. While the odds don't look great on any one dimension, these are only the odds of any one bad thing happening. We have not tried to answer quantitatively the question that is more worrisome: What are the odds that at least one of these six threats will be realized in one's life? That is, what are the odds that one will be born into a poor family *or* suffer from cancer or heart disease or many other diseases less frequently encountered *or* die early *or* be disabled *or* lose one's job many times *or* outlive one's savings? You get the picture: it is quite likely that an American will confront several such threats in his or her lifetime.

How have America's public institutions thought about and addressed these possibilities? That history is the subject of our next chapter.

Table 2.2 The Six Threats

Threat	Probability	Consequences
Birth into a poor family	25–30%	At greater risk for violence, poor health, school dropout, incarceration, economic immobility
Ill health		
Cancer	10% working life	Medical bills of $25,000–$100,000+, greater risk of death or disability
Heart disease	10–20% working life	Medical bills of $10,000–$100,000+, greater risk of death or disability
Early death	10% working life	Reduced family income by 50–100%, greater child-care expenses
Total disability	5–10% working life	Reduced family income by 50–100%, greater health care expenses
Involuntary unemployment	90% of one or more spells	Reduced family income by 33–100%, increased risk of losing home, health insurance
Outliving one's savings	45%	Loss of independence, risk of becoming a ward of the state

"We should make it past the rocks by nightfall, provided our luck holds."

Source: Matthew Diffee/The New Yorker Collection/www.cartoonbank.com

3

Philosophies, Policies, and Public Budgets

A PHILOSOPHY—OF LIFE, OF ONE'S OCCUPATION, OF SPORT, of social welfare—is a set of stable, fundamental beliefs about what is worth doing and how to do it. A shared philosophy of social policy—or social insurance— does not rule out some differences over details or the implications of particular policies. But understanding social welfare policy does require attention to the underlying philosophical premises that are expressed in social policy—that is, our customary practices, our social and political norms, and America's legislative and administrative arrangements.

In democratic societies, different philosophies compete to influence the decisions of elected and appointed leaders, and the programs pursued reflect compromise as well as conviction. We end up with programs with many purposes, some of which conflict.

So we begin our examination of American social welfare policy by asking what different fundamental beliefs are in conflict about the purposes and modes of social policy. Multiple philosophical roots, some more powerful than others, find expression in American social policies. We examine them in turn to get a sense of their character and their influence on current policy.

PHILOSOPHIES OF SOCIAL WELFARE

What are the major philosophies of social welfare policy? On what important dimensions do they vary? What are their historical roots in Europe and America? We will characterize five philosophical conceptions. We borrow the shorthand label for each from its literature: behaviorism, residualism, social insurance, opportunity enhancement, and egalitarian populism. We first review each independently, suggesting its connection to programmatic expressions. American practices, as well as relevant polling data, reveal commitments that diverge sharply from those that dominate the evening news and the political debates that dominate public discussion.

The Behaviorist Conception of Social Welfare Policy

The behaviorist vision of social welfare policy has deep roots in the European poor laws that preceded the twentieth-century development of the modern welfare state. The poor laws evolved over four hundred years, creating and modifying the rules about how societies help—but do not encourage the dependency of—the indigent.[1] Reformers tried to distinguish between the deserving poor—children, the sick, and the aged—and the undeserving, able-bodied poor. National and local governments built and maintained poorhouses (and workhouses). At times they provided *outdoor relief,* essentially cash payments, to the indigent. These institutions pleased few. They were costly according to their critics and inadequate from the perspective of those sympathetic to the poor.

Social welfare policy, according to the behaviorist view, is mainly concerned with inducing the poor to behave in more socially acceptable ways. The able-bodied should work at whatever jobs are available. Families should assume responsibility for the care of the young, the old, and the disabled. Everyone should look to his or her own future, providing for both expected and unexpected reductions in earning power. Behaviorists believe that if everyone conformed to this ideal, social welfare programs could be limited to charitable relief for victims of truly exceptional circumstances. Indeed, private charity might reasonably be expected to perform this task without the assistance of the state. On this view, the undeserving poor are without enough income—and suffer from a lack of medical care, food, housing, and security—because they do not behave as they should. Humaneness requires that suffering be partially relieved, but generous assistance, it is assumed, reinforces the very behavior that causes poverty in the first place.

In particular, public assistance should be denied when the behavior at issue is immediately correctable. The able-bodied poor, for example, need only submit themselves to the discipline of the labor market. Long-term assistance may be necessary when behavioral change is not possible, as with children or elderly paupers without family or savings. Such assistance, however, should be marginal, even punitive, to discourage fraudulent appeals for help. Recall Charles Dickens's portrayal of the orphanage in *Oliver Twist!*

The behaviorist point of view has considerable contemporary expression, never more apparent than when the television is tuned to the programming of Fox News. Writers such as Charles Murray argue that by supporting the poor and promoting dependency, governmental social welfare does more harm than good, and a substantial number of Americans—24% in a recent survey—apparently agree.[2] Workhouses and poorhouses vanished in the United States by the early twentieth century, but echoes of the behaviorist perspective are commonplace. The 1996 welfare reforms are a major recent example. In 1996, President Bill Clinton and Congress replaced Aid to Families with Dependent Children (AFDC), a sixty-year-old program that had many behaviorist features itself, with the program Temporary Assistance for Needy Families (TANF). The reform focused on moving recipients from welfare assistance to work by eliminating the statutory entitlement to cash subsistence-level payments for poor families with children. While TANF relies on counseling and sanctions to promote work, subsidies were also a part of the reform strategy.[3] A key parallel development to TANF was an expansion of the Earned Income Tax Credit (EITC), which is designed to provide a government subsidy to the poor. The EITC can be claimed, however, only by deserving individuals who earn some income from employment. An individual who does not earn any income from employment is ineligible to claim the EITC.

The Residualist Conception of the Welfare State

The view we term residualist trades on the metaphor of the safety net. The net of social welfare programs is meant to rescue the casualties of capitalism and the business cycle; its aim is to give a modest level of financial relief to those unable to provide for themselves or their families. This conception also emerged from the poor law tradition, but it now more nearly reflects the legacy of philanthropic humanitarianism. In this tradition, charity is a moral duty for those whose incomes permit them to help the downtrodden.

Those who think of the welfare state as "residual" typically believe its financial assistance should be temporary and its administration highly decentralized, much like the private charity that it supplements. They envision a distribution of relief closely supervised by officials thoroughly familiar with the circumstances of their clients' lives. Localism is a means to ensure that only the deserving poor receive assistance. The metaphor of the safety net suggests the key features of appropriate welfare policy. The net is close to the ground, with modest levels of benefits. Subsistence standards might well vary widely based on local conditions.

The clientele are the unfortunate, the down and out. Eligibility criteria are designed to sort out the truly needy from the rest. There is here an important conception of potential waste that it is important to understand. Aid to those who could help themselves is considered simple inefficiency. Minimal adequacy, selectivity, localism, and tests of need constitute the residualist's standard bases for evaluating the welfare state.

The residualist imprint on American social provision is visible in many means-tested programs. The prominent illustrations include food and nutrition aid (originally known as the food stamp program, now the Supplemental Nutrition Assistance Program, or SNAP) and housing (public housing and Section 8 rental assistance). Similar programs such as health insurance for the poor aged, blind, and disabled (Medicaid) and poor children (State Children's Health Insurance Program, or SCHIP) are substantial items in public budgets, particularly for state and local governments.

The Welfare State as Social Insurance

Residualist convictions differ sharply from what we term the social insurance conception of what the welfare state should embrace. The basic purpose of the welfare state, according to this view, is to provide economic security. It is intended to *prevent* individuals—and their families—from falling into destitution rather than to rescue them after they have already fallen. (In *The Great Risk Shift,* political scientist Jacob Hacker aptly distinguishes "forward-looking" social insurance from "backward-looking" means-tested relief.)

The threats to economic security are the risks we described earlier—birth into a poor family, early death of a family breadwinner, sickness, involuntary unemployment, disability, and outliving one's savings. Welfare states have provided for these eventualities at different times, in different sequences, and with considerable variation in generosity and terms of administration. Yet, irrespective of the form and level of payment, social insurance programs have rejected as inferior the "means testing" common to many American welfare programs. Social insurance programs typically condition benefits on some level of prior contributions toward the support of the programs. The more universal both contributions and benefits are, the closer the program is to the social insurance model.

The central image of social insurance is the earned benefit for which all similarly situated persons are eligible because of their financial contributions to the program. The contributions may sometimes be made in the form of income taxes. Typically, proportional taxes support the programs, as with the Federal Insurance Contributions Act (FICA) payroll tax, which we will discuss in subsequent chapters. Whatever the arrangement for finance, the idea is for a beneficiary to contribute through taxation while working in exchange for protection while out of work. Equitable treatment, not the equalizing of incomes, is the controlling standard.

Redistribution of income is clearly one consequence of such programs, but it is not their primary aim. The model of redistribution is not intended to be from rich to poor, but rather from lucky to unlucky (non–burn victims to burn victims), or over the life cycle of individuals (contributions while young, pensions when old or disabled). The relevant question for the proponents of social insurance is the adequacy of citizen preparation for the predictable risks of modern industrial societies. Looked at this way, social insurance simply extends the security aims of private insurance to circumstances where either risks are uninsurable privately or the purchase of adequate levels of commercial insurance is unlikely.

In contemporary America, the philosophy of social insurance is evident in the Social Security Act's Old-Age, Survivors, and Disability Insurance (OASDI) programs, Medicare, and workers' compensation and unemployment compensation programs. These programs protect beneficiaries against the changing fortunes so characteristic of capitalism. They do so prospectively, placing a platform under family income, rather than subjecting beneficiaries to tests of means or assets. In that sense they are "entitlements," benefits recipients believe they are owed, with obligations that are regarded as legitimate claims on future governmental revenues.

Opportunity Enhancement as Public Policy

The first three conceptions presented above focus on either the currently threatened or those who will as a matter of statistical probability face risks of being financially threatened. The view we term opportunity enhancement emphasizes instead the programs and pathways that help citizens achieve their intellectual and economic potential. Such policies, proponents argue, improve national welfare by providing citizens, among other benefits, the skills to compete in a demanding world economy. The idea (attributed to Confucius, King David, Mark Twain, and surely many others across time) is captured in the familiar adage: "Give a man a fish, feed him for a day. Teach him how to fish, feed him for a lifetime."

While the idea of education is old, mandatory universal public education is mostly a modern phenomenon. Early in America's history, Thomas Jefferson emphasized the "need for an educated citizenry," and a proposal for a "national university" was part of George Washington's legislative agenda. Schooling became and has remained primarily a state and local responsibility in the United States. The federal government provides only about 10 cents of every dollar spent on education. Local governments fund and operate public primary, secondary, and vocational schools; states provide localities with school funding and give policy direction through their departments of education. States play an important role in postsecondary education, operating large community college systems and public universities. All three levels of government fund and administer a mélange of job training programs for adults.

Free public education from kindergarten to the twelfth grade remains the most prominent example of the opportunity-enhancing idea of what the modern American welfare state should provide. Beyond that, hundreds of other programs at the state, local, and federal levels assist some of the disadvantaged to enter the mainstream of American economic life. The social services, such as job search assistance and retraining and rehabilitation services, attached to many income-support programs marry the opportunity enhancement idea to other notions of social provision.

Egalitarian Populism

So far we have not emphasized the redistribution of wealth and power in our brief survey of social welfare beliefs. In the behaviorist model, the powerful correct the faults of the weak. In the residualist ideal, the powerful take care of the deserving weak. In the opportunity enhancement model, the powerful give the weak tools to become more like them. Social insurance offers a measure of economic security to the entire population, but it does not attempt directly to transform the society's economic stratification or power relations.

An egalitarian conception of the welfare state holds that all citizens should share equally in the burdens and benefits of their society. Policies that would reduce or eliminate disparities in income or social standing express this conviction. The aim of egalitarian populists is social change, not a safety net or opportunity for individual improvement. What social insurance advocates count as generous provision is, for the most critical egalitarian populist, a glossing over of the inequities of modern capitalism.

The egalitarian's aim is not programs for the people, but programs by the people. Advocates of egalitarian populism have made their mark on American public policy mostly through universal public education. It was not until the twentieth century that the public finance of education was adopted in all states. In its absence, social mobility and empowerment were almost surely less possible in the United States.

Table 3.1 Social Welfare Philosophy Matrix

	Behaviorist	Residualist	Social Insurance	Opportunity Enhancement	Egalitarian Populist
Purpose	Change behavior of poor	Help deserving poor	Shield from risks	Build skills to compete	Redistribute power
Metaphor	Workhouse	Safety net	Earned benefit	Diploma	May Day
Current policy	TANF Shelters	Medicaid SNAP	Social Security Medicare	Job training EITC	Public defenders Public schools

Here opportunity enhancement and desires for a more egalitarian society are complementary. But stronger egalitarian ideas find expression in programs and constitutional protections designed to promote civic, not economic, equality.[4] Steep income and wealth taxes to support generous "demogrants" for all families are not typically a part of American social welfare provision. Americans tend to be liberal, not social, democrats.

To fix the ideas discussed above, consider the matrix in Table 3.1. But do not get too fixed. Most programs have some elements of each philosophical tradition built into their structures. Social welfare programs are legislative compromises, not philosophy texts.

THE AMERICAN EXPRESSION OF SOCIAL WELFARE PHILOSOPHY

To hear popular debates concerning social welfare policy is to imagine that behaviorist and residualist programs dominate American social welfare provision. Concerns about the integrity (read "waste, fraud, and abuse") of residualist programs such as Medicaid or food stamps (now SNAP) loom large in press and television coverage of American welfare state operations. Criticism of America's large social insurance programs—Social Security and Medicare—often includes the residualist lament that they are wasteful because they are not means-tested.

But if we inspect American public expenditures, a quite different picture emerges of what American social welfare policy actually does. And these expenditures mirror Americans' preferences, according to many years of opinion polling. With both their money and their mouths, Americans strongly support welfare state programs featuring social insurance and opportunity enhancement. (This chapter's appendix provides a high-level overview of American government spending at the federal, state, and local levels. The tables and figure within the appendix are referenced in the analysis that follows.)

Consider the following: Social Security (including old-age, disability, and survivors insurance) and Medicare are two of the top five expenditure categories in the national budget. Together they accounted for just over one-third of all federal direct expenditures in 2012 (see Figure 3A.1). By any account, those are programs that respond to the philosophy of social insurance with hardly a trace of behaviorist, residualist, or other beliefs. They are two of the most popular and broadly supported programs ever adopted at the national level.[5] Social Security and Medicare have long been termed "the third rail of American politics." Any legislator touching those programs—other than to expand them—risks, according to current lore, political fury.

In addition to direct expenditures, we must consider what are known as tax expenditures. These are created when the Congress decides to forgo tax revenue from companies or individuals in return for their purchasing specified products that support a policy goal. Federal tax subsidies for employment-based pensions rank among the largest and most popular tax expenditures in the national budget (see Table 3A.1). More than $100 billion is spent annually to encourage retirement saving. This is really social insurance provision via the tax code. (We will examine the range of protections against outliving one's savings in Chapter 10.)

Moreover, the contemporary (and historical) political struggles over universal health insurance coverage mask two important facts. First, Americans overwhelmingly support universal health insurance as a national goal.[6] Second, even before the recent enactment of the complex and broadly misunderstood Affordable Care Act, a collection of programs at federal and state levels funded or subsidized health insurance for the vast majority (approximately 85%) of Americans. And again that is where the money goes. Medicaid represents more than 8% of the federal budget and about 18% of state budgets (see Figure 3A.1 and Table 3A.2). Federal tax expenditures play a large role as well. Revenue forgone to subsidize the purchase of employment-based private health insurance constitutes the largest single tax expenditure—at $177 billion in 2011—in the national budget (see Table 3A.1). Add in state, local, and federal expenditures for veterans' health insurance, direct expenditures for hospitals and public health clinics, and medical coverage under workers' compensation laws, and the total is staggering.[7]

The United States does not yet have universal health insurance coverage, and it can be a disaster for an American to slip between the cracks of existing arrangements. But that is largely due to the fragmented nature of our programs, not a repudiation of the idea of national health insurance. Americans overwhelmingly support closing the gaps in our health insurance arrangements, and they claim to be ready to spend enough to get the job done (more on this in Chapters 4 and 7). In short, while among public health insurance programs only Medicare (and indeed only Part A of it) is a pure model of a social insurance program, support for universal coverage expresses similar aims.

Finally, Americans undeniably support opportunity-enhancing public programs. Providing fishing instructions rather than (or in addition to) fish strikes a chord in American social consciousness. We do not always act on our philosophical commitments, but the United States does spend a lot on opportunity-enhancing programs. K–12 and higher education account for just over a quarter of state and local spending nationwide (see Table 3A.2).[8] Vocational education and training and employment programs add billions more. More than $100 billion in federal funds supports these state and local efforts.[9]

Indeed, when all levels of governmental spending are considered, it becomes clear that "American welfare state" is partly a misnomer. Of all public, social, and welfare expenditures, about three-quarters go toward social insurance and opportunity enhancement programs (see Table 3.2). The United States has built what we have called an insurance-opportunity state. While the term *welfare* in American usage refers generally to "means-tested" or residualist programs, those programs account for a minority share of U.S. social welfare spending. Cash welfare payments are, for all intents and purposes, extinct as a matter of public policy.

This does not mean, we acknowledge, that the American insurance-opportunity state tightly matches public sentiment, is well understood by the person on the street, or functions as well as it might. If 24% of Americans believe too much welfare causes poverty in the United States, they cannot be conversant with what American social policy actually does. Our current arrangements reflect the legacy of incremental growth, fractious politics, constitutionally designed institutional inertia, shifting national economic circumstances, and the vagaries of historical circumstances. Knowing something of that history is crucial to understanding where we are now and thinking realistically about the future. Providing that essential background is the task of Chapter 4.

APPENDIX: PUBLIC EXPENDITURE IN THE UNITED STATES

When national, state, or local governments pay cash to a beneficiary directly or to a service provider, we say an expenditure has been made. Governments can also adopt policies that reduce the amount of tax owed by a citizen who spends cash on a qualifying expenditure, such as mortgage interest payments or charitable donations. We call these tax

Table 3.2 Public Spending by Social Welfare Philosophy Category

Program	U.S. Federal ($)	State and Local ($)	All ($)	% Total
Social insurance programs				
Social Security: retirement and survivors	612		612	
Social Security: disability	128		128	
Medicare	566		566	
Government employee retirement	197	205	402	
Veterans health care	51		51	
Workers' compensation		12	12	
Unemployment insurance	132	135	267	
Total social insurance	**1,686**	**352**	**2,038**	**53.1**
Opportunity enhancement programs				
Elementary, secondary, vocational education	78	574	652	
Job training and employment, social services	30			
Higher education	1	243	244	
Total opportunity enhancement	**109**	**817**	**926**	**24.1**
Means-tested residualist programs				
Medicaid/SCHIP health insurance	285	129	414	
Food and nutrition assistance	106		106	
Assistance to students	58		58	
Earned Income Tax Credit	55		55	
Supplemental Security Income (SSI)	49		49	
Housing assistance	69		69	
Temporary Assistance for Needy Families (TANF)	21		21	
Public assistance (noncash)		82	82	
General assistance (cash)		22	22	
Total means-tested residual	**643**	**233**	**876**	**22.8**
Total social welfare program expenditure	**2,438**	**1,402**	**3,840**	**100.0**

Source: Authors' analysis of federal data for fiscal year 2011 from U.S. Census Bureau, *Statistical Abstract of the United States* (Washington, DC: Government Printing Office, 2012), Tables 473 and 474, http://www.census.gov/compendia/statab/2012/tables/12s0474.pdf; and state and local data for 2010 from Table 3A.2, this chapter. State spending growth between 2010 and 2011 was negligible, so we did not adjust the data.

expenditures. Both types of expenditures count as public policy efforts and imply certain, sometimes mixed, philosophical views.

We implicitly raised the subject of American *federalism* when we noted the substantial involvement of the individual states in running and funding social welfare programs and the emphasis on localism in the residualist vision. Government power in the United States is diffused across levels of government. National (often called federal), state, and local governments take on separate responsibilities or share responsibility for certain types of service provision. (This is not to be confused with *separation of powers,* in which the power of any one of those levels of government is split among the legislative, executive, and judicial branches.) Thus when we ask, "On what do we spend our tax dollars?" separate levels of analysis are required to clarify the answer, because Americans fund public spending through all the three levels of government.

Federal Expenditure

In fiscal year 2012, the U.S. national government spent $3.54 trillion, 68% of which went to five areas: Social Security, Medicare, Medicaid, national defense, and interest on the nation's debt (see Figure 3A.1).

The "all other" category funds many government functions and programs: the federal courts, domestic security, air traffic control, veterans' hospitals, disaster relief, international affairs, environmental protection, health research, farm subsidies, the National Aeronautics and Space Administration, national parks, and a variety of relief programs for the impoverished, which will be discussed in Chapter 5. Most of these programs are considered "discretionary" in nature, as there is no legal right, or citizen "entitlement," to the programs. Congress decides whether and

Figure 3A.1 Fiscal Year 2012 Federal Outlays (in billions of $)

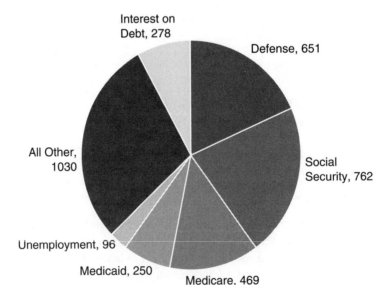

Source: Congressional Budget Office, "Monthly Budget Review: Fiscal Year 2012," October 5, 2012.

at what level to fund these programs during an annual budget process and then presents a bill to the president for approval. (You will see that even where entitlements exist, only those persons who meet the statutory criteria qualify for the program benefits.)

Federal Tax Expenditures

To encourage progress toward the attainment of a public policy goal, governments may offer special tax treatment to certain types of citizen expenditure. These policies reduce the amount government collects, but only in proportion to the extent that citizens make the preferred expenditure. These amounts are called tax expenditures. While such policy exists at all levels of government, its weight is greatest at the federal level. Table 3A.1 shows the largest current federal tax expenditures. They total $641 billion, which likely constitutes 80% of the total tax revenues forgone by all tax expenditures. (A complete thirteen-page list of tax expenditures is available from the congressional Joint Committee on Taxation.)[10]

The collective size of these expenditures is equal to close to one-fifth of total direct federal expenditures. Their impact as a tool of public policy is profound and often unrecognized.

State and Local Expenditure

State and local governments spend collectively an amount similar to that spent by the federal government. In 2010, this sum amounted to $3.1 trillion. Table 3A.2 presents a breakdown of state and local spending.

Table 3A.1 Largest Tax Expenditures in Fiscal Year 2011 (in billions of $)

Expenditure	Amount
Exclusion for employer-sponsored health insurance	177.0
Mortgage interest deduction	104.5
401(k) plans	67.1
Deduction for state and local taxes other than property tax	46.5
Step-up basis of capital gains at death	44.5
Lower rate on capital gains	44.3
Charitable deduction (other than education and health)	43.9
Pensions (defined benefit)	44.6
Exclusion of net imputed rental income	37.6
Capital gains exclusion on home sales	31.3
Top 10	641.3

Source: Catherine Rampell, "Tax Breaks: A Primer," *New York Times,* February 22, 2012.

Note: Provisions are ranked based on five-year total cost, fiscal years 2011–2015.

Table 3A.2 State and Local Government Expenditure, 2010 (in billions of $)

	State	%	Local	%	State and Local	%
Total direct expenditure	1,944	100	1,667	100	3,115	100
Elementary and secondary education	8	0.4	566	34.0	574	18.4
Medicaid	345	17.7	6	0.4	351	11.3
Higher education	203	10.4	40	2.4	243	7.8
Employee retirement	167	8.6	38	2.3	205	6.6
Highways	93	4.8	63	3.8	156	5.0
Hospitals	59	3.0	84	5.0	143	4.6
Unemployment compensation	135	6.9		0.0	135	4.3
Interest on general debt	47	2.4	72	4.3	119	3.8
Police protection	12	0.6	83	5.0	95	3.0
Health	40	2.1	41	2.5	81	2.6
Electric power	12	0.6	65	3.9	77	2.5
Correction	46	2.4	27	1.6	73	2.3
Water supply		0.0	61	3.7	61	2.0
Noncash/non-Medicaid assistance	46	2.4	35	2.1	82	2.6
Cash assistance payments	13	0.7	10	0.6	23	0.7
All other categories	718	36.9	476	28.6	697	22.4

Source: Jeffrey L. Barnett and Phillip M. Vidal, *State and Local Government Finances Summary: 2010* (Washington, DC: U.S. Census Bureau, 2012), Table A-1, http://www2.census.gov/govs/local/summary_report.pdf.

Note: Numbers do not always add to 100% due to rounding and intergovernmental spending.

Local governments play a major role in funding and providing primary and secondary education—that is, kindergarten through twelfth grade in the public schools. State governments focus on postsecondary education and often run vast systems of community colleges and state universities. The federal role in education funding is small, less than 10 cents of every dollar spent. Over a quarter of state and local spending goes toward education.

Other significant roles for state government include the maintenance of public infrastructure—roads, bridges, and mass transit—and management of state employee pension funds. In tandem with the federal government, states provide health insurance to poor kids, senior citizens, and the blind or disabled. Local governments maintain neighborhood and city infrastructure and provide protection to residents through police, fire, and emergency "911" services.

Chapter

4

The Historical Development of American Social Insurance and Its Associated Programs

THE HISTORY OF AMERICAN SOCIAL INSURANCE IS INTERESTINGLY COMPLEX. Here we offer only a brief account, one sufficient, we hope, to inform the more detailed discussion of contemporary programs in Part II of this book. Details matter, but four major themes should be kept in mind.

First, while most Americans today could probably not offer a working definition of *social insurance* or identify the programs that best fit that definition, earlier generations understood and debated the concept as a crucial issue in domestic politics. Strangely enough, as programs of social insurance were enacted and then expanded to occupy the prominent place in public budgets that we have recounted in Chapter 3, Americans' understanding (and even recognition) of the term *social insurance* atrophied. Indeed, the term has virtually disappeared from public discourse, as Figure 4.1 illustrates.

Second, an understanding of the competing philosophies of social welfare provision, as discussed in Chapter 3, is crucial for an understanding of the deeply ideological politics that have marked debates over America's programs of social insurance, whether that label is used or not. Residualists, who favor smaller government and market solutions based on individual initiative and effort, remain prominent in our public social policy conversations. Social insurance advocates have had to defend both social insurance proposals and established programs from intermittent charges of "socialism" and, in recent years, from steady attacks on social insurance programs' contribution to "big government." These political battle lines are well entrenched and spring from profound ideological differences.

Figure 4.1 Newspaper Articles with "Social Insurance" in the Title, 1900–1990

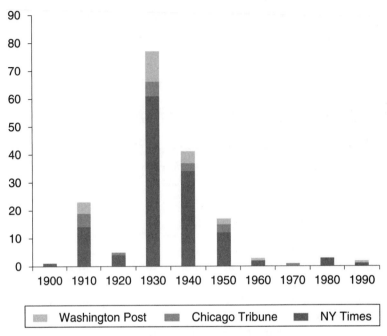

Source: Authors' search of the archives of the *Washington Post, Chicago Tribune,* and *New York Times.*

Third, while the ideological nature of social policy politics promotes apocalyptic claims and political demagoguery, there is often surprisingly strong bipartisan support for the national legislation that passes. While Democratic presidents have strongly supported social insurance expansion, Republican presidents—including Theodore Roosevelt, Dwight Eisenhower, Richard Nixon and George W. Bush—have proposed or signed into law improvements in social insurance programs. In part this is the result of a fourth feature of American social insurance politics—namely, overwhelming public support for social insurance programs based on worker contributions or otherwise "earned" through attachment to the workforce or military service.

Finally, and somewhat paradoxically, this widespread support for enacted social insurance programs hides a complex political environment, in which many proposals die and most require decades of incubation and compromise to become operational programs. The history of American social insurance has taken a highly variable path. Shifting combinations of partisan electoral fortunes, general economic

"In Washington today, the sun rose over Capitol Hill and received broad bipartisan support."

Source: Robert Mankoff/The New Yorker Collection/www.cartoonbank.com

conditions, and the state of federal and state budgets have yielded dramatically different results from one time period to the next.

THE FORMATIVE YEARS

The genesis of American social insurance conventionally is associated with the Great Depression of the 1930s and the administration of President Franklin Delano Roosevelt. Americans elected Roosevelt, a Democrat, as their thirty-second president in 1932. The former governor of New York faced tremendous challenges: an economy that had shrunk by 40% in the prior four years, a breakdown of the banking industry as citizens lost trust that their deposits were safe, an unemployment rate of 25%, and high levels of impoverishment among Americans of all regions and ages.

When addressing these challenges, FDR did not turn immediately to social insurance solutions. He instead called for programs of economic "relief and recovery," a "New Deal." He proposed public works to put citizens back to work and restore economic growth. He asked for new regulatory protections against a "return of the evils of the old order," including "supervision" of the financial industry and an end to "speculation with other people's money."[1] In short order, Congress passed most elements of his plan.

Fifteen months later, in June 1934, the president praised Congress for its work on "relief and recovery."[2] Then, he asked legislators to shift their focus to the longer-term "reconstruction"—a process in which social insurance protections were to play a large part.

When calling for this new legislation, Roosevelt returned to a theme of his inaugural address: "Our task . . . does not require the creation of new and strange values," he said. "It is rather the finding of the way once more to known, but to some degree forgotten, ideals and values."[3] Chief among these was the aspiration for economic security:

> Security was attained in the earlier days through the interdependence of members of families upon each other and of the families within a small community upon each other. The complexities of great communities and of organized industry make less real these simple means of security. Therefore, we are compelled to employ the active interest of the Nation as a whole through government in order to encourage a greater security for each individual.[4]

The president argued that all Americans "want some safeguard against misfortunes which cannot wholly be eliminated in this man-made world of ours."[5] The safeguard he had in mind was social insurance.

Like most "new" policy proposals in American political life, social insurance was not really an innovation in 1934. The earliest mention of social insurance in the American press appears to have been in a 1906 opinion piece in the *Chicago Daily Tribune* by University of Chicago professor Charles R. Henderson. According to Henderson, "Advocates of social insurance . . . [were] not asking for charity nor for class legislation and special privileges."[6] Like most early advocates of American social insurance, Henderson held up Germany as a model of how to proceed. Where social insurance was present, he argued, "we observe the advance in the condition of German workmen, their improved health and lowered mortality, their individual savings in banks."[7]

German social insurance had begun under Chancellor Otto von Bismarck, who united Germany in the late nineteenth century after leading a series of successful Prussian wars against Denmark, France, and Austria. His program evolved to include worker health insurance (1883), worker accident insurance (1884), and invalidity and old-age insurance (1889). Protections for involuntary unemployment were absent until the 1920s. The German government required workers to contribute to these funds across time, and then they received payments as their circumstances required. Popular U.S. press accounts of the German system of social insurance were frequent in the early decades of the twentieth century.

When Henderson wrote, discussion of the German system and social insurance had become "timely" and politically salient, in part because of the growth of "Progressivism" in America. The Progressive Party represented a wide-ranging movement whose partisans sought to reduce corruption in government and regulate corporate excesses. Its successes between 1890 and 1920 included universal women's suffrage, prohibition, the direct election of senators, food and drug safety laws, compulsory schooling, and antitrust laws. In many ways, the movement was a response to a growing awareness that workers and their families were too often faring poorly in the new industrialized economy. Social insurance protections were one obvious response to this diagnosis.

Among Progressivism's leaders was the war hero and former Republican U.S. president Theodore Roosevelt. In 1912, the Progressive Party nominated him as its candidate for president. (That election would prove to be the only one in the twentieth century in which the Republican and Democratic candidates were not the top two vote-getters.) At the nominating convention, Roosevelt gave a stirring speech that outlined starkly the problems of the new economy and his plan of reform through social insurance:

> It is abnormal for any industry to throw back upon the community the human wreckage due to its wear and tear, and the hazards of sickness, accident, invalidism, involuntary unemployment, and old age should be provided for through insurance. This should be made a charge in whole or in part upon the industries[,] the employer, the employee, and perhaps the people at large, to contribute severally in some degree. Wherever such standards are not met by given establishments, by given industries, are unprovided for by a legislature, or are balked by unenlightened courts, the workers are in jeopardy, the progressive employer is penalized, and the community pays a heavy cost in lessened efficiency and in misery. What Germany has done in the way of old age pensions or insurance should be studied by us, and the system adapted to our uses, with whatever modifications are rendered necessary by our different ways of life and habits of thought.[8]

Theodore Roosevelt's support for social insurance was the first voiced by a twentieth-century U.S. president. But he did not win in 1912, and it would be two decades before a federal scheme of social insurance was prominent on the agenda of another Roosevelt, Theodore's distant cousin, President Franklin Delano Roosevelt.

That did not mean that public officials ignored the problems Teddy Roosevelt outlined. Over the course of the next two decades, some, but not all, state governments implemented plans of "workmen's compensation." These "no-fault" laws allowed injured workers to receive timely financial relief when injury occurred on the job, and to avoid the uncertainty and delays of litigation. And while some pilloried social insurance as socialist, others, such as Rufus Potts, superintendent of insurance in Illinois, lauded such programs as a defense against desperate workers joining the "ranks of radicals" (code for socialists or communists).[9] Potts, like the pioneering Bismarck and many others, saw European-style social insurance programs as a solution to social unrest. Potts argued that the "respective merits" of the European systems should be studied and "a new system adaptable to the conditions peculiar to the United States" developed.[10] But social insurance's time did not come until the cataclysmic economic collapse of the 1930s made the need for new initiatives plain to almost everyone.

THE NEW DEAL ARRIVES

In a radio address on June 28, 1934, President Franklin Roosevelt revealed his plan to study and then create programmatic safeguards to protect American families' economic security. The president understood that social insurance could be characterized as a radical idea, warning Americans that opponents of social insurance will sometimes "call it 'Fascism,' sometimes 'Communism' . . . sometimes 'Socialism.' But, in doing so, they are trying to make very complex and theoretical something that is very simple and very practical."[11] Portraying his program as a practical, pragmatic approach to concrete problems was consistent with President Roosevelt's overall New Deal political strategy. Social insurance theory and foreign experience were downplayed in favor of concrete information about America's needs and specific programs to tackle these obvious problems. To make social insurance more politically feasible, the term itself was not regularly deployed. "Economic security" became the watchword for the president's proposals.

The next day, Roosevelt appointed the Committee on Economic Security, composed of five cabinet officials—the secretaries of labor, agriculture, and the Treasury; the attorney general; and the federal emergency relief administrator. They were to be assisted by an advisory council comprising leaders from all facets of American life and a technical board of policy experts. The president charged the committee simply to "study problems related to the economic security of individuals and . . . report . . . recommendations concerning proposals which in its judgment will promote greater economic security."[12] For the next six months, the committee studied and deliberated. In early January 1935, it produced a report to the president that outlined the nature of the economic insecurity Americans faced and presented its recommendations for legislation.[13]

The committee described insecurity "in every stage of life." Children constituted 40% of the 18 million Americans on emergency relief. Ten million working-age adults, no longer able to "carry the burden of current production," were unemployed; many more had lost their savings and were working at reduced incomes. In 1933, not an atypical year, almost 70,000 workers had been killed or permanently disabled on the job. And for "those now old," the committee saw insecurity "as doubly tragic, because they are beyond the[ir] productive period."

While these problems were particularly acute during the Depression, the committee insisted they were present at all times, even in "the 'normal' times of the prosperous twenties."

> The one almost all-embracing measure of security is an assured income. A program of economic security, as we vision it, must have as its primary aim the assurance of an adequate income to each human being in childhood, youth, middle age, or old age—in sickness or in health. It must provide safeguards against all of the hazards leading to destitution and dependency.

The committee's report offered five major categories of recommendations. First, the federal government needed to do everything in its power to assure full employment: "We regard work as preferable to other forms of relief where possible." This meant policies encouraging high rates of private employment. And, if and when private efforts proved insufficient, the committee recommended "the provision of public employment for those able-bodied workers whom industry cannot employ at a given time." Advance planning and coordination between federal and state governments would be required "to avoid the evils of hastily planned emergency work."

Second, the committee urged a joint federal and state government program of insurance against involuntary unemployment: "While we favor unemployment compensation in cash, we believe that it should be provided for limited periods on a contractual basis and without governmental subsidies."[14] This meant that workers and their employers ought to contribute small percentages of current wages to a pool that would pay out funds when workers lost jobs. The program would build upon existing state efforts, most of which had proven wholly inadequate during the economic turmoil of the Depression. And it would ensure that one state did not gain a competitive advantage over another by failing to provide unemployment insurance to workers.

Third, the committee recommended a three-part approach to address the insecurity of old age. A system of cash assistance, known as Old Age Assistance (OAA), would support those elderly people unable to work and without their own pensions. This means-tested program would be phased out over time as a second program for workers—Social Security's now familiar mandatory contributory pensions—built up its resources and began distributing pension payments to retirees who had contributed over time. Workers' contributions to the Social Security program were to be matched by their employers. A final plan, ultimately rejected by the Congress, was a voluntary contributory program that would allow self-employed individuals not qualifying for either of the first two programs to build up pensions.

Fourth, the committee considered the security of children. The programs of employment assurance and unemployment compensation would not help children without fathers or those in families without breadwinners. So the committee recommended grants-in-aid to existing but inadequately funded state government programs providing "mothers' pensions." The program was established and came to be known as Aid to Families with Dependent Children. Other recommendations included funding to "protect and care [for] homeless, neglected, and delinquent children and for child and maternal health services especially in rural areas . . . and . . . for transportation, hospitalization, and convalescent care of crippled and handicapped children."

Anticipating the antagonism and political importance of organized physicians' groups, the committee refrained from calling for a program of health insurance. Instead, it declared that a number of committees would produce recommendations within two months. Ultimately, the committee recommended only a federal grants-in-aid program to the states for the development of "preventative public health programs."

Two days after he received the committee's report, the president forwarded it to Congress along with a letter of strong support. He made no mention of the employment provisions, focusing instead on the four enumerated social insurance protections. He emphasized that "the system adopted, except for the money necessary to initiate it, should be self-sustaining. . . . the payment of insurance benefits should not come from the proceeds of general taxation."[15] The states—following federal standards—would administer all programs with the exception of "old-age insurance." The federal government would ensure "sound financial management" of the funds through responsible trustees. An American version of social insurance had been crafted and proposed for adoption.

Public reaction in the press and from interest groups spanned a wide range—from fervent support to bombastic opposition.[16] But in Congress the various titles of the Social Security Act received swift action and strong support. Committees made only relatively minor changes to the bill as introduced. On April 19, 1935, the House passed the committee bill without alteration by a vote of 372–33.[17] Two months later, the Senate passed a similar bill 76–6.[18] A House-Senate Conference Committee reconciled differences in the two versions in July, and both chambers approved the final version by voice vote in early August. The following day's *New York Times* front-page headline read "Social Security Bill Voted; Will Benefit 30,000,000."[19] On August 9, President Roosevelt signed the Social Security Act of 1935 into law. From this point forward, "social insurance" in America would be synonymous with Social Security, a development that would eventually confuse rather than clarify the topic for many Americans.

EARLY EXPANSION

In 1937, workers and their employers began making what would later be known as FICA (Federal Insurance Contributions Act) payments into the Social Security "reserve" fund. The original contribution rate for the old-age pension program was set at 1% of worker wages for both employer and employee. No one was slated to receive benefits until 1942. This would allow the reserve balance to build up to a level that would be regarded as actuarially sound.

During the first four years of the program, contributions swelled the reserve fund to levels much higher than its planners had anticipated. In response, the Social Security Advisory Committee recommended a number of modifications in the program, and President Roosevelt forwarded them on to Congress.[20]

Roosevelt called for more generous pension benefits to the elderly and urged that payments begin immediately. He sought to expand the reach of social insurance by extending benefits to dependents of qualifying workers, specifically their wives and children. He asked Congress to "extend our Federal old-age insurance system so as to provide regular monthly benefits not only to the aged but also to the dependent children of workers dying before reaching retirement age."[21]

In June of 1939, the House of Representatives passed the expansion plan in a bipartisan vote of 361–2.[22] Two weeks later, the Senate passed a similar bill 59–4. After a two-month delay caused by a dispute between two Democratic senators over the size of old-age assistance program matching grants to poor states, both chambers passed the conference report and sent the bill to the president for his certain approval.[23]

The 1939 amendments to the Social Security Act expanded both the number of beneficiaries and the scale of benefits. "Instead of a straight old-age retirement system," the *Washington Post* reported, "the amendments create a combination old-age retirement and insurance plan for more than 46,000,000 workers and their dependents." Social Security Board chairman Arthur Altmeyer called the new program a "group insurance program."[24] Another foundational element of American social insurance, survivors insurance, had been added: protections to family income now extended to the risk of early death of a breadwinner.

CONSOLIDATION AND CONFLICT

Although elected by an overwhelming majority in 1940 to an unprecedented (and now unconstitutional) third term, President Franklin Delano Roosevelt was unable to patch the obvious holes in the social insurance programs enacted during his first two terms. Two months before the surprise Japanese attack on Pearl Harbor, Roosevelt proposed "a single, all-inclusive, national social insurance system."[25] By all-inclusive, Roosevelt meant that existing protections against old age, unemployment, and early death of a family member would be combined with new protections against disability. Also, in emphasizing "national," he highlighted the desirability of making the unemployment insurance program available to all Americans.

In the midst of World War II, these proposals languished, but Harry Truman, who succeeded Roosevelt upon his death in April 1945, carried on the struggle for a more comprehensive social insurance scheme. Just three months after the Japanese surrendered, Truman proposed expanding American social insurance programs to include both sickness and disability.[26] Acutely aware of the American Medical Association's deep hostility toward both health insurance and disability payments based in part on medical examination, President Truman used his message to throw up anticipatory defenses. He assured physicians and hospitals that they would be reimbursed at levels consistent with "the best they have received in peace time years," and he repeated like a mantra that he was not proposing "socialized medicine." As Truman explained his proposal, health care providers and patients respectively would continue to provide services and choose their providers in private markets. The government would be involved only in financing care. As Truman put it: "Socialized medicine means that all doctors are employees of the Government. The American people want no such system. No such system is here proposed."[27]

The AMA response, through Dr. Morris Fishbein, the organization's president, was swift and hyperbolic:

[This] is the first step toward the regimentation of utilities, of industry, of finance, and eventually of labor itself. This is the kind of regimentation that led to totalitarianism in Germany and the downfall of that nation. . . . no one will ever convince the physicians of America that the . . . bill is not socialized medicine.[28]

Fishbein appealed to Americans to lobby their representatives to defeat Truman's proposals, and, while the proposals remained popular with the public, the congressional balance of power favored conservative positions after the end of World War II. Congress failed to act.

Although the Republican Party, riding on the shoulders of General Dwight Eisenhower, supreme commander of Allied forces in World War II, won the presidency and both houses of Congress in 1952, attempts to strengthen America's social insurance system did not cease. Eisenhower, following the lead of his secretary of health, education, and welfare, Oveta Culp Hobby, took a more incremental approach. The administration proposed merely to extend the Social Security pension system to self-employed professionals and to remove the penalty—built into the way Social Security pensions were calculated—that radically reduced the benefits of workers who became disabled before retirement age.[29]

Conscious of the need to win over his own party, as well as business groups, President Eisenhower characterized the federal social insurance system as a base upon which "each individual has a better chance to achieve for himself the assurance of continued income, after his earning days are over and for his family after his death."[30] Once again the administration had to confront charges of socialism. Administration officials were sent forth to sell the president's program. Before the Capital Press Club, Undersecretary Arthur Larson lamented the confusion of socialism with social insurance.[31] Larson called the conflation of these two philosophies "one of the most widespread and baseless misconceptions in history":

We are told over and over again that all this sort of thing is creeping socialism, and that it can lead in the end to a society in which we are all reduced to a mass of soulless, cringing dull-eyed slaves gratefully accepting our support from the beneficent but all-powerful state. It never seems to bother these speakers that there is not one bit of concrete proof or evidence that income-insurance really makes Americans soft and lazy.[32]

Incrementalism and the administration's full-court press prevailed. The House approved Eisenhower's plan 356 to 8, and the Senate voted it out in a voice vote.[33] A year later, Eisenhower was able to add cash payments for disabled workers over the age of 50. Five years later, Congress removed the age-50 limitation, making disability insurance available to all workers who had contributed to the Social Security system in a sufficient number of calendar quarters. Thus the basic elements of a comprehensive social insurance system—Old-Age, Survivors, and Disability Insurance (OASDI), unemployment insurance (UI), and state and federal workers' compensation (WC) programs—have been in place for more than a half century. By 1960, only health insurance and some form of universal non–means-tested support for families with children remained as gaps in America's social insurance regime.

Since 1960, American social insurance arrangements have been largely stable. Aside from health insurance, which we discuss in the next section, most amendments have strengthened social insurance legislation by addressing economic, fiscal, and demographic contingencies that have threatened existing programs. Means-tested programs for the aged, blind, and disabled have been nationalized under the Supplemental Security Income program, which unified eligibility standards. Social Security retirement pensions have been tied to changes in the cost of living, and the pension system's finances have been shored up by increases in tax levels and shifts in the normal retirement age. The initially popular but subsequently deeply controversial AFDC program has been supplanted by Temporary Assistance for Needy Families, combined with a significant broadening of the Earned Income Tax Credit for the working poor. All of these developments are important in their own way and have their own politics and political histories. But none of them changed the main lines of development of social insurance provision in the United States.

In sum, the basic threats to family economic security recognized in the early years of the twentieth century have by the twenty-first been moderated by public programs directed separately at each threat. But, as we shall see in more detail in Part II, none of these largely social insurance programs is simple in either its structure or its administration, and no two are exactly alike.

Complexity in American social insurance arrangements is the offspring of political compromises. Those compromises have been made necessary by crosscutting commitments, all of which had political support. Indeed, virtually all Americans believe in both protection for the economically vulnerable and individual responsibility; both an active government and a small one; both national solutions for national needs and local control and state administration. Add in shifting economic fortunes, feast and famine in public accounts, and the usual partisan wrangling that attends any governmental initiative, and you have a formula for incremental, complex, and occasionally incoherent public action. The piecemeal emergence of universal, or near-universal, health insurance is a similar story, but, if anything, an even more complicated one in both its politics and its ultimate programmatic expression.

THE BATTLE FOR UNIVERSAL HEALTH INSURANCE

The federal government's involvement in health care or health insurance for Americans can be traced back to the 1790s, when Congress enacted a special tax on seamen to support a system of seamen's hospitals to provide for their care. But we need not press our story back that far. Fast-forward to the late 1940s, when President Truman proposed (and failed to have adopted) a general scheme of publicly financed health insurance.

By the time of Truman's proposal, the federal government was already subsidizing private employer-provided health insurance. Although this is now the principal method through which working-age Americans receive health care coverage, the expansion of subsidized, employment-based health insurance was, in part, inadvertent. Responding to, or perhaps one should say evading, wartime wage and price controls, employers during World War II began to provide company pensions and health insurance benefits, which were not counted as wages. Competition for labor during the postwar economic boom and similar wage controls during the Korean conflict accelerated the adoption of employment-based health insurance. Union support provided an additional boost for employer-provided health insurance.

Wage and price controls aside, other considerations made this an attractive bargain for both employers and employees. These benefits were not counted as income to employees, although they could be deducted as costs to the employer on a company's income tax returns. This implicit public subsidy—a tax expenditure in budgetary terms—could be divided between employers and employees. A dollar in wages was a dollar in cost to the employer and a dollar of taxable income to the employee, but a dollar's worth of health insurance benefits was the equivalent of an after-tax dollar for the worker. For an employee paying income tax at a 20% rate, an employer need only provide 80 cents' worth of health insurance to provide the equivalent of a dollar in wages. If the worker, or a workers' union, bargains for 90 cents' worth of health insurance, both employer and employees are better off substituting health insurance for cash.

U.S. Treasury regulations also helped to broaden employee participation. Recognizing that the government was now subsidizing something of value to American workers, the federal government assumed the responsibility of insuring that employers did not limit this subsidized insurance to only a favored few in the workforce. Hence the Treasury's so-called nondiscrimination rules, which condition the deductibility of insurance costs to the employer on broad coverage of the company's employees. Employment-based plans came to have the further benefit of freedom from state insurance regulation because of the federal Employee Retirement Income Security Act of 1974 (ERISA).

This approach to health insurance coverage has expanded greatly since the 1950s. In 2011, 170 million people, 55.1% of all Americans, received some form of health insurance coverage through the workplace.[34] This included 115.4 million "working-age" Americans (those between 18 and 65 years old), or 59.7% of the total.[35] But retired Americans, unemployed Americans, and those who work in low-wage industries not offering health insurance coverage derive no benefits from this scheme. What about them?

Until 1965, these categories of Americans were left to the private insurance market, where individual policies were generally unaffordable. Those without health insurance and the ability to pay for their care depended on charity provided by public and private hospitals and uncompensated care from physicians and other health care providers. Then, as part of the tsunami of social legislation that constituted President Lyndon Baines Johnson's "Great Society" programs, the aged, disabled, and impoverished began receiving publicly provided health insurance through the new Medicare and Medicaid programs.

Although enacted together in a sort of grand compromise between liberals and conservatives, Medicare and Medicaid have quite different political underpinnings. Medicare, which now covers the aged and disabled, was put forward as a necessary completion of the existing Social Security pension system. Because seniors have much higher average medical costs than those under 65, health care expenses were threatening the security that Social Security pensions provided. Medicare was also, of course, a step toward public provision of universal health insurance—at least that is what many of its proponents believed.

In statements made when signing the Medicare legislation, President Johnson noted both themes. On universal health insurance, he said:

> It was a generation ago that Harry Truman said, and I quote him: "Millions of our citizens do not now have a full measure of opportunity to achieve and to enjoy good health. Millions do not now have protection or security against the economic effects of sickness. And the time has now arrived for action to help them attain that opportunity and to help them get that protection." Well, today . . . we are taking such action—20 years later.[36]

But, of course, Truman was proposing universal health insurance, not health insurance only for the aged.

In partially explaining why the aged were the focus of concern in the Medicare legislation, Johnson emphasized how health care costs undermined the economic security that private savings and the social insurance system sought to provide. As Johnson put it:

> No longer will illness crush and destroy the savings that they have so carefully put away over a lifetime so that they might enjoy dignity in their later years. No longer will young families see their own incomes, and their own hopes, eaten away simply because they are carrying out their deep moral obligations to their parents, and to their uncles, and their aunts.[37]

In mentioning the burden on younger families, Johnson folded Medicare into the overall scheme of social insurance designed, ideally, to provide some measure of security to families over the life cycle.

Johnson's extension of health insurance coverage to retired Americans no longer covered by employment-based insurance was hugely controversial.[38] The AMA remained adamantly opposed. The organization, and others opposed to social insurance, regarded Medicare as the first step toward government control of health care provision. Moreover, opponents of "big government" could portray the Medicare enactment as a major expansion of the government's role and a dangerous incursion into "private markets." A potential legislative stalemate was averted, oddly enough, by the addition of another program to the mix. Medicaid was largely the work of Medicare's opponents, their attempt to frustrate the future expansion of Medicare to additional populations.[39]

Whatever the Medicaid program's strategic political origins, its history of considerable political support has been something of a mystery. Middle-income families have difficulties maintaining health insurance and meeting the costs of co-payments and deductibles under employment-based private insurance plans. Why should they not resent substantial public expenditures for "medically needy" Americans, many of whom might be imagined to have brought their neediness on themselves? The answer is that, to some extent, they do, but other factors are at work. First, a substantial portion of Medicaid dollars pay for the health services used by poor children and the poor aged. Americans historically view these groups as among the "deserving poor" and are prepared to provide aid to them, particularly in-kind aid like health care. Second, remember President Johnson's remarks concerning the effect on young families of having to take on the burden of the health expenses of their parents. This is particularly important where the expenses are for very costly nursing home care, covered under Medicaid, but not through Medicare. According to a Met Life survey, in 2012 the average annual cost of nursing home care in a semiprivate room was more than $81,000.[40]

Third, and crucial to the support of some conservative members of Congress, localities, both cities and counties, have long run charity hospitals. Many private and nonprofit hospitals have also provided uncompensated care to those unable to pay their medical bills, and employers understand that uncompensated care gets compensated in part through the premiums that they pay for their employees' health insurance coverage. These considerations have provided a coalition of incidental beneficiaries of the Medicaid program who were and are important to conservative legislators. In the peculiar politics of American social provision, somehow making big government bigger by adding Medicaid to Medicare produced a package that was more attractive to Americans. Congressional representatives and senators who did not share their liberal colleagues' commitment to social insurance found means-tested and state-administered Medicaid more to their liking. Equally or more important, Medicaid made the liberal effort to expand Medicare to the rest of the population more problematic. After all, the elderly and most of America's poor were now protected, removing the most obvious objectives of reform.

This was hardly the first or the last time that American social provision has produced strange political bedfellows. Other examples include the urban liberal and rural conservative coalition that banded together to enact the initial food stamp program; a similar story can be told about the Clinton-era welfare reforms. That episode combined residualist and behaviorist approaches (TANF) to cash assistance for low-income families with a very substantial broadening of eligibility and benefits for families who could qualify for the EITC. And, of course, stitching together coalitions of very different ideological predispositions tends to produce compromise programs. Such compromises often result in puzzling gaps and inadequacies in protection, which helps to explain the conventional description of American social policy as a patchwork quilt with a number of the patches ragged or missing.

As of 1965, the missing patches in the American health insurance quilt could be fairly easily identified: families of working-age adults not poor enough to qualify for Medicaid who were either unemployed or employed in occupations or with companies that did not offer employment-based health insurance coverage. Some members of that group may be covered if they are eligible for veterans' health benefits, the only truly socialized medicine available in the United States. The Veterans

Administration provides not health insurance but health care services through its hospitals and outpatient clinics.

Medicare's original proponents had believed that once that program was established it was only a matter of time before it would insure most, if not all, Americans. Medicare for all, or something very like that, has been the consistent goal of universal health insurance advocates from Harry Truman's time to the present. Once some health insurance program or other covered most of the population, however, filling the remaining gap has proved remarkably difficult. The explanation for this hotly contested movement toward universality must be based on the peculiarities (one might say the ironies) of American political life.

Virtually all Americans say they believe that everyone should have access to decent health care and the access to health insurance that would pay for such care. Moreover, virtually every administration since 1965, both Democratic and Republican, has made proposals, and often enacted legislation, that would strengthen and enlarge both Medicare and Medicaid. Yet the grand bargain that would cover the uninsured has remained elusive. The Clinton administration failed spectacularly after making universal health insurance its signature domestic policy proposal.

In 2010, President Barack Obama and his congressional allies managed to enact the Patient Protection and Affordable Care Act, a statute that promises to cover virtually all the uninsured. But that legislation is so complex and compromised that it threatens to unravel before it can be fully implemented. Twenty-six states along with others sued to have the statute declared unconstitutional in whole or in part. The Supreme Court's decision was, essentially, split: the mandate requiring individuals to buy insurance was upheld, but the expansion of Medicaid was weakened.[41] Polling has repeatedly found that a majority of Americans dislike the statute, either because they think it goes too far or because they think it does not go far enough.[42] Administrators charged with implementing the law have found some provisions to be essentially unworkable. Why, more than a half century after Harry Truman first proposed universal health care insurance coverage as a national responsibility, should this "successful" effort at achieving that dream leave Americans with a patchwork of programs, the most recent of which is widely misunderstood, unpopular, and potentially unworkable?

Interest group politics provide one explanation. Although the medical profession is no longer unified in opposition to national health insurance, the insurance industry is. A health insurance industry campaign against the Clinton health insurance proposals helped to derail that effort in 1993–1994. Determined to avoid Clinton's disappointment, the

Obama administration built its reform around private health insurance. The result was a complex set of arrangements involving new federal regulation of private health insurance firms, state-operated insurance "exchanges" (essentially marketplaces), mandates on both employers and individuals to provide or acquire insurance or suffer tax penalties, subsidies for health insurance acquisition by those unable to afford it, and a large set of potentially useful but unproven and easily mischaracterized initiatives to control medical care costs.

The popular provisions in the Affordable Care Act—such as the ability to keep children on their parents' health insurance policies until age 26 and the prohibition against refusing to insure individuals because of preexisting conditions—coexist with other features that many Americans find objectionable. The individual mandate is thought by many to be un-American, and the cost-cutting proposals have been mischaracterized in ways that have left many Americans hesitant, with some believing, erroneously, that the legislation contemplates "death panels" that will decide whether it is worth it for insurance to pay for needed health care services that might save their lives. Moreover, precisely because the vast majority of Americans are covered by some form of health insurance, many worry that any changes brought about by the new law will make them worse off. To summarize, the Affordable Care Act of 2010 ended up as a gap-filling solution that is too complex for most Americans to understand and for many to fully support. We will look more closely at the act and its prospects in Chapter 7.

ACCOMPLISHMENTS AND CHALLENGES

Over the past one hundred years, the American aspiration for social insurance protection against the common, indeed universally shared, risks to family economic security has been in large part fulfilled. We now have programs or groups of programs that address all of those risks and that in their combined coverage are very nearly universal. This does not mean that they are adequate or work well all of the time or for all Americans. It does not mean the current programs should be retained without modification, but how much has been accomplished should not be overlooked. In 1959, before Social Security was fully phased in for most workers and before Medicare had been adopted, the poverty rate for persons over 65 years of age was 35%. By 1979, it had dropped to 15.2%, and by 1996 to 10.8%. A substantial portion of this improvement was the direct result of Social Security and Medicare.

Do Americans Still Support Social Insurance Programs?

Strong public support for social insurance is not a relic of the past. In a 2013 poll commissioned by the National Academy of Social Insurance, respondents overwhelmingly reported strong support for the Social Security retirement program, a willingness to pay more to sustain or increase benefits, and eroding confidence that Congress will make the adjustments that they favor. The report's conclusion summarizes its findings:

> Seventy-eight years after Social Security began, Americans maintain strong support for it. Many Americans lack confidence in Social Security's future but when given accurate information are much more likely to consider Social Security's financing to be a manageable problem or not a problem at all. Americans of all racial and ethnic groups want to strengthen Social Security's finances and are willing to contribute more to the program. African Americans and Hispanics, who are more reliant on Social Security benefits in old age, express higher levels of confidence in and particularly strong support for Social Security. Americans across racial and ethnic lines clearly want to close the system's projected financing gap and ensure that the program will protect future generations. But rather than doing so in part by reducing benefits, they prefer a package of changes that closes the gap without benefit cuts—and pays for benefit improvements. Americans' willingness to pay more for Social Security shows that they view it as vital insurance that provides essential economic security for themselves, their families and their communities.

Note: The National Academy of Social Insurance is a federally chartered honorary organization patterned on the National Academy of Sciences. Members of the academy are drawn from the ranks of academic scholars of social insurance and social insurance professionals in government and the private sector. For a description of the survey cited above, see Jasmine V. Tucker, *Strengthening Social Security: Views among African Americans, Hispanic Americans, and White Americans* (Washington, DC: National Academy of Social Insurance, May 2013), http://www.nasi .org/sites/default/files/research/Views_Among_African_Americans_Hispanic_Americans.pdf.

Despite the heated rhetoric that now dominates partisan debate, most of the extensions and improvements of America's social insurance programs have been bipartisan affairs. Much social insurance legislation has passed Congress with overwhelming majorities, sometimes unanimity. The leadership on social insurance improvement has typically come from Democratic administrations, but Republican administrations have led some reforms and, in time, accepted most. It is worth reflecting on the statements of conservative Republican presidents.

President Richard Nixon, when signing the Social Security Amendments of 1972, said it gave him "very great pleasure to sign . . . legislation that will end many old inequities and will provide a new uniform system of well-earned benefits for older Americans, the blind, and the disabled." He added that the law "contain[ed] many improvements and expansions of the social security, Medicare, and Medicaid programs which this Administration recommended and is proud to bring into reality today."[43] Ronald Reagan, when signing the Social Security Amendments of 1983, emphasized:

> These amendments reaffirm the commitment of our government to the performance and stability of social security. It was nearly 50 years ago when, under the leadership of Franklin Delano Roosevelt, the American people reached a great turning point, setting up the social security system. . . . Today we reaffirm Franklin Roosevelt's commitment that social security must always provide a secure and stable base so that older Americans may live in dignity.[44]

The first President Bush, in his State of the Union Address in 1990, claimed there was one thing he hoped would be agreed upon:

> I'm talking about Social Security. To every American out there on Social Security, to every American supporting that system today, and to everyone counting on it when they retire, we made a promise to you, and we are going to keep it. We rescued the system in 1983, and it's sound again by bipartisan arrangement. Our budget fully funds today's benefits, and it assures that future benefits will be funded as well. The last thing we need to do is mess around with Social Security.[45]

And President George W. Bush, on signing the act that provided prescription drug coverage under Medicare, described the program as "a great achievement of a compassionate government" and stated, "Each generation benefits from Medicare. Each generation has a duty to strengthen Medicare, and this generation is fulfilling our duty."[46]

That these conservative presidents, backed by equally or more conservative legislators, should have supported America's programs to protect the aged, poor, and disabled is, in one sense, not too surprising. The programs that they mentioned and supported were and are enormously popular with the American public. Moreover, all of these presidents recognized at some level that social insurance was and is a deeply conservative idea. Early social insurance advocates never doubted that capitalism was a superior means for organizing economic activity and that most Americans would get most of their income from productive work. What they saw was that the movement from an agrarian to an industrial economy created risks that would threaten economic security and could undermine acceptance of a capitalist market economy.

The aim of social insurance was to cushion workers and their families from the many threats to economic security that capitalism produces while, at the same time, permitting the market economy to produce its undeniable gains in national income. Social insurance has always been a program for political moderates. It occupies a middle position between egalitarian efforts to equalize economic results and narrower conservative programs that rely on charity, means-tested programs with minimalist benefits, and behavior modification. Americans are mostly political moderates, and our social insurance schemes, broadly speaking, are consistent with that picture of our political culture.

But this history is not just a success story. As we shall see in more detail in the next six chapters, compromises have produced programs that are often less than adequate and sometimes, at the extreme, dysfunctional. Moreover, as the political process addressed particular economic security risks, the conversation changed from an overarching vision of family economic security to debates about particular program features and the possibilities of coalition building through compromise. An earlier social insurance vision that proceeded from a common understanding of recognized risks has fragmented. The ideological underpinnings of social insurance regularly get lost in the political discussion, which takes place program by program or program feature by program feature.

This is no trivial loss. In recent decades, the ideological commitment to private markets and individual responsibility has strengthened. Social insurance programs now face critics arguing for the "privatization" of what they consider unsustainable entitlement programs.[47] Rather than being seen as supporting a capitalist system by cushioning its inevitable risks, social insurance arrangements are portrayed as undermining private markets and personal responsibility, or as threatening the overall fiscal health of the nation. With little public understanding of how social insurance programs fit together, the prospects for individual programs are more uncertain. We will have more to say about these issues in Part III when we take up the subject of America's major social insurance programs in the context of contemporary budgetary concerns. For now, we will put aside these broad concerns to look more carefully at the programs that make up the American insurance landscape.

Part

I I

Threats and Protections

We turn now to a review of America's programmatic protections against the six threats to adequate family income. Those protections take various forms: near-universal social insurance programs, federal block grants to states, tax expenditures, and means-tested social assistance programs. Both public and private organizations play substantial roles in the over-all provision of protection, with national, state, and local officials active in both policy development and administration.

We proceed chronologically, in effect applying a "life-cycle" model to the protections.[1] First is the period of childhood, when an individual largely depends on the income of family members or guardians. Two threats predominate in this period—birth into a poor family and the early death (or disability) of a family breadwinner. Then we consider the period of working age, when adults are primarily responsible for providing their families' incomes. Ill health, involuntary unemployment, and disability are the major threats. Finally, we turn to retirement, when outliving one's savings constitutes the major threat to adequate income. The increased likelihood of expensive medical and long-term care services is a fact of retirement years. Absent astute planning and good luck, ill health can quickly deplete a lifetime of savings.

5

The Threat of Birth into a Poor Family

THE STUBBORNLY PERSISTENT REALITY OF CHILDHOOD POVERTY in the United States stands in stark contrast to the nation's successful reduction of poverty among senior citizens. When Lyndon Johnson declared "war on poverty" in 1964, 30% of the elderly were impoverished; by 2011, less than 9% were (see Figure 5.1). Poverty rates for children have waxed and waned over time, but they have stayed between 15% and 22%. If we imagine the war on poverty as focused on the two largest groups not in the workforce, the young and the old, this has been a war on two fronts but with victory in only the battle against poverty in old age. There the war has been waged primarily through the Social Security and Medicare programs.

More than 16 million American children, more than one in five, live in families with incomes below the federal poverty level.[1] Over time, some poor families with children will rise out of poverty, but others not currently considered poor will suffer spells of impoverishment. Families below or near the poverty level fail to earn adequate income to ensure proper nutrition, shelter, and health care for their children. Other important wants, such as access to preschool education and day care while parents work, often go unmet.

Being born into a poor family is the strongest predictor of persistent childhood impoverishment. As we have seen, poor children are much more likely than their better-off counterparts to become victims of violence, high school dropouts, teenage parents, or prison inmates. Although some will lead productive, successful adult lives, a much greater percentage of middle- and upper-class children will do so. The deck is simply stacked against children born into poverty. Where one starts is a strong predictor of where one ends up. Sadly, the gradient appears to be steepening.[2]

Figure 5.1 Poverty Rates by Age, 1959–2011

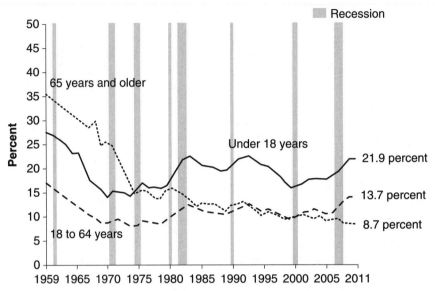

Source: Carmen DeNavas-Walt, Bernadette D. Proctor, and Jessica C. Smith, *Income, Poverty, and Health Insurance Coverage in the United States: 2011* (Washington, DC: Government Printing Office, 2012), 15.

The United States, among the richest nations in human history, possesses the wherewithal to eliminate childhood poverty. But doing so would require eliminating the poverty of parents as well. Any agreement among Americans on the lofty goal of ending childhood poverty quickly falls apart with this realization. We want to help the deserving poor, which children surely are, but we are not so sure about their parents or caretakers. We worry about programs that, by ending a child's impoverishment, may encourage the dependency of adults in the same household. Struggling with our own family bills, we aren't anxious to subsidize those who have children but can't support them.

On the other hand, once blameless children are born into poverty, none of us believe that they are unworthy of community support. We believe adequate provision ought to be made to ensure that children are well fed, educated, and safely housed, and that they have access to necessary medical services. We suspect that many of those children's parents and grandparents were born into similarly disadvantaged circumstances and may have suffered from racial or ethnic discrimination. There is a persistent nature to poverty in America. And, finally, we know that poor families tend to be ones headed by women, where men either cannot or do not provide for their offspring (see Figure 5.2).

Help could come in the form of social insurance. All children—future workers—could be insured against birth into poverty, in effect receiving

Figure 5.2 Distribution of Families by Income, 2009

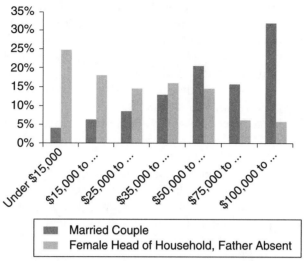

Source: U.S. Census Bureau, *Statistical Abstract of the United States: 2012* (Washington, DC: Government Printing Office, 2012), Table 698.

benefits when young in return for the expectation of future contributions into the pool. Many industrialized nations provide children's allowances— or "demogrants"—to all families with children. Although such programs "target" many non-needy families, this seeming "waste" is mostly recovered through progressive taxation. Such programs have never been popular in the United States. When George McGovern proposed a demogrant program in his 1972 quest for the presidency, he was almost laughed off the campaign trail. Instead, America has relied primarily on means-tested social assistance for poor families with children.

Cash assistance programs—never lucrative to parents or poor children—have changed greatly in character over the past decade. As we saw in Chapter 3, in 1996, a Republican Congress and Democratic president, Bill Clinton, did away with the national means-tested Aid to Families with Dependent Children. Under AFDC, states were required to provide aid to all eligible families as defined in part by federal standards. Funding was provided by states and the national government according to a formula that favored subsidies to the states with the largest populations of poor families. AFDC was replaced by Temporary Assistance for Needy Families, a state-based social assistance program. Under TANF, the federal government provides a fixed amount, a block grant, to states, which now determine eligibility criteria. Even those who qualify under their states' programs are not guaranteed cash assistance; rather, they receive services designed to promote entry into the workforce. Cash assistance, where available, is limited to five years. One of the principal purposes of the 1996 welfare reform was "to encourage work." But, as TANF moved toward stringency and work promotion, other work-subsidy and in-kind programs became somewhat more generous. President Clinton fought for and signed into law a bill that provided an expanded refundable tax credit (the Earned Income Tax Credit) to low-income workers, in effect providing a wage bonus to those working sufficient hours to qualify. Over the 2000s, Congress expanded other social assistance programs for poor families, including food stamps and health insurance. None of these programs provokes the same level of concern about dependency that plagued cash benefits under AFDC. The EITC is available only to those already working, and Americans are prepared to attack hunger (through food stamps, now the Supplemental Nutrition Assistance Program, or SNAP) and childhood illness (through the State Children's Health Insurance Program, or SCHIP, formerly the Children's Health Insurance Program, or CHIP) without too much concern for these in-kind benefits' effects on work incentives. These broader programs, targeted primarily at poor families with children, combine with a host of other in-kind transfers, opportunity-enhancing services, and tax code provisions to create a complex landscape of assistance to children born into poverty.

Yet high levels of childhood poverty persist. Understanding why requires that we examine these programs individually and collectively to appreciate the nature and limits of America's commitment to some of its most vulnerable citizens, children born into poor families.

MEASURING POVERTY IN AMERICA: A BRIEF DISCUSSION

But first, what is poverty? More specifically, how is the federal poverty level (FPL) determined? Is the definition one that, if scrutinized, would command broad public support?

Critics from both sides of the political spectrum argue that the FPL is a poor measure of underlying want, both understating and overstating the extent of poverty in the United States. There is much truth to these critiques. The FPL measure fails, for example, to consider cash and non-cash government benefits received by poor families, thus overstating poverty. Analysts from the conservative Heritage Foundation estimate that these amounts average about $9,000 per year to "every poor and low-income American."[3] In a 2008 report, two liberal think tanks estimated the per capita federal spending on all children at $2,895. Poor children, in fact, receive much more.[4]

Other factors lead to underestimations of poverty. The FPL is a measure of gross rather than net income. Expenses that draw cash from poor families, such as payroll taxes and expenses for health care and work-related child care, are not considered. Moreover, the FPL makes no adjustments for geographic variation in housing and other costs. Accordingly, poverty is underestimated in high-cost areas and overestimated in low-cost regions. The federal poverty calculation is indeed a crude, imperfect measure of the condition it aims to describe.

Beyond the mix of understatement and overstatement of actual poverty, there is a more fundamental issue: Does this measure make sense in twenty-first-century America? The Department of Agriculture established the basic approach of the FPL in the 1950s. Estimating that lower-income families spent roughly one-third of their incomes on food, the department priced a basket of food items that could sustain a family, at least temporarily, without endangering the family's nutritional adequacy. It multiplied this number by three and arrived at the so-called poverty level for families of various sizes. Adjustments have since been made to reflect higher food prices, but the basic approach to the FPL has remained constant ever since. Students of poverty have long recognized that the mix of family expenditures has shifted substantially since the 1950s. Food now represents considerably less than one-third of family living costs, and the "temporary emergency" food basket priced in the original Agriculture Department computation was a lowball estimate to begin with.

In 1995, a study panel convened at the nonpartisan National Academy of Sciences concluded that a new poverty measure was needed.[5] The original formula required expansion to include the costs of shelter, clothing, and "a small additional amount." The new measure also needed to take into account government benefits that increased and taxation that reduced the family income available for consumption. Finally, adjustments had to be made for regional variations in the cost of living and to account for the reality of substantial out-of-pocket expenses for things like medical services and child care.

In 2011, researchers at the Census Bureau compared the traditional poverty rate calculation with that recommended by the National Academy of Sciences.[6] Using this new (and presumably more realistic) measure, they found a lower rate of poverty among children but somewhat higher rates among adults, especially older Americans (see Figure 5.3). The EITC, SNAP, and housing subsidies produced most of the measured improvement, but FICA taxes, work expenses, and out-of-pocket medical payments counteracted their effects.

For children, then, the more robust measure suggests a number closer to one in six, rather than one in five, living in poverty. Perhaps more strikingly, the Census Bureau found that one in twenty American children live in families with incomes at 50% or less than the refined poverty level.[7] The array of poverty programs we describe below clearly fails to provide much assistance to this cohort. These children live in

Figure 5.3 U.S. Poverty Rates Using Two Measures for Total Populations and Age Group, 2010

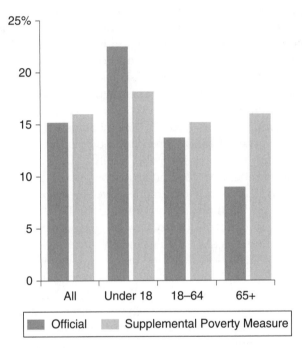

Source: Kathleen Short, *The Research Supplemental Poverty Measure: 2010,* Current Population Reports P60-241 (Washington, DC: U.S. Census Bureau, November 2011), 5, Figure 1, http://www.census.gov/prod/2011pubs/p60-241.pdf.

abject poverty. Moreover, the poverty level has no magical properties. An income that just exceeds that figure does not suddenly make a family well-off. Indeed, living in a family whose income is near the poverty level but not below it is still a substantial disadvantage. According to Census Bureau data, 35% of American children live in families having incomes no more than 150% of the poverty threshold.[8] Because many social programs use the poverty level as a condition of eligibility, these families are excluded from assistance.

CASH ASSISTANCE

From AFDC to TANF: The Disappearance of Welfare as We Knew It

In 1996, more than 12.6 million poor Americans—8.7 million of them children—qualified for and received cash payments under AFDC.[9] The average family benefit was $374 per month.[10] Total program funding was $20 billion, of which $15 billion was provided as matching funds to states by the federal government.[11]

That year, the Congress passed and President Clinton signed the Personal Responsibility and Work Opportunity Reconciliation Act. The act ended the legal right to cash assistance for poor families under the Social Security Act of 1935. As noted earlier, AFDC was replaced by a federal block grant program—Temporary Assistance for Needy Families—with broader aims than direct financial relief. Among them were the prevention of out-of-wedlock births, the encouragement of two-parent families, and the elimination of the "dependence of needy parents on government benefits."[12] The means of doing so included job preparation and a clear time limit—five years—on the duration of benefits. In terms of the approaches to social welfare provision discussed in Chapter 3, the predominantly residualist approach of AFDC was replaced by a strongly behaviorist program.

The block grant funding was set at $16 billion in 1996, and that figure has remained constant. The effect as of 2012 was a reduction of program funding, in real terms, of 28%.[13] Unlike the AFDC program, in which the vast majority of funds found their way into the wallets of poor families, only 29% of TANF funds end up as direct "cash assistance" to program beneficiaries.[14]

"Welfare" caseloads and benefit levels have fallen dramatically. As of the end of 2011, the total caseload was 1.95 million families, a decline of just over 50% from when AFDC ended in 1996.[15] The average monthly beneficiary payment reported for 2009 was $389,[16] almost identical to the 1996 AFDC benefit in nominal terms, but some 25% less in real terms.[17]

Has the program had its intended effects? In its 2009 report to Congress, the U.S. Department of Health and Human Services boasts of the program's success in its first decade: "Millions of families have avoided dependence on welfare in favor of greater independence through work. Employment among low income single mothers . . . has increased significantly . . . child poverty rates have declined substantially."[18] A closer look at the report's data, however, suggests celebration should be restrained. While 57% of single mothers with children were employed in 2006, the report acknowledges that number as only "6 percentage points higher than in 1996."[19] The average monthly earnings of employed people increased from $599 to $707 over the decade, an increase that leaves families with one breadwinner well below the poverty threshold.[20] Childhood poverty did fall from 20.5% to 17.4% during TANF's first ten years, which was a time of significant growth in the American economy,[21] but these gains were erased during the recession of 2009. By 2011, childhood poverty had risen to 22%, higher than when TANF began in 1996.[22] Finally, out-of-wedlock births increased from 32.4% to 35.8% of all births during the decade.[23] Any success TANF had in its goal of reducing such births is not apparent.

TANF's major success seems to have been the reduction of program caseloads. Many states have erected difficult bureaucratic hurdles for program participation. Some require participants to engage in extensive job searches, even at times when unemployment is very high and new jobs nonexistent. Other states fingerprint and photograph applicants— ostensibly an antifraud measure, but one that also increases stigma and deters applications.[24] Most states failed to ease program qualification criteria during the economic crisis that began in 2008 (see Figure 5.4).

One would hope, even expect, that "temporary assistance for needy families" would rise in unison with declining American economic performance. This has not been the case. The number of needy families rises, but assistance barely budges. In both its design and its effects, TANF is primarily an antidependency program and not an antipoverty or economic security program.

Three Tax Benefits for Families with Children

The Earned Income Tax Credit

TANF is not the only program providing cash assistance to children in poor families. The Earned Income Tax Credit typically reduces the

Figure 5.4 TANF Cases, 1994–2010

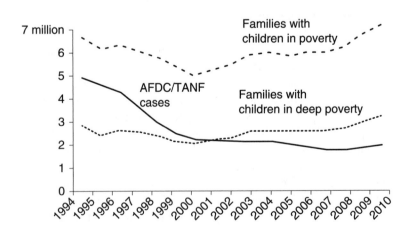

Source: Center on Budget and Policy Priorities, *Chart Book: TANF at 16* (Washington, DC: Center on Budget and Policy Priorities, August 22, 2012), 1, http://www.cbpp.org/files/8-22-12tanf.pdf.

amount of tax owed by working parents by $3,000 to $5,000 per year. The total cost to the U.S. Treasury in fiscal year (FY) 2011 was $64.7 billion.[25] At $250–$400 per month, this is comparable to the average TANF benefit. But the EITC reaches more than thirteen times as many American families, some 27 million in 2009.[26]

The EITC in practice is a program that supplements wages. Here is a somewhat simplified example of how it works: Consider a working parent who has two children and earns minimum wage, $7.25 per hour. On a full-time basis, this amounts to close to $15,000 per year before taxes. Since some federal taxes begin with even the first dollar of income, this worker would owe about $850 in payroll taxes. The EITC maximum benefit for a single parent with two children is close to $6,000, so the full $850 is returned to the taxpayer. Because the EITC is a *refundable* credit and the worker has earned $15,000 in income, she receives the full $6,000. Her work income has grown from $15,000 to $21,000. According to the conventional definition of the FPL, this family is lifted out of poverty. Using this standard measure of poverty, the EITC undoubtedly has substantial antipoverty effects.

The actual tax formula is much more complicated, however, because the EITC phases out as family income reaches middle-income levels. EITC benefits rise in value as family income grows from zero to $10,000–$20,000, depending on family unit size and composition. The benefit stays the same until family income reaches about $25,000 and then gradually falls to zero for incomes between $40,000 and $50,000. See Figure 5.5 for a graphic depiction of how the benefit changes with increases in income.

The Center for Budget and Policy Priorities has estimated that the EITC lifted 3.3 million children out of poverty in 2010.[27] About half the fifty states have followed the federal government's lead in passing state EITC's that reduce state tax liabilities and supplement work income. Of course, the tax credit relies on the availability of work. When unemployment rates rose from under 5% to more than 10% during the recession of 2009, many families lost both their income and EITC benefits at the very time they were most needy.

The Child Tax Credit

The EITC is not the only tax credit available to families with children. Approximately 35 million families claimed the Child Tax Credit (CTC) on their federal income tax returns in FY 2011.[28] The maximum benefit per child was $1,000. The cost to the U.S. Treasury was about $52 billion.

Unfortunately for poor children, families in the lowest income quintile receive only 8% of the program's tax expenditure. Like the EITC, a complicated formula makes CTC benefits phase out at higher incomes.

Figure 5.5 Value of Federal Earned Income Tax Credit, 2012

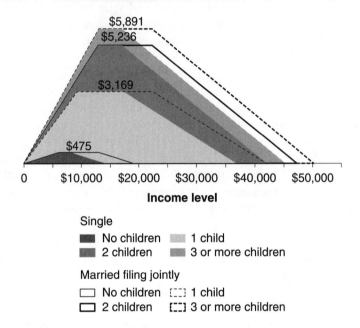

Source: Center on Budget and Policy Priorities, *Policy Basics: The Earned Income Tax Credit* (Washington, DC: Center on Budget and Policy Priorities, February 1, 2013), 1, http://www.cbpp.org/files/policy basics-eitc.pdf.

Unlike the EITC, however, that formula does not favor families with no or low tax liability. It is essentially a middle-income tax benefit.

Figure 5.6 shows the distributional character of the program. Families in the middle three quintiles receive benefits at three to four times the level of their poorer and richer counterparts. The CTC benefits a much larger percentage of middle-class families than of poor families.

Still, the program helps some poor families. The Center on Budget and Policy Priorities has estimated that in 2010 the CTC protected 2.6 million people, including 1.4 million children, from poverty and lifted 1 million children above the poverty level.[29] Many more could be helped given the same "tax expenditure" were the program formula changed to favor low-income families.

The Dependent Exemption

Another tax provision, the dependent tax exemption, reduces taxable income on families with dependent children. The program cost the Treasury $38 billion in 2010 and benefited 48 million families.[30] At first glance, it would appear to be a substantial benefit to poor families with children.

Figure 5.6 Families Eligible for the Child Tax Credit: Average Credit and Percentage Receiving the Credit, 2011

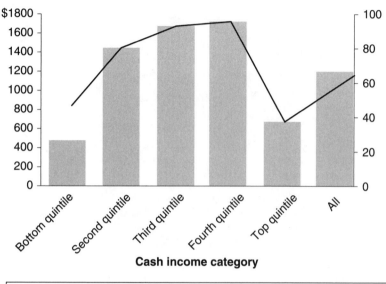

Cash income category

― Average Benefit for People Benefiting (left axis)

░ Percent of Families with Eligible Children Receiving CTC (right axis)

Source: Tax Policy Center, Urban Institute and Brookings Institution, *The Tax Policy Briefing Book: A Citizens' Guide for the 2012 Election and Beyond* (Washington, DC: Tax Policy Center, 2012), II-1-4, http://www.taxpolicycenter.org/briefing-book/TPC_briefingbook_full.pdf.

The basic idea is a $3,650-per-child reduction in taxable family income—not in taxes, but in taxable income. This crucial difference means the ultimate cash benefit to the family is a function of the marginal tax rate—the tax levied on the final $3,650 earned. The U.S. income tax code is progressive in nature, with seven tax rates, beginning in 2013 at 10% for taxable family income up to $17,850 and peaking at 39.6% for income over $450,000.[31] A poor family that pays a 10% marginal tax rate receives a benefit of $365 per child, while a high-income family that pays the highest 35% rate receives $1,278 per child. While there are other aspects of the tax code that may reduce the benefit to higher-income families, a very small portion of the program's benefit goes to families in the lowest quintile of income earners (see Figure 5.7). Consequently, few American children are lifted out of poverty by this $38 billion tax expenditure. In fact, 43% of the benefits flow to the top 40% of income-earning families, which is no surprise; deductions from taxable income are not designed to help poor families.

Figure 5.7 Dependent Exemption Benefit Share by Income Quintile

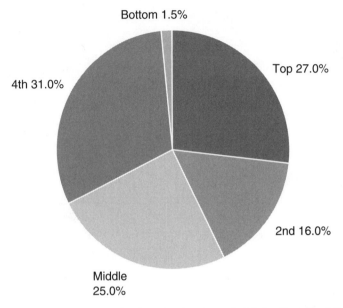

Bottom 1.5%

Top 27.0%

4th 31.0%

2nd 16.0%

Middle
25.0%

Source: Elaine Maag, "Who Benefits from the Dependent Exemption?," *Tax Notes* (Tax Policy Center, Urban Institute and Brookings Institution), December 20, 2010, 1, http://www.taxpolicycenter.org/ UploadedPDF/1001478-Tax-Facts-Dependent-Exemption-Maag.pdf.

FOOD ASSISTANCE

Supplemental Nutrition Assistance Program (formerly food stamps)

During the 2012 Republican presidential primary election campaign, former Speaker of the House Newt Gingrich repeatedly said that Barack Obama was "the best food stamp president in American history."[32] The numbers suggest that Gingrich was correct: during the president's first three years in office, the number of beneficiaries of the Supplemental Nutrition Assistance Program grew from 31.9 million to 46.4 million, and the average monthly benefit increased from $113 to $135 per person. In FY 2011, annual SNAP spending reached $72 billion, more than twice the amount of four years earlier.[33]

But the numbers tell only part of the story. SNAP—whose food stamp predecessor antedates the Obama presidency by four decades—was designed to expand during times of economic hardship and contract upon recovery. The financial crisis that began in 2008 cost the American economy 8.7 million jobs by the end of 2009.[34] Economic crisis made certain a rapidly rising SNAP caseload, no matter what President Obama might have done.

Over time, enrollment in SNAP has tended to rise and fall in line with the performance of the economy. Notice how the lines depicting unemployment and SNAP enrollment generally track each other in Figure 5.8. An exception to this was the period 2002–2005, when the unemployment rate fell but enrollment rose. That rise was explained by the Farm Bill of 2002, signed by President George W. Bush, which expanded enrollment by restoring benefits to legal aliens, who had been cut in the 1990s, and simplifying the application process.[35] Program participation rates—a measure of the share of the eligible individuals actually enrolling—grew from 54% to 72% as a result.[36]

The combination of enrollment gains from 2002 and the economic troubles of 2008 largely explains the program's expansion. Speaker Gingrich's suggestion that President Obama was somehow to blame for SNAP's enrollment growth was obviously well off the mark.[37] His implicit belief that SNAP is not a popular program with the conservative voters he was wooing was more nearly correct.

Figure 5.8 SNAP Participation, Poverty, and Unemployment

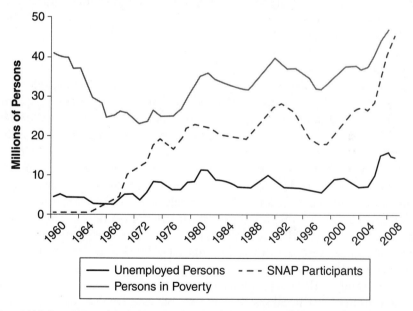

Source: U.S. Department of Agriculture, Food and Nutrition Service, Office of Research and Analysis, *Building a Healthy America: A Profile of the Supplemental Nutrition Assistance Program* (Alexandria, VA: U.S. Department of Agriculture, April 2012), 4, http://www.fns.usda.gov/ora/MENU/Published/snap/FILES/Other/BuildingHealthyAmerica.pdf.

Although state officials administer SNAP, the federal government sets both benefit funding and the standards for qualification. To qualify for benefits, a family of four must have household monthly income below 130% of the FPL, $2,422 in 2012.[38] In 2010, almost half of SNAP beneficiaries were children (47%); another 8% were poor seniors, and 6% were nonelderly disabled people.[39] Almost half the qualifying households had incomes of less than 50% of the FPL. Only 15% had incomes at or higher than the federal poverty level.

The Census Bureau estimates that SNAP lifted 1.7 million children out of poverty in FY 2011.[40] This has become a vitally important subsidy to poor families, especially after the cash benefits of the AFDC/TANF program dwindled (see Figure 5.9). Less than 10% of SNAP households now receive "welfare" cash benefits.

Other Food Programs

Three other federal food programs target poor children. Collectively, they are less than one-fifth the size of SNAP. One is the Special Supplemental Nutrition Program for Women, Infants, and Children, known as WIC (pronounced "wick"). This program provides nutritious food to low-income pregnant and postpartum women and infants and children who are certified by caregivers as "at risk" for inadequate nutrition. In FY 2011, the average benefit provided cost $47 per month. The overall program budget was $7.2 billion.[41]

Eligibility requires that household income be less than 185% of the poverty level.[42] Unlike SNAP (but like TANF), WIC is not an entitlement program—that is, a program where benefits are owed to all eligible families unless and until the program's statute is changed. Congress allocates WIC funding to state agencies, which administer the program. When the money runs out, benefits stop, even if qualified applicants apply. In FY 2010, WIC provided food to 9.17 million beneficiaries each month; 4.86 million of the beneficiaries were children.[43] Enrollment increased only 10% from prerecession levels, more likely a result of program design than a reflection of the growth in true underlying need.[44] In fact, in 2003, researchers estimated that 33% of pregnant and postpartum women, 27% of infants, and 62% of children ages 1–4 who were eligible for WIC did not receive benefits.[45]

Two other federal child nutrition programs—the National School Lunch and School Breakfast Programs—provide free (to children from families with income less than 130% of the FPL) or reduced-price (to children from families with income of 130–185% of the FPL) meals to schoolchildren up to 18 years of age.[46] In 2011, 31.8 million children

Figure 5.9 Percentages of SNAP Households Receiving TANF, 1989–2009

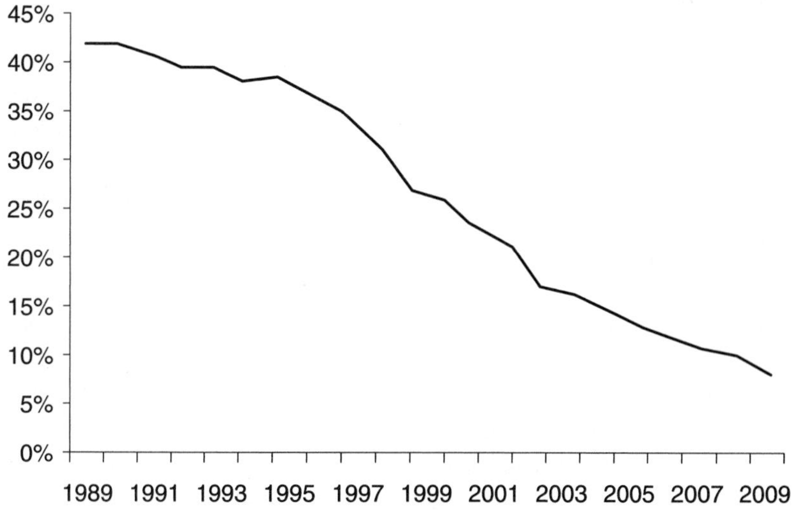

Source: U.S. Department of Agriculture, Food and Nutrition Service, Office of Research and Analysis, *Building a Healthy America: A Profile of the Supplemental Nutrition Assistance Program* (Alexandria, VA: U.S. Department of Agriculture, April 2012), 26, http://www.fns.usda.gov/ora/MENU/Published/snap/FILES/Other/BuildingHealthyAmerica.pdf.

received lunch and 12.1 million received breakfast under the programs.[47] Together, the two programs cost $14.1 billion in FY 2011.[48]

ACCESS TO HEALTH CARE FOR POOR CHILDREN

Medicaid/CHIP Health Insurance

Low-income families without individual or employment-based health insurance rely on two public programs for coverage. President Lyndon Johnson signed the first, Medicaid, into law in 1965. To qualify for federal matching funds, states must agree to meet certain conditions, including providing insurance coverage to particular groups. Among these groups are school-age children in families with incomes less than the FPL and younger children in families with incomes up to 133% of the FPL. The second program, the Children's Health Insurance Program, passed in 1996, built on Medicaid. It provides more generous terms—higher levels of federal matching funds—to entice states to cover children not qualified for traditional Medicaid. States may include children in families with incomes up to 300% of the FPL.[49]

Together, the two programs have pushed the rate of health insurance for children up to 90.6% in 2011 from 88% in 1999.[50] This progress is especially noteworthy since it occurred during a time when rates of private insurance coverage were falling.[51] Figure 5.10 shows the divergence in coverage trends for adults and children during the period. Absent CHIP (now SCHIP), the two curves would likely have mirrored each other.

The over-90% success rate still leaves nearly 7 million children without coverage, however.[52] It has been estimated that about two-thirds of them are eligible for public coverage, but their parents do not apply.[53] In part this is because of varying efforts by states to enroll eligible children. The range spans from 96.0% in Massachusetts—with a universal coverage program for state residents—down to 62.9% in Nevada.[54]

It is important to note that health care coverage for children is relatively inexpensive. Medicaid expenditures were $389 billion in FY 2010, more than $6,000 per beneficiary. Although children made up 49% of beneficiaries, they accounted for just 21% of the costs, about $82 billion. The average cost per child, $2,313, was understandably much lower than the cost per aged ($13,186) or disabled ($15,453) beneficiary.[55] Although some have enormously expensive health problems, children are mostly healthy.

Five programs—TANF, SNAP, the EITC, Medicaid, and CHIP—represent by far the largest federal and federal/state efforts to help poor children or poor families with children. Other smaller programs, plus public K–12 education, contribute to the economic well-being of children born into poor families. The next three sections briefly describe those programs that have national funding components.

ACCESS TO CHILD CARE AND EDUCATION FOR CHILDREN OF POOR FAMILIES

An explicit goal of the 1996 welfare reform was to encourage employment and end "dependency." For parents with young children, this means an expectation of work outside the home. But, oddly, welfare reform rolled back not only the right to cash assistance for poor families but also a concomitant entitlement to free child care.[56] Given the (correct) belief that a decent job is the most effective path out of poverty and the fact that affordable child care is often a crucial determinant of a parent's ability to find and hold a job, this was an odd policy choice. What provisions are made for the care of young children of poor working parents?

Child Care and Development Block Grant

Prior to 1996, the AFDC program provided three funding streams for child-care expenses. They differed for differently situated groups—current

Figure 5.10 Proportion of U.S. Population with Health Insurance by Age Group, 1997–2011

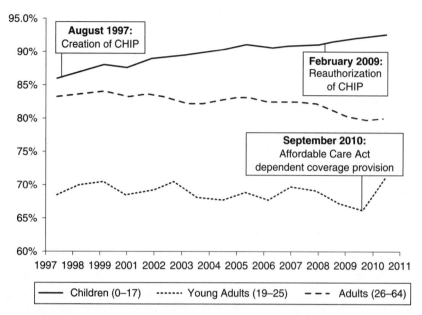

Source: Benjamin D. Sommers, *1.2 Million Children Gain Insurance since Reauthorization of Children's Health Insurance Program,* ASPE Issue Brief (Washington, DC: U.S. Department of Health and Human Services, December 22, 2011), 2, http://aspe.hhs.gov/health/reports/2011/CHIPRA/ib.pdf.

AFDC families, families that had recently left AFDC, and families at risk of qualifying for AFDC. Welfare reform consolidated these into one block of mandatory funding under the amended Social Security Act. Another funding stream, created by Congress and President George H. W. Bush in 1990, provided discretionary funds for child-care assistance to families unconnected to the AFDC system. It was called the Child Care and Development Block Grant (CCDBG).

At present, the federal government provides both mandatory and discretionary funds to the state agencies that administer the CCDBG. The annual spending approaches $5.2 billion. As in the TANF program, states are not required to cover all eligible individuals. The only significant federal condition is that states may subsidize child care only for families below 85% of the state's median income (SMI). This leaves states free to set even lower thresholds, and many do.[57] All in all, the CCDBG program covered a total of 998,600 families (with 1.69 million children) in FY 2009.[58] The average subsidy per child was about $250 per month.[59]

The total served is a small percentage of poor families in need. Measured against the federal maximum standard of families with incomes below 85% of SMI, 18% of eligible children were served.[60] If the standard is the percentage of preschool children living under the FPL, well below half of their families received this subsidy.[61] Welfare reform's expectation of work omits strong support for needed child care. And as we have seen, the employment and poverty reduction gains of welfare reform remain very modest indeed.

Head Start

Head Start is a federally funded, locally run program to help 3- and 4-year-olds prepare for school. It aims to improve "the social and cognitive development of children through the provision of educational, health, nutritional, social, and other services to enrolled children and families."[62] In the 2007–2008 program year, Head Start served approximately 1.06 million children; of these, 825,241 came from families with incomes below the poverty level.[63] The cost was $6.89 billion, which amounted to more than $7,000 per child.[64]

While that seems very expensive, academic evidence suggests that Head Start "generates about 80 percent of the benefits of [model, highest-quality preschool] programs at about 60 percent of the cost."[65] Those model programs, which typically cost more than $10,000 per child, are the exclusive domains of children from well-to-do families. The long-term benefits of Head Start include educational improvement, less repeating of grades, and reductions in special education services. A number of academic studies have estimated the long-term benefit to society of Head Start at approximately $180,000 per student, a large return on an investment of not quite $14,000 per child.[66]

The apparent wisdom of the investment has not led to the provision of Head Start to all 3- and 4-year-olds who are eligible. Less than two-thirds of the children living below the poverty level are enrolled in the program.[67] A U.S. Government Accountability Office (GAO) report showed that 92% of the sampled Head Start programs had waiting lists, in many cases populated by families with incomes higher than 130% of the FPL and unable to qualify.[68]

Public School for All at Age 5

While public education is not targeted at poor families, American public schools serve almost all poor children. The cost in 2011 for America's nearly 50 million K–12 students was $571 billion, more than $10,000 per child.[69] The cost of educating the 15 million children from poor families was on the order of $150 billion in 2011.

CHAPTER 5 BIRTH INTO A POOR FAMILY 89

Public education is, as noted earlier, primarily a state and local government responsibility. Federal funds amount to only about 13% of total education spending.[70] This reliance on local resources, of course, places great burdens on poor communities in poor states. They cannot provide schools with resources comparable to those in wealthier communities in higher-income states. Demonstrating this, significant variation exists around the national average per pupil expenditure of $10,000—in 2010, state per pupil spending ranged from $7,106 to $18,667.[71]

ACCESS TO SHELTER

The federal Department of Housing and Urban Development spends three-fourths of its annual budget on three major programs designed to help poor families obtain housing. This is of great importance to children in poor families: many fall in and out of homelessness over the course of time. The federal Department of Education found that "939,903 homeless students were reported enrolled" in public schools during the 2009–2010 school year.[72] HUD reports that on any given night, there are about 650,000 "sheltered and unsheltered homeless nationwide," and over the course of a year, almost 1.6 million persons experience homelessness.[73]

Section 8 Tenant-Based Rental Assistance

At $19 billion annually, Section 8 tenant-based rental assistance (TBRA) is the nation's largest housing program.[74] Low-income families apply to state housing agencies for federally funded vouchers that pay any gap between 30% of their income and market rents of approved units. Currently 2.2 million families participate, and the program provides an average benefit of approximately $653 a month in reduced rent.[75] The median income of an assisted household is $10,200.[76]

By statute, families with incomes up to 50% of the area median are eligible, but three-quarters of the vouchers must go to families with less than 30% of area median income.[77] Demand vastly outpaces supply, and long waiting lists are ubiquitous.[78]

Project-Based Rental Assistance

The rules for project-based rental assistance (PBRA) are similar to those for TBRA, but in PBRA vouchers must be used for privately owned, multifamily developments. Currently 1.2 million families receive such assistance, at an annual budgetary cost of approximately $8.44 billion; thus the average benefit is $586 per month in reduced rent.[79] The guarantee of the rental subsidy motivates some increase in supply of housing stock built by private for-profit and nonprofit developers.

Public Housing Operating Funds

The federal government provides on the order of $5 billion annually to local housing authorities to operate and maintain 1.2 million units of public housing. The funds are used for rental subsidies and general maintenance. The average subsidy per unit is about $314 per month.[80]

Together, the three programs described above spend more than $30 billion annually on housing programs designed specifically for low-income households. This total pales in comparison to the $105 billion FY 2011 tax expenditure for the mortgage interest deduction, which, in effect, allows home buyers to pay interest with pretax rather than posttax income. Almost half of this sum goes to aid families with incomes above $200,000.[81]

PROGRAMMATIC SUMMARY: ASSISTANCE TO POOR FAMILIES

Table 5.1 presents a summary of the costs and distribution of assistance in the programs described in this chapter. While each program has a mix of purposes, at least one of those purposes is to assist poor families with children. That support is often conditioned on more than a simple assessment of need, and the level of support available is often far from sufficient to serve all in need.

What might be said of these programs and policies collectively? First, the commitment to poor families with children is substantial, though not generous. Although the days of cash welfare payments are well behind us, a wide variety of in-kind benefits and tax incentives designed to encourage work are available to poor families. Primary education and health insurance are, for all intents and purposes, universally available to poor children. (Their parents could not begin to afford these huge costs—close to $25,000 annually for a family with two school-age children.) Most poor kids receive free school breakfasts and lunches during the school year, and a substantial proportion of their families receive SNAP benefits. A poor child might live in a rent-subsidized apartment, albeit not in an expensive section of town, and if the child's parent or parents can find sufficient work, the first $25,000 of income would be essentially tax-free because of EITC benefits.

By our calculation, the average annual value of these benefits is close to $10,000 for every poor person in America. Collectively, the individual programs' per family costs add up to much more, but all poor families do not receive benefits from all programs.

Second, note the mix of these benefits in Figure 5.11. Almost 90% is for food, housing, education, and health care. Cash benefits to

Table 5.1 U.S. Public Spending on Families with Children in Fiscal Year 2011

Program/Policy	Type	Total $ (in billions)	%	$ to Poor Families (in billions)	%	% to Poor Families
TANF	Cash/child care	16	1.1	16	3.5	100
Earned Income Tax Credit	Tax expenditure	65	4.7	33	7.2	51
Child Tax Credit	Tax expenditure	52	3.7	4	0.9	8
Dependent exemption	Tax expenditure	38	2.7	1	0.2	3
SNAP (food stamps)	Food	72	5.2	61	13.4	85
WIC	Food	7	0.5	7	1.5	100
School lunch/ breakfast	Food	14	1.0	5	1.1	36
Medicaid/CHIP	Health	411	29.5	136	29.7	33
Child Care and Development Block Grant	Child care	5	0.4	5	1.1	100
Head Start	Education	7	0.5	7	1.5	100
Public education K–12	Education	571	40.9	150	32.8	26
Section 8 tenant-based rental assistance	Housing	19	1.4	19	4.2	100
Project-based rental assistance	Housing	8	0.6	8	1.8	100
Public housing funds	Housing	5	0.4	5	1.1	100
Mortgage interest deduction	Tax expenditure	105	7.5	0	0.0	0
Total public spending	All	1,395	100	457	100	33

Source: FY 2010 program data, authors' analysis.

poor families make up a small sliver of the pie, approximately $3,000 per year, and well over half of that figure comes only with work income.

Third, despite the fiscal significance of these programs and policies as a whole, many needy children do not receive adequate assistance. They suffer material deprivation, especially those with parents who are absent or fail to work enough to earn significant tax benefits. As we have seen, the percentage of poor families receiving TANF benefits barely budged during the Great Recession of 2008. Policies that encourage and reward

Figure 5.11 U.S. Public Assistance by Type to Poor Families with Children, Fiscal Year 2011 (in billions of $)

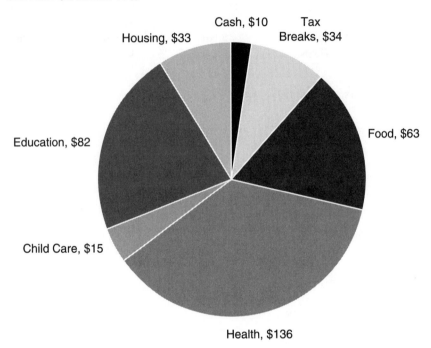

Source: Authors' calculations from programmatic data.

work—desirable in times of prosperity—leave many of the most desperate without aid in times of widespread economic trouble.

From our individual program analysis, one can see that where there is a means-tested *entitlement* to assistance, such as with SNAP and Medicaid/CHIP, or a universal public system, such as the public schools, the vast majority of poor families receive the assistance or services they and their children require. Where there are block grant programs with ample state discretion, such as TANF, Section 8 rental assistance programs, and CCDBG, many eligible for assistance fall through the cracks—often large, gaping cracks—and many families with children are left impoverished.

How many? The Center for Budget and Policy Priorities estimates that the overall collection of programs cuts family poverty almost in half.[82] According to the U.S. Census Bureau, however, the programs still leave some 46.2 million Americans, including 16.1 million children, under the poverty level.[83]

REFORM DIRECTIONS

American rates of childhood poverty are indeed quite high when viewed against international experience. As Figure 5.12 shows, the U.S. rates are

Figure 5.12 Poverty Rates for Children and Total Population in Selected Countries, 2008

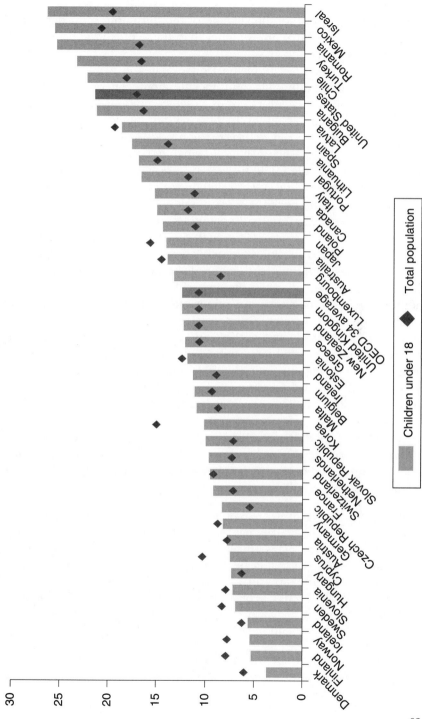

Children under 18 ◆ Total population

Source: Organisation for Economic Co-operation and Development, Social Policy Division, Directorate of Employment, Labour and Social Affairs, OECD Family Database, last revised October 20, 2011, http://www.oecd.org/els/family.

twice as high as those of the average of the thirty-four most developed nations, and four to five times higher than those of Nordic nations with U.S.-level per capita incomes.

These countries differ from the United States in a number of ways. Some have more ethnically and racially homogeneous populations, which may make it easier for citizens to see common risks as demanding common or universal solutions. In these nations, higher levels of taxation are generally accepted in return for higher levels of public service. In comparison with the United States, a "small government" ideology plays a somewhat lesser role in the welfare state politics of most of the OECD countries. Few are federal systems with historically divided and contested responsibility for the health and economic welfare of their citizens. The inhabitants, especially in Nordic countries, often view health care and child care as entitlements of national citizenship. For them, generous child tax credits and subsidies are stable features of the policy landscape.

Despite these differences, there are lessons we might learn from the successes of these nations in limiting childhood poverty. First, there is nothing inconsistent about the provision of strong support for child welfare and solid economic performance. The Nordic economies are among the most productive in the world. This economic performance is attributable in part to child-care subsidies, which enable women to work in the economy without much worry about the care of their children. Second, national-level funding of programs at amounts sufficient to cover all eligible families—much as in our EITC or SNAP—ensures that the promise of assistance is not a false one. The assistance is not a case of geographic good fortune. Finally, the Nordic experience shows that higher levels of social mobility are associated with lower rates of childhood poverty. As the *New York Times* reported, even some of America's leading conservatives have taken note:

> Former Senator Rick Santorum of Pennsylvania, a Republican candidate for president in the primary battles of 2012, warned that movement "up into the middle income is actually greater, the mobility in Europe, than it is in America." National Review, a conservative thought leader, wrote that "most Western European and English-speaking nations have higher rates of mobility." Even Representative Paul D. Ryan, the Wisconsin Republican vice presidential candidate in 2012, wrote that "mobility from the very bottom up" is "where the United States lags behind."[84]

The lesson seems to be this: economic security and economic opportunity can march hand in hand. Insuring more adequately against the threat of being born into a poor family could have large payoffs for the whole of American society.

Chapter

6

The Threat of Early Death
of a Family Breadwinner

THE BIRTH OF THE MODERN REPUBLICAN PARTY MIGHT BE traced to 1994, when
fifty-four freshmen swept into Congress committed to new Speaker
Gingrich's conservative political blueprint, the Contract with America.
Among them was a youthful Air Force reservist and plaintiffs' lawyer
from South Carolina, Lindsey Graham. One expects congressmen from
South Carolina to be conservative, and Graham did not disappoint
his red-state constituents. He was reliably "pro-gun, pro-life, and
pro–tax cut," earning a score of 91 from the American Conservative
Union, a watchdog organization that tracks the voting performance
of members of Congress on issues of importance to the right wing
of the political spectrum.[1] Perhaps most noteworthy, Graham led the
1996 impeachment prosecution against President Clinton during the
scandal that surrounded the president's involvement with a White
House intern.

But to view Graham simply as a partisan conservative is to miss
important aspects of his nature. In an act of courage—and some would
say foolhardiness—for a junior congressman, he led a failed revolt
against Speaker Gingrich's leadership. Fiercely independent, he voted
against what was seen as the most substantive of the House Judiciary
Committee's four articles of impeachment, the perjury claim. "If that's
what it is about, an extramarital affair with an intern, and that's it,"
Graham concluded, "I will not vote to impeach this President no matter
if 82% of the people back home want me to because we will destroy
this country."[2]

He showed as well a willingness to acknowledge the value of
programs his party colleagues abhorred. A member of the House
Subcommittee on Workforce Protections, which has responsibility for

the Occupational Health and Safety Administration (OSHA), the young Congressman Graham defended OSHA's underlying purposes, if not its scope. He remembered the mill workers who frequented his parents' bar, the Sanitary Café, "their shirts covered in cotton, white as they could be . . . a finger missing on every other person."[3]

South Carolina voters rewarded Graham with a promotion to the Senate in 2002. There, he maintained his standing with the American Conservative Union, but, unlike most of his conservative colleagues, he also sought alliances across the aisle. Working with Senate Majority Leader Tom Daschle, a Democrat, he tried to improve health care benefits for military reservists. After Daschle lost his Senate seat in 2004, Graham took up the cause with Senator Hillary Clinton.

Two years later, recently reelected President George W. Bush proposed major changes in Social Security. The president promoted the idea of replacing the traditional program's conservative investment strategy and earned-benefit structure with personal retirement accounts. Citizens could choose to invest their money in riskier but potentially higher-returning stocks and bonds. This push for what the president called an "ownership society" tickled ideological conservatives and Wall Street interests that stood to gain tens of millions of new customers.

Others were worried—among them, Senator Graham. While supportive of adding private accounts to the Social Security program, he knew that such accounts would do nothing to shore up Social Security's long-term finances, which continued to trouble program trustees. "The one thing we're not doing as Republicans," Graham emphasized, "is asking anybody to pay for anything."[4] He proposed doubling the amount of personal income subject to Social Security's payroll tax from $90,000 to $200,000,[5] while lowering the rate from 12.4% to 11.9%.[6] If implemented, these changes would shift the program's financial burden from lower-income to higher-income earners. Graham argued as well that the formula used to calculate benefits should be made less progressive. He asserted that this step would reduce Social Security's long-term deficit of $3.7 trillion by about $1 trillion.[7] Republican leaders, viewing private accounts as the only solution to the problem they had diagnosed, rejected Graham's ideas and scolded him for his outreach to Democrats.[8]

What explains Senator Graham's political courage—his willingness to take on his party and President Bush? In part, his reasons were personal. While a college student three decades earlier, Graham saw his parents, Millie and FJ, die within a year of each other. His aunt and uncle took in his 13-year-old sister, Darlene. Both were retired. They depended solely on their Social Security pensions. Graham told a group of reporters that his aunt and uncle "worked in that Cotton Mill, they busted their ass for 44 years. This is not money somebody gives them. This is money they earn[ed]."[9] He understood at a personal level how Social Security helps retirees make ends meet. He sought, like Alan Greenspan and some other Republican leaders before him, to strengthen the program so future generations would enjoy its protections.

But it was a lesser known aspect of Social Security—survivors benefits—that helped Lindsey and Darlene Graham directly in their time of loss and need. Their parents had no life insurance, but Social Security, it turns out, is America's biggest life insurance policy. The program paid monthly benefits for the care of his sister until she reached adulthood. Those checks helped Graham's aunt and uncle pay the new bills they had never expected to encounter. "As a 22-year-old college student with a 13-year-old sister to raise," Graham humbly recalled, "survivor benefits meant the world to me and our family."[10]

In Chapter 2, we reviewed available evidence on the incidence of early death in the United States. Between 15% and 20% of Americans will die prior to retirement age. Many, like the Grahams, will leave dependent children without resources sufficient for their care. Of the six threats to family income, early death of a family breadwinner would seem the easiest with which to cope. More than nine hundred companies—among them some of the world's largest financial services firms—compete in the thriving market for private life insurance. Prices for such insurance have fallen over time as life spans have increased. By purchasing a policy while young, an individual can lock in a relatively low price for decades.

We begin our analysis of the protections in place against the threat of premature death of a family breadwinner with a look at private life insurance. As with health insurance, the federal government encourages employers to purchase group life insurance plans by offering special tax treatment. We will then examine the place of Social Security survivors insurance in complementing or substituting for private protection purchased either by individuals or by employers on their behalf. Indeed, given the size and scope of survivors insurance, it may be more accurate to describe private life insurance as supplementing the Social Security program.

PRIVATE LIFE INSURANCE

In 2010, American families and companies paid $105 billion in annual premiums for $18.4 trillion of life insurance coverage. Individuals purchased 57%, $10.5 trillion, and employers purchased the remaining

*"Life Insurance. You know, just in case—God forbid—
something should ever happen to you."*

Source: Michael Maslin/The New Yorker Collection/www.cartoonbank.com

$7.8 trillion on behalf of their employees.[11] The amount of total life insurance in force is down almost 10% since the prerecession peak of $19.5 trillion in 2007.[12] Employers have cut back on employment-based life insurance, and cash-strapped workers have allowed their policies to lapse or cashed them in if they had a cash value. Even after that downturn, the level of life insurance, nonetheless, was more than $60,000 for every man, woman, and child in the United States.

As of 2011, 284 million policies were in force, which equated, on average, to more than 2 policies per family.[13] But, as Figure 6.1 shows, the number of policies has been falling, particularly since the 2008 recession began. This trend has been particularly evident in employment-based group plans.

Group Life Insurance

The federal government encourages the purchase of life insurance through work by not taxing workers for the in-kind compensation that employer-provided life insurance represents. As with employment-based health insurance, employees buy group life insurance with pretax dollars, in contrast to those without access to employer benefits, who must spend posttax dollars to purchase life insurance. This policy costs the U.S. Treasury more than $2.1 billion annually.[14]

As companies pared back their workforces or failed outright during the recession, the number of Americans covered by employment-based group life insurance fell dramatically. These plans, historically a staple

Figure 6.1 Life Insurance Policies/Certificates in Force (in millions)

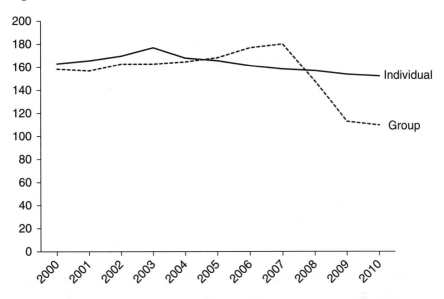

Source: American Council of Life Insurers, *2011 Life Insurers Fact Book* (Washington, DC: American Council of Life Insurers, 2011), 73, Table 7.9.

of American employment, usually provide a basic benefit of one year of annual salary in the case of early death. Typically, the benefit is offered at no cost to the employee, unless he or she wants to add to the basic coverage. This explains both the high "take-up rate," 97% across both private- and public-sector employees,[15] and the median benefit level of 100% of salary. (The average benefit is higher, 1.4 times annual salary, suggesting that a certain minority of risk-averse employees buy coverage beyond even two years of salary.)[16]

A high take-up rate is not to be confused with universal access to a benefit. In fact, in 2011, only 61% of workers received life insurance benefits through their jobs.[17] In the private sector the number was even lower, 57%.[18] The average individual insured by a group plan has coverage of $102,300.[19]

A final caveat about group insurance plans is that seven in ten have maximum benefit amounts that override any full salary benefit. These provisions limit employer cost but may produce inadequate protection for employee beneficiaries. Of plans with limits, one in four defines the maximum benefit as $50,000 or lower.[20] While surely better than nothing, a benefit of this amount will not provide anything approaching long-term sustenance for most beneficiary families.

Employment-based life insurance plays an important role in most families' protective arrangements. Because of its limitations, however, families are wise to supplement employer-provided policies with individual plans. As many families discovered during the recession that began in 2008, benefits linked to employment can disappear or become costly quite quickly. At that point, older or sick workers are likely to find that most individual coverage is unavailable or prohibitively expensive.

Individual Life Insurance

Life insurance comes in a wide variety of forms. The two fundamental products are known as *term life* and *whole life* insurance. Both require regular, often annual, premium payments. Term life protects for a defined period (ten, twenty, thirty years) and promises a defined death benefit to survivors (ranging from as little as $1,000 to as much as many millions of dollars). There is no benefit payout if the policy "lapses" (that is, the premium goes unpaid) or the period ends without the death of the policyholder. Whole life insurance, on the other hand, is essentially a savings and investment program that pays upon the death of the policyholder. If the policy lapses, some built-up "surrender value" is paid to the policyholder. When the policy payout is held constant, term life is typically much less expensive to buy than whole life.

In 2010, Americans purchased just over 10 million new individual life insurance policies. They spent after-tax income on these plans, which collectively provide $1.7 trillion in coverage.[21] The term life plans purchased provide on average $289,000 of protection, while the "whole life" plans provide much less—$86,000.[22] On balance, the new purchases in 2010 provide an average of $165,000 in protection, a falloff from the historical trend of increasing values (see Figure 6.2).

The new purchases of individual life insurance in 2010 were more than exceeded by the number of lapsed policies no longer in force. As shown in Figure 6.1, total policies in force fell by 1 million, to 152 million. This is still more than one policy per American family, on average.

The available data on the average number (and distribution) of family policies and amount of life insurance in force tell us that 30% of Americans have no life insurance coverage.[23] Of the 70% that have insurance, 26% have only employment-based group coverage. As we have seen, this is often of insufficient level and always at risk in a turbulent economy.

The reality, however, is worse than these numbers suggest. A *Wall Street Journal* reporter with access to a 2010 industry association survey wrote that "among households with children under 18, 4 in 10 respondents said they would immediately have trouble meeting living expenses if a primary wage earner died, and another 3 in 10 would have trouble keeping up

Figure 6.2 Average Face Amount of Individual Life Insurance Policies Purchased, 1990–2010 (in thousands)

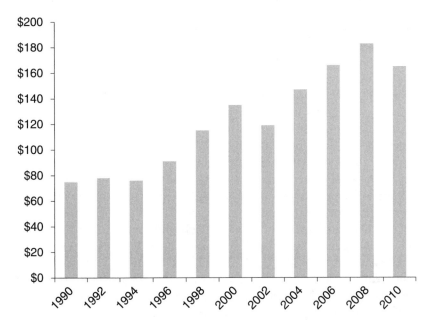

Source: American Council of Life Insurers, *2011 Life Insurers Fact Book* (Washington, DC: American Council of Life Insurers, 2011), 67.

with expenses after several months."[24] Whether they know it or not, 70% of families with dependent children who lose their primary breadwinners will rely on survivors benefits from the Social Security program.

SOCIAL SECURITY SURVIVORS BENEFITS

Survey data on this topic are not publicly available, but we think few Americans are aware that Social Security has its own life insurance program. A Social Security Administration website posting suggests that the program's administrators are well aware of this ignorance—it states, "And you thought Social Security was just for retirement!"[25]

Those in the unfortunate sliver of the American public that learns firsthand about Social Security survivors benefits must be pleasantly surprised. A young widow with two children qualifies on average for a monthly benefit of $2,543.[26] That's $30,000 per year, the first $25,000 of which is tax-free for a widow or widower filing as an individual.[27] When the first child turns 18, benefits are reduced. When the second turns 18, benefits end, although in many cases, the widow will eventually collect the retirement benefits earned by the deceased spouse.

These streams of monthly cash payments, while different in form from the traditional lump-sum life insurance benefit, are the financial equivalent of a very large life insurance policy payout. Consider the average parent with two elementary school–age children whose spouse dies. The benefit of about $30,000 per year continues for a decade. That amounts to a life insurance policy worth approximately $300,000—well in excess of the average individual life insurance plan in force in America.

Of course, if the breadwinner earned more than $30,000 a year in after-tax income, his or her death will still cause an income loss to the family. Further, benefits to children end at 18 years of age, so college tuition is still a large issue for the family. Consequently, there is indeed a strong case for supplemental term life insurance atop Social Security's foundation-level protection. But the worst outcome—impoverishment or unexpected dependence on family and friends—is thwarted by Social Security survivors insurance.

Figure 6.3 demonstrates the wide reach of the program. In December 2011, Social Security sent payments to the remaining parent of more than 1.9 million "surviving children" of deceased workers. The total amount spent monthly on this cohort is approximately $1.5 billion. Another $5 billion per month is spent on the widowed spouses themselves, who qualify for benefits while their children are under 18 and again after the spouses reach age 60 (or 50 if they are disabled and unable to work).[28] In 2012, 4.4 million beneficiaries, mostly women, fell into this category.[29] The Social Security survivors program paid out about $105 billion in 2010.[30] Collectively, private life insurance companies paid out $58 billion that same year.[31] Both Social Security and private life insurance are important components of family security, but the program with the largest payouts, the Social Security survivors insurance program, ironically is virtually invisible to its potential beneficiaries.

Following the terrorist attacks on New York City and Washington, D.C., on September 11, 2001, much was made of the special compensation system Congress established to aid the victims of the attacks and their families. But there was also considerable controversy about the fairness of a scheme heavily weighted toward compensating higher-earning households, and the receipt of benefits was years in coming. Meanwhile, virtually no notice was paid to the rapid response of the Social Security survivors insurance program. The first checks were sent to families on October 3, 2001. Within a few months, 3,000 children and surviving spouses were receiving payments totaling $2.8 million each month.[32] As with all aspects of the OASDI program, higher earners received higher benefits, but less well-paid workers' families were compensated at a higher replacement rate for their lost income. A family whose breadwinner earned $48,000 per year received

Figure 6.3 Social Security Surviving Child Beneficiaries by Monthly Benefit, December 2011

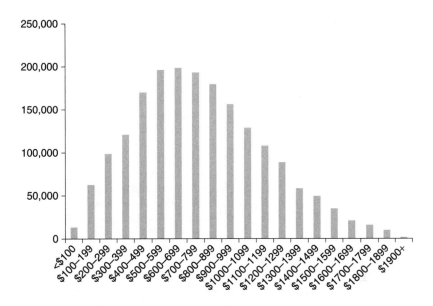

Source: Social Security Administration, "Surviving Child Beneficiaries in Current Payment Status at the End of December 2011, Distributed by Benefit Level and Sex of Worker," accessed November 20, 2012, http://www.ssa.gov/oact/ProgData/benefits/sc_mbc201112.html.

about 56% of the lost earnings; for a family whose breadwinner earned $90,000 per year, the replacement rate was 38%.[33]

INTERNATIONAL COMPARISONS

The U.S. program for survivors benefits is consistent with the approach taken by the vast majority of developed European and Asian countries, but there are two significant differences. Both payroll tax rates and survivor benefit levels are low in the United States in comparison with its international counterparts. The payroll tax rate that finances all Social Security benefits in the United States—pensions, disability benefits, and survivors benefits—is lower than that of almost any other developed nation and a little over half the rate of the international average of 22.9% (see Figure 6.4).

Although the United States ranks high among nations in per capita income, these relatively low payroll tax rates mean that Social Security benefits are bound to be generally lower than the benefits provided in higher-taxing nations. In particular, U.S. spending on survivors benefits is on the low side in international comparisons (see Figure 6.5).[34]

Figure 6.4 Contribution Rates for Social Security Programs, Old Age, Survivors, Disability, 2010 (in %)

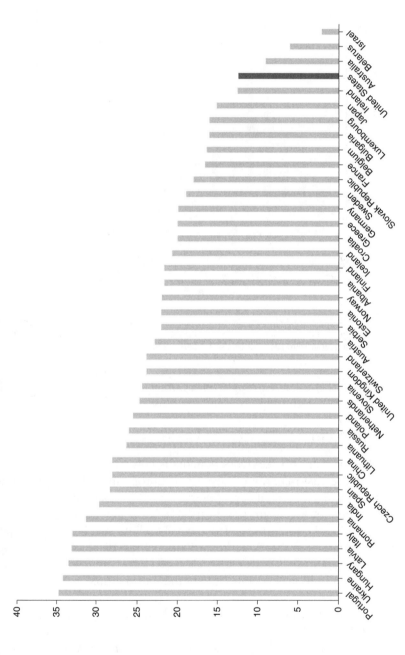

Sources: U.S. Social Security Administration, *Social Security Programs throughout the World: Europe, 2010* (Washington, DC: Government Printing Office, 2010), Table 4; U.S. Social Security Administration, *Social Security Programs throughout the World: Asia and the Pacific, 2010* (Washington, DC: Government Printing Office, 2010), Table 4.

Figure 6.5 Public plus Mandatory Private Expenditures on Survivor Benefits as Percentage of GDP, 2003

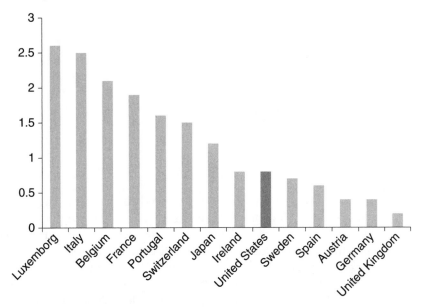

Source: Estelle James, *Rethinking Survivor Benefits* (Washington, DC: World Bank, 2009), 63.

The United States could (and arguably should) increase payroll tax rates and survivors benefit levels commensurately. That no major politician has, in recent memory, proposed such a reform in no way reflects the adequacy of current policy. For an American family, survivors benefits replace only a portion of lost income at a time when expenses for the family rise in unexpected ways. The average funeral in the United States costs more than $6,500, an amount greater than the average family holds in current savings.[35] The remaining parent, if there is one, must find work or better-paying work if he or she can. Child-care expenses are almost certain to rise.

Americans who end up in the unfortunate position of losing a family breadwinner, as did Senator Lindsey Graham and his sister, Darlene, and families whose breadwinners were victims of the 9/11 attacks know the value of Social Security survivors benefits all too well. If more Americans understood both the magnitude of the threat of losing a family breadwinner and the relatively modest cost of improving the adequacy of the survivors benefits program, reform might find its way onto the national political agenda.

7

The Threat of Ill Health

Forty-year-old single mom Robina Castaut worked for the same successful Fortune 500 company for fifteen years. In 2010 the company promoted her to assistant manager at its Fairfield, Connecticut, office. Customers knew her as friendly and conscientious. Robina loved her job.

During a self-examination in the summer of 2011, Robina felt a lump in her breast. Weeks of doctor visits, imaging studies, and a needle biopsy followed. In August, doctors at Yale's Smilow Cancer Center told Robina she had metastatic breast cancer. Her medical team implemented a grueling course of treatment over the next six months, including a double mastectomy, ten rounds of chemotherapy, and weeks of radiation therapy. Robina endured the pain and side effects, all while doing her best to tend to her kids. She looked forward to the day her life would "return to normal" and she would go back to work. Her employer-sponsored health insurance covered most of the tens of thousands of dollars of medical expenses, which, she said, made a "tough time bearable."

For six months Robina labored on, following her physician's advice that she get plenty of rest and appropriate nutrition. Then, on January 27, 2012, the day of Robina's final chemotherapy treatment, a human resources manager for the company Robina worked for called the Yale cancer center. He demanded that an oncologist sign off on Robina's readiness to return to work in February at "110% capacity"—otherwise, she would be "terminated." The Yale medical team refused to make any assurances and informed Robina about the call.

Anxious and tearful, Robina spent the next days bedridden from the devastating effects of the chemotherapy. Finally mustering the strength to walk to her computer, she e-mailed the human resources manager a short note, stating that "according to the doctors, the end of June was a more reasonable expectation for a return to work."

The next day, Robina's doorbell rang, and a courier delivered an over-nighted envelope. It contained a notice of termination. Also included was an invoice for $1,500, the new monthly cost of the family health insurance that the former employer was legally bound to maintain in force, provided the ex-employee paid the premium. The same coverage had previously cost Robina $300 a month, when she had a job and her health.[1]

Robina's case is not unusual. Who among us hasn't seen a flyer for a bake sale or spaghetti supper being held as a fund-raiser to help some-one with their medical bills? Read any newspaper, watch the local news, and you will find that tragic cases are commonplace, a predictable con-sequence of the fragmented and expensive $2.7 trillion American health "system." Our task here is to describe the arrangements now in place to protect American family incomes from the costs of illness. Any such effort must contend with an ever-changing landscape.

Source: Mick Stevens/The New Yorker Collection

In 2010, President Obama signed into law the Patient Protection and Affordable Care Act, which, he assured his audience, will help those like Robina:

The stories of everyday Americans and, more importantly, the courage it took to share those stories is what kept this effort alive and moving forward even when it looked like it was lost. They are why we got this done.[2]

The law promises progressive change as it is implemented over the next decade: near universal insurance coverage, "innovations" in insurance products, reforms in how care is paid for, and new models for delivering medical care. The Congressional Budget Office even predicted some small savings in the federal budget ($210 billion over the period 2012–21) as it estimated the rate of growth of health care expenditures.[3]

The public share of total health care financing in the United States is much larger than most people seem to realize, more than half of the $2.7 trillion estimated to have been spent in 2012. This public funding includes not only the major programs discussed below but also other federal programs that include coverage for Native Americans and members of the armed services, local health clinics, and, importantly, the tax expenditures that subsidize employment-based coverage for working Americans.

The problems of access to health care have worsened in the past decade and a half, with growth in the numbers of uninsured and underinsured. The estimated number of uninsured at any given time within a two-year period is, it should be emphasized, nearly twice the 50 million noted below. Medical inflation (the annual growth rate of health expenditures in relation to a fixed market basket of health care services) has generally been higher in the United States than in any other industrialized country since the early 1970s. Moreover, as we discuss below, medical bills remain a major cause of personal bankruptcy among American families.[4]

The most striking features of American medical care, then, are its fragmentation, high costs and continued high level of medical inflation, uneven access to health services, and unfair distributive consequences.[5] In the past three decades, facing high rates of medical inflation, American employers have become more reluctant to offer (private) insurance coverage to their employees. They have cut costs by offering lower-priced plans with restricted coverage and high deductibles. Private insurers have imposed more and more restrictions on the choices of the insured. Federal and state governments have sought ways to restrain medical care expenditures, which have persistently outdistanced revenue growth.

AMERICAN HEALTH CARE REFORM: MAKING SENSE OF THE AFFORDABLE CARE ACT'S ORIGINS, FATE, AND FUTURE

As of the summer of 2012, two dozen states had been disappointed in their efforts to overturn the Affordable Care Act (ACA) through legal challenges. By a 5–4 vote in June 2012, the U.S. Supreme Court decided that the requirement that all uninsured American citizens purchase health coverage or be subject to a penalty is constitutionally permissible.[6] At the same time, a different Court majority held that the federal government cannot press states to expand their Medicaid programs by threatening to withdraw all Medicaid funds from states that balk at making their programs available to a broader population. Whatever the impact of the Court's decision, the political forces that gave rise to the challenges will continue. Pressure to repeal the ACA or defund its parts is certain to remain an element in American health politics despite the results of the 2012 and subsequent elections. Disputes will continue over the factors that drive health care costs, quality, and access problems and what constitute acceptable remedies. It is likely to be a debate without end.

The aim of expanded health insurance has been a widely shared goal for decades, and the accomplishment of such expansion would close a major gap in America's social insurance protections. But even if fully implemented, the 2010 act leaves in place many worrisome features of current arrangements. The costs of health care will certainly remain high and likely will continue to increase faster than national income. Health insurance coverage will not be universal. The ACA's experimental techniques for reforming the delivery of medical care rely on either untested or, remarkably, tested-but-unsuccessful models for reducing health care costs.[7] Critics who say social insurance protections are unaffordable will not find much in the ACA to allay their worries.

We advise attention to but not anxiety about whether the reforms laid out in the ACA continue or are blocked. We will review the features of the Affordable Care Act later in this chapter, but we start with the more important task of describing the health care "system" that is its object and the economic and political forces that propelled its evolution.

The chapter concludes with a summary of successful international experience. Almost all developed nations provide social insurance–style coverage against the threat of ill health's costs to 100% of their citizens, and they do so at a cost 30–50% lower than the expenditure on health care in the United States, prereform or postreform. That experience was all but ignored during the reform debate between 2007 and 2010.

THE NATURE OF THE THREAT AND ITS COST

Individual ill health arises from both avoidable and unavoidable causes. Babies may be born with disease or developmental difficulties. Doctors diagnose children with an array of common but, left untreated, life-threatening illnesses. Workers exposed to dangerous industrial environments suffer occupational accidents and diseases. In 2011, more than 30,000 Americans died and 2 million more suffered injuries in motor vehicle accidents.[8] Both genetic predisposition and risky behavior—smoking, illicit drug use, overconsumption of food and alcohol—put individuals at risk for heart disease, cancer, and stroke. Chronic diseases strike all age groups in increasing numbers, for reasons known (e.g., diabetes) and unknown (e.g., asthma). Medical errors and prescription drug side effects harm hundreds of thousands annually. Natural aging is typically accompanied by a gradual breakdown in health status. The causes of ill health are many.

So are the means of cure and care. Since World War II, American private firms and federal, state, and local governments have invested trillions of dollars in medical research and the building, equipping, and maintaining of more than 5,000 hospitals and rehabilitation and convalescence facilities. State and local governments have built and maintain "911" systems to respond to accidents and episodes of health emergencies. The federal government subsidizes the training of physicians, a mostly private sector workforce that now exceeds 700,000. The American Recovery and Reinvestment Act of 2009 (also known as the Stimulus Act) provided $20 billion to encourage doctors and hospitals to deploy privately developed health information technology systems. Government and private investors finance the development of drugs as well as medical devices, imaging, and other medical technologies.

Annual U.S. health care costs to patients and payments to providers—two sides of the same coin—represent 18% of the American economy. This is an amount larger than the entire economies of all but four of the world's nations. The United States spends more than $8,000 per citizen per year on health care, well in excess of even the second-biggest spender, small but wealthy Switzerland (see Figure 7.1). The average American incurs $400,000 in health care expense over a lifetime. Women, by virtue of maternity expenses and longer life spans, can expect to spend closer to a half-million dollars.[9]

The costs of treating serious disease in the United States are staggeringly large, well beyond the capacity of the savings of the vast majority

Figure 7.1 Growth in Total Health Expenditure per Capita, United States and Selected Countries, 1970–2008

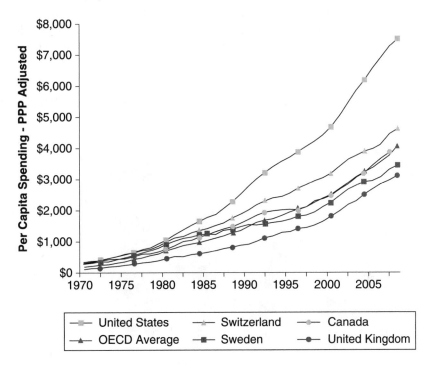

Source: Organisation for Economic Co-operation and Development, "OECD Health Data," OECD Health Statistics (database), 2010.

of American families. Recall from Chapter 2 that a bout with cancer or heart disease costs in the range of $50,000–$200,000. Recall also that 80% of families have less than $10,000 set aside in current savings for such surprises.

What do we know about the distribution of individual health care costs? Over a given year the likelihood of individual ill health is quite low. This year half of Americans will spend next to nothing on health care, but those who do get seriously ill or are badly injured will spend a great deal. Each year just 1% of the population accounts for 20% of all health care spending; the top 10% accounts for half of all such spending. But, of course, the people who make up the 1% or 10% change over time. Over a lifetime, the chances of a person's being one of the high health care utilizers is a near certainty (see Figure 7.2). The logic of having health care insurance is obvious: pay a premium reflecting average costs and enjoy insurance protection against devastating costs from a risk whose incidence is a near certainty but whose timing is unpredictable. (The selfish economic logic of the free rider, who doesn't pay but gains access to emergency care when needed, is also clear. These are among the individuals that the ACA mandate seeks to bring into the health insurance system.)

Figure 7.2 Concentration of U.S. Health Expenditures, 1987, 1996, and 2002

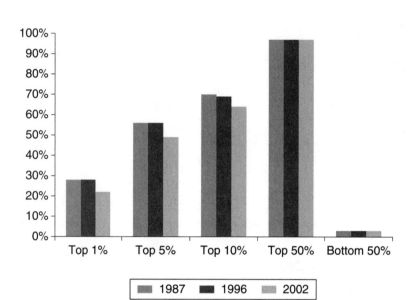

Source: Agency for Healthcare Research and Quality, Center for Financing, Access and Cost Trends, National Medical Expenditure Survey, 1987, and Household Component of the Medical Expenditure Panel Survey, 1996 and 2002.

Over the long run, the pattern of medical expenses becomes much more actuarially predictable. As people age, their average health care costs increase with every passing decade (see Figure 7.3). Buried within the increasing averages is the wide variation in the short run. But few can avoid ill health over the long run. Modern public health measures and improvements in medical care—vaccinations against infectious diseases, sanitation, preventive screenings, seat belt and speed limit laws, and advances in prescription drugs, surgical techniques, and many other areas—have helped push the average life span in the United States into the late 70s. At the onset of the twentieth century, Americans' average life spans were in the 40s. Now early deaths are much rarer, and the chronic illnesses of old age are much more common. Vastly expanded capacities for prevention, treatment, rehabilitation, and cure are part of the explanation for the increasing costs of this improvement.

Figure 7.3 U.S. per Capita Health Spending by Age Group, 2004

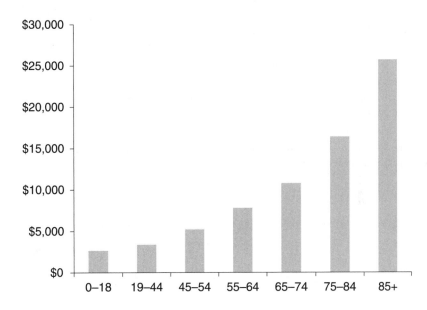

Source: Centers for Medicare & Medicaid Services, Office of the Actuary, National Health Statistics Group, Age Tables 2004, http://www.cms.gov/Research-Statistics-Data-and-Systems/Statistics-Trends-and-Reports/ NationalHealthExpendData/downloads/2004-age-tables.pdf.

THE PROTECTIVE ARRANGEMENTS IN PLACE

For five decades, the typical pattern for health care access in the United States has been coverage by employer-sponsored health insurance during a person's working life, and then protection by the federal government's social insurance program, Medicare, after age 65. For those workers whose employers do not offer health insurance benefits, three possibilities exist. About 30 million Americans buy individual health insurance of varying cost and quality. For some of those unable to afford such plans, joint federal-state social assistance programs, Medicaid and the State Children's Health Insurance Program (SCHIP), may be available. Today, 60 million Americans qualify for those programs. Finally, for those unable to buy health insurance or qualify for Medicaid—almost 50 million Americans at present—there is no protection from the threat of ill health except the ability to pay directly for medical care or trust that charity care will be available. This is poor protection in two senses: first, many uninsured or inadequately insured families find their finances devastated by health care expenses;[10] and second, the uninsured are sicker, are more likely to forgo necessary care, die sooner, and receive lower-quality medical care even when under the care of providers.[11]

Almost 170 million Americans received coverage through their employers in 2011. This is a large but shrinking majority of the working-age population.[12] And while the number of Americans covered by public programs—Medicare, Medicaid, and Veterans Administration health services—has grown, the number of uninsured has grown as well (see Figure 7.4).

Figure 7.4 Sources of Health Insurance for Americans without Employment-Based Coverage (numbers in thousands)

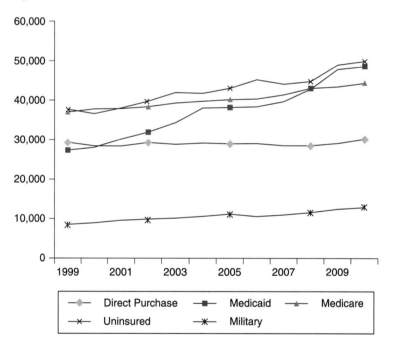

Source: U.S. Census Bureau, Current Population Survey, Annual Social and Economic Supplements, 2011, "Health Insurance Historical Tables," Table HIB-1, http://www.census.gov/hhes/www/hlthins/data/historical/HIB_tables.html.

EMPLOYER-SPONSORED COVERAGE

Why are the majority of Americans insured through employment-based coverage? First, virtually everyone wants health insurance, and being part of a large insurance pool lowers the cost for most workers when compared with trying to buy insurance in the private individual market. Second, as described in Chapter 4, long-standing tax policy encourages employer provision of health insurance. This "tax expenditure" is estimated to cost the U.S. Treasury an average of $132 billion per year in the period 2010–2014.[13] Third, the Employee Retirement Income Security Act facilitates employer provision of health insurance. Large, multistate employers typically self-insure rather than pay for an insurance company to bear the financial risks of their employee coverage. Under ERISA, these employers can avoid state government oversight of their plans and, potentially, as many as fifty different schemes of regulation. Despite these advantages, rising costs have recently caused many large firms to shift an increasing share of health insurance costs to their employees, raising both their premiums and their out-of-pocket costs. Critics of the trend regard this as the "hollowing out" of necessary coverage, while supporters laud the movement toward something closer to catastrophic health insurance. Such insurance would cover only large expenditures, and thus, supporters argue, would make patients more "cost-conscious" in their use of routine health care services.

Whatever the resolution of these debates, employment-based health insurance is in trouble. The average costs of employer coverage have doubled over the past decade, to $5,400 for an individual and $15,000 for a family (see Figure 7.5). Worker incomes in real terms have stagnated as health insurance inflation has consumed most of the gains from increased productivity.[14] Workers at the low end of the wage spectrum have been especially hard-hit as a growing global economy has allowed employers to move jobs overseas or to low-cost areas of the United States, where they often can hire workers without offering any health insurance benefits at all. The percentage of American workers covered by employers' health benefits fell from 63% in 2000 to 56% in 2012.[15] In addition, health care coverage for retirees is fast disappearing, with only 25% of large firms offering such benefits, down from 66% in 1988.[16]

An employee with family coverage through work faces directly only a fraction of the typical plan's overall $15,000+ annual premium cost. In 2009, this amounted to a cost per worker of $3,926 in large firms and $5,134 in small firms.[17] Workers often pay this $300–$400 a month through direct deduction from their paychecks. Individual employees who do not add family members to their coverage typically pay closer to $100 per month.

Figure 7.5 Average Annual Premiums for Single and Family Health Insurance Coverage, 1999–2011

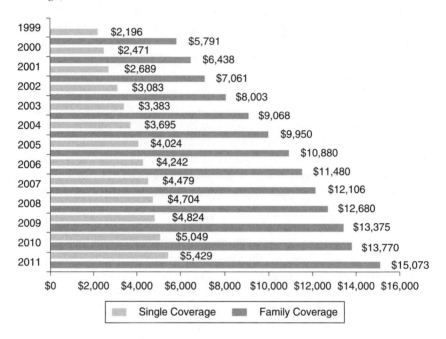

	Single Coverage	Family Coverage
1999	$2,196	$5,791
2000	$2,471	$6,438
2001	$2,689	$7,061
2002	$3,083	$8,003
2003	$3,383	$9,068
2004	$3,695	$9,950
2005	$4,024	$10,880
2006	$4,242	$11,480
2007	$4,479	$12,106
2008	$4,704	$12,680
2009	$4,824	$13,375
2010	$5,049	$13,770
2011	$5,429	$15,073

Source: Kaiser Family Foundation and Health Research & Educational Trust, *Employer Health Benefits,* annual surveys (Menlo Park, CA: Kaiser Family Foundation, 1999–2011).

As required by the terms of the Consolidated Omnibus Budget Reconciliation Act of 1985, workers who leave or are fired from jobs may continue to receive the same health coverage they had before for eighteen months, provided they are willing to pay the full premium costs. This is known as COBRA coverage—perhaps appropriately, since it carries a bite. Many, like Robina Castaut, are shocked to get a bill for three times the monthly premium they were paying, or more. This "bite" is $1,300–$1,500 per month per family.

High and rising premiums are bad enough, but employment-related health insurance itself has changed for the worse, becoming less protective of family income. Employers, as mentioned, are increasingly shifting a portion of costs onto employees in the forms of higher deductibles and medical visit co-payments. In 2006, only 10% of firm plans for individuals required deductible payments of $1,000 or more before insurance payment began. By 2011, 34% of all and 49% of small firm plans did.[18] Just under half of these plans have deductibles of $2,000 or more.

It doesn't end there. A relatively recent "innovation," the high-deductible health plan, carries with it a deductible of at least $5,000 per family. The good news is that those who choose such plans may set up corresponding health savings accounts (HSAs), in which they can deposit funds to be devoted to health expenses and deduct those funds from gross income. This allows families, in effect, to pay for their out-of-pocket health expenses with pretax dollars. It is one health care–targeted tax break atop another—at least for those workers who can afford to make HSA contributions from their current income.

This increased cost sharing, however, causes a number of problems. One in ten insured patients claim to have used most or all of their savings paying their medical bills. Others report that they are unable to pay for other basic necessities because of high medical bills. When patients cannot or will not pay, physicians and hospitals provide increasing levels of charity care or bear more bad debt expense. Increased bad debt leads some physicians and hospitals to call in collection agencies, which in turn hassle those insured patients who are unable or unwilling to pay their share of the cost of care (see Figure 7.6). It also leads medical professionals to increase the price of services for those who can pay, thus

Figure 7.6 Financial Consequences of Medical Bills by Insurance Status, 2009

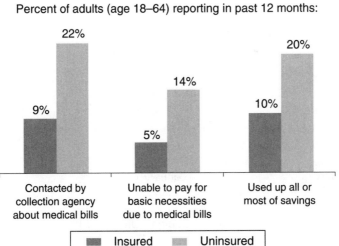

Source: Kaiser Family Foundation Health Tracking Poll, August 2009.

raising insurance and out-of-pocket costs for everyone who is insured. Of course, the problems of America's 50 million chronically uninsured are even worse. One in five uninsured adults report collection agency contact and depleted savings accounts in a given year.

These symptoms of financial trouble often lead to bigger problems. In a 2007 study funded by the Robert Wood Johnson Foundation, 29% of those filing for bankruptcy cited medical bills as the cause. The researchers classified another 28% of respondents as having "medical bill problems."[19] While other researchers have persuasively contested the magnitude of the problem, none have argued that medical costs are an insignificant factor in the incidence of personal bankruptcies.[20]

In the two years prior to their declaration of bankruptcy, more than one-third of those sampled in the 2007 study cited above reported health insurance coverage lapses. These periods were likely associated with job loss and exposed many to potentially ruinous health care expenses. Indeed, lapses in coverage are common for those who do

Figure 7.7 Among Adults Insured in January 2006, Percentage Uninsured in Each Month, January 2006 to December 2007

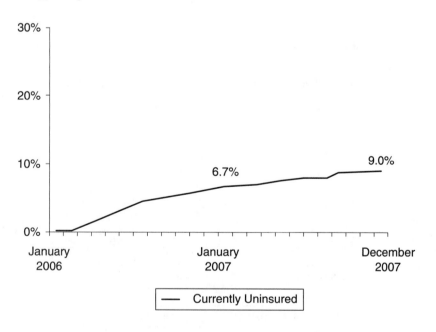

Source: Kaiser Family Foundation analysis data from U.S. Department of Health and Human Services, Agency for Healthcare Research and Quality, Medical Expenditure Panel Survey, 2006 and 2007.

have employment-based health insurance. A Kaiser Family Foundation analysis shows that for adults covered in January 2006, 6.7% lost coverage over the next year. By the end of two years, 9% had lost coverage (see Figure 7.7). The numbers were somewhat worse for those covered by "nongroup" or individual health insurance plans (7.3% and 11.5%) and much worse for those covered by the means-tested Medicaid program (20% and 23.7%).

The reasons for loss of coverage differ among these insured groups. In the employer-sponsored group market, job transitions and unaffordable COBRA coverage are the major issues. In the individual market, which is regulated by the government of the state in which the policyholder lives, there may be no guarantee of renewal once a policy term ends. Insurance companies use the practice of "medical underwriting"—the assessment of likely costs for a covered individual—to determine whether they will provide or continue providing coverage and on what terms. Insurers deny or offer only extremely high-priced coverage to the seriously ill or those seemingly at risk of becoming seriously ill.[21] In response, some state legislatures passed "community rating" and "guaranteed issue" laws to attempt to ensure that insurance companies offer affordable coverage to all individuals on similar terms. However, without a mandate that everyone carry health insurance, as in Massachusetts, these state efforts have been unsuccessful.[22] This is a problem that the ACA seeks to eliminate with its individual mandate and its prohibition on insurers rejecting coverage for preexisting conditions.

MEDICAID

Medicaid beneficiaries need not worry about medical underwriting or the affordability of coverage, but they may lose coverage for a number of reasons. Among these, the most troubling circumstance involves the beneficiary who finds marginally better paid work. Why? Because Medicaid is what policy experts call a "lumpy" benefit. Earning a few dollars more than the income figure necessary to qualify for the program's financing means the loss of all benefits.

As a $400 billion–plus joint federal-state social assistance program, Medicaid is designed to help some but not all of the poorest among us. Medicaid has nominally quite broad coverage. It pays for hospital care, physician services, personal care, prescription drugs, and nursing home stays. (Almost one-third of the dollars spent for Medicaid go for nursing home care of impoverished seniors.) One can qualify by meeting two strict criteria: (1) being "categorically eligible" (eligible groups are pregnant women, children, the aged, the disabled, and parents with dependent children) and (2) not making enough income. Alternatively, adults without dependents can qualify as "medically needy" by virtue of spending down their income on medical costs and becoming poor enough. State governments define these categories and income levels within a range determined by the federal government, which provides matching funds. Most states provide Medicaid to working parents only if their income is below the federal poverty level (see Figure 7.8). For a family of three, that is an annual income of about $19,000.

Recall that a full-time minimum wage job pays about $15,000 per year. Remember too that low-paying jobs with employer-provided benefits are increasingly rare. Thus the seemingly sensible decision to leave a

Figure 7.8 Medicaid Eligibility for Working Parents by Income, 2011

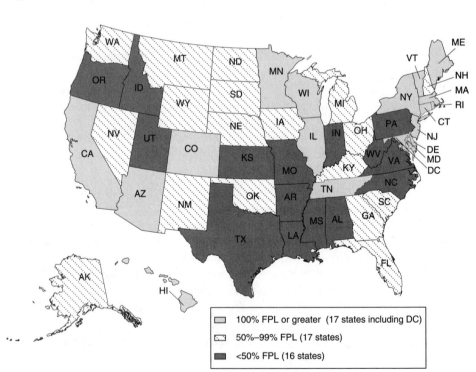

Source: Kaiser/Georgetown Medicaid Eligibility Enrollment Survey, 2011.

minimum wage job for a better-paying one is complicated by the likelihood of losing one's Medicaid health benefits and entering the ranks of
America's 50 million uninsured.

MEDICARE

Medicare beneficiaries need not worry about losing their social
insurance–style protection because of changes in employment status
or medical underwriting shocks. Benefits begin at the age of 65 or
two years after the onset of a qualifying disability. Coverage is broad
but not complete. It includes three of the four major categories of
medical expense: hospital care (Part A), physician services (Part B),
and pharmaceuticals (Part D). Not included is long-term care, where
private savings, family support, and, in the worst-case scenario of
total asset depletion, Medicaid fills the gap. (Nursing home care costs
between $50,000 and $100,000 per year, well beyond the means of all
but the wealthiest.) Medicare expenditures were $551 billion in 2011,
and in that year the program served 49 million aged and disabled
beneficiaries.

One qualifies for Medicare by virtue of a lifetime of payroll contributions, now at 2.9% of income, split evenly between employer and
employee. These contributory taxes are accounted for in what is known
as the Medicare trust fund; some portion of the fund pays for the care
of current beneficiaries, while the rest is invested in long-term Treasury
notes. Qualifying citizens receive Part A Medicare coverage without
additional charge, but to receive benefits under Parts B and D they must
pay additional premiums. These direct costs are affordable for most beneficiaries because about three-quarters of the funding for Parts B and D
comes from general tax revenues.[23]

About 75% of seniors receive Medicare through the traditional
government-run, fee-for-service, free-choice-of-provider program.
The rest choose to participate in for-profit Medicare "Advantage"
health plans (Part C). These plans tend to restrict choices of providers somewhat, but they offer additional benefits. The two prevalent
forms of organizations offering Advantage plans are health maintenance organizations (HMOs), in which members must use in-network
providers, and preferred provider organizations (PPOs), in which
beneficiaries may use out-of-network providers but must pay more
to do so. Advantage plans entice beneficiaries to sign up by offering
them lower out-of-pocket costs and coverage not provided by traditional Medicare, such as dental, hearing, and vision services. (Despite

the original rationalization of greater efficiency in competitive private plans, Part C plans have ended up costing taxpayers more per person than the traditional program.)[24]

The fiscal problems of Medicare are in large part the problems of American health insurance generally. There is ample evidence of underutilization of effective care, overutilization of care not known to be effective, and wide regional variation in patterns of care and costs that seem to have little impact on health outcomes.[25] In both public and private health insurance, per enrollee spending growth has been well in excess of general inflation. Compared to private health insurance, however, Medicare has actually done a marginally better job of controlling cost growth over the past three decades (see Figure 7.9).

The biggest fiscal challenge facing Medicare arises from American demographics. The post–World War II spike in birthrates produced a large generation known as the Baby Boomers, and the members of this generation are now beginning to retire and qualify for Medicare.

Figure 7.9 Annual Percentage Change in per Enrollee Medicare Spending and Private Health Insurance Spending, 1970–2008

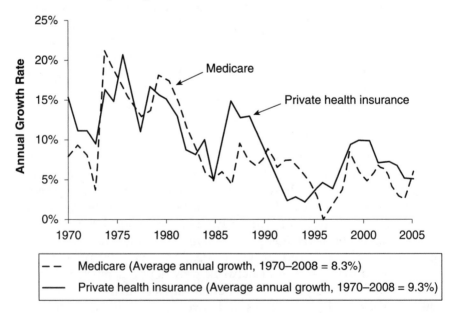

Source: Kaiser Family Foundation, *Medicare Chartbook,* 4th ed. (Menlo Park, CA: Kaiser Family Foundation, 2010), 83, citing Centers for Medicare & Medicaid Services, Office of the Actuary, National Health Statistics Group, 2010.

They are also living longer than previous generations. Thus the number of workers paying into Medicare per beneficiary receiving Medicare has fallen from 4 in 2000 to 3.4 in 2010. It is projected to fall to 2.3 by 2030.[26] Combined with health care cost increases expected to be well in excess of general inflation, this demographic shift will necessarily require increases in tax payments to the Medicare trust fund—or reductions in Medicare benefits. We will explore proposals for balancing Medicare's income and expenses further in Chapter 12.

Projections of future costs are difficult to make. The future is by definition uncertain, so assumptions must be made about program costs, provider payment rates, economic growth, employment, and so on. A history of the Medicare trustee projections shows wide variation year to year (see Figure 7.10), and for any one projection, tweaking those assumptions slightly can easily add years to or subtract years from the life of the trust fund.

Critics contend that Medicare is on the verge of "bankruptcy." This is neither true in the short run nor likely in the long run. What we do

Figure 7.10 Solvency Projections of the Medicare Hospital Insurance Trust Fund, 1970–2011

Projected number of years to insolvency and projected year of insolvency

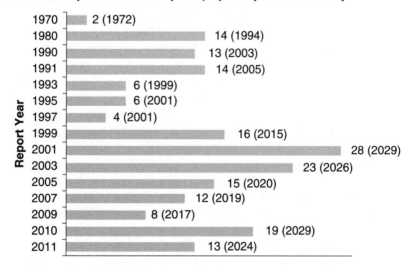

Source: Intermediate projections, 1970–2011, from the annual reports of the Boards of Trustees of the Federal Hospital Insurance and Federal Supplementary Medical Insurance Trust Funds.

know is that modest adjustment will be necessary in order for Medicare to withstand a period of Baby Boomer and medical inflation–induced strain. The Affordable Care Act has made a start in this direction—it both reduced the Medicare program cost growth formula and increased modestly the cost sharing of wealthy beneficiaries, adding eleven years to the Trust Fund's expected solvency.

THE AFFORDABLE CARE ACT

In approximately 1,000 dense pages, the ACA sets in motion many changes to health insurance coverage and health care delivery in the United States. A full summary of the act is not possible here, but we will examine the extent to which the law changes the nature of America's substantial but incomplete protections against the threat of ill health to adequate family income.

The act maintains three main components of American medical financing—employer-sponsored insurance, Medicare, and Medicaid— and tinkers with them only at the margins. Its focus is providing coverage options for the many who lose or cannot obtain employment coverage and do not have incomes low enough to qualify for Medicaid. Most of the act's major provisions were scheduled to be implemented by 2014.

Medicaid expansion is one pillar of the reform. Parents with dependent children in most states must have incomes below the poverty level to qualify. In 2014, anyone with family income of up to 133% of the poverty level is supposed to qualify for Medicaid. If this provision of the act is implemented, and there is no certainty of that, no longer will poor adults without dependent children have to spend down their assets to become medically needy before qualifying for coverage. The federal government is willing to pay the entire cost of new beneficiaries in the period 2014–2017. The federal government's contributions will then decrease slightly until they reach a steady state of 90% federal/10% state funding for 2020 and thereafter. The provision of increased federal funding for Medicaid's expansion recognizes that the program puts a great strain on many states' finances.

The fate of Medicaid expansion has been uncertain since the Supreme Court's decision in June 2012. The Court's decision removed the federal government's ability to threaten to deny Medicaid funding for current beneficiaries for states unwilling to expand their programs. Whether the financial terms of the reform will be sufficient to induce participation is, at this writing, uncertain.[27] What is clear is that the road to Medicaid expansion will be bumpy.

For those above 133% of the FPL but unable to gain health insurance coverage from an employer, a second pillar of the plan will help. At its center is an individual mandate to purchase private insurance and a combination of mechanisms designed to make the financial burden affordable and ensure that insurance is available. States, with federal funding, will create "health insurance exchanges," essentially marketplaces where individuals can shop among an understandable array of insurance plans that provide comprehensive packages of "essential benefits" as defined by the federal government. Sliding-scale subsidies for purchase of insurance in the form of refundable tax credits will be available to families with incomes up to 400% of the federal poverty level ($88,000 for a family of four in 2010). Small businesses may qualify as well for tax credits for up to 50% of their cost of providing employee coverage. Government officials predict that close to 30 million Americans will purchase coverage through health insurance exchanges by 2018.[28]

Insurance market reforms are the third pillar of the plan. By 2014, private insurance practices such as exclusions for preexisting conditions, annual and lifetime benefit limits, and revoking of coverage will be illegal. "Mini-med" plans that provide modest health care benefits but no coverage for high-cost, financially ruinous expenses should be relics of the past. Plans will be required to return funds to beneficiaries if the insurers spend less than 85% of large group or 80% of small group premiums on health care. The operational goal is to force plans to compete by providing citizens what they really need—continuous access to reliable health insurance. The theory is that regulated competition among plans for this large market segment will lead to downward pressure on price, but not to a decrease in the quality of coverage.

What evidence exists to suggest that this theory will work in reality? Not much. We know that Medicare Advantage plans cost more than traditional government-provided benefits, and we know that Medicare has done a slightly better job over time than private insurance in restraining growth in health care costs. Neither fact suggests cause for optimism. And it is likely to be the case that the performance of the plans offered by health insurance exchanges will be similar to the performance of private plans. States may even choose to retain the current market segmentation of individual, small group, and large group markets. Many, urged on by insurance and provider groups, will do so. If this occurs, fragmentation among insurance plans will continue, and weak buying power on their part will provide little downward pressure on prices.[29]

On the other hand, there are medical care organizations, such as Kaiser Permanente in California and the Geisinger Health System in Pennsylvania, that have done a better job than average in restraining health care cost growth while providing high-quality care.[30] These organizations both provide insurance and deliver care. Their numbers are small, however, and the available evidence of success is scant. Most important, they are organizations that select professionals who are drawn to their mode of operation. This selection bias makes it unrealistic to imagine the general expansion of these innovative institutions. We can hope that through a strategy of imitation, thousands of nonintegrated insurers and care delivery providers will be transformed into more efficient and effective providers of care.

In summary, the Affordable Care Act does move the United States somewhat toward the ideal of universal social insurance that protects family income from the economic consequences of ill health. Perhaps 30 million of the 50 million currently uninsured will gain coverage, and many more citizens will avoid losing coverage because of job loss or the onset of illness itself. But the cost of such coverage—already 30–50% higher than anywhere else on Earth—will most likely continue to rise. Little if anything in the ACA addresses the fundamental causes of the rampant inflation in medical care that has consumed greater portions of Americans' income over past decades.[31] Medical inflation will likely continue to plague public, personal, and corporate budgets. Claims that protection is unaffordable will grow in tandem with the rising cost of care. Efforts to repeal the act and reduce Medicare and Medicaid coverage are likely to continue. Despite virtually no evidence of cost-control success, the plea to let market competition work its wonders will remain a refrain of American medical care debates.

BASIC HEALTH CARE ECONOMICS

The general appeal of market solutions in American politics is unsurprising. We live in the wake of the collapse of the Soviet Union and most other Cold War communist states. There can be no question that their strategies of one-party-led government—ownership of the means of production, replete with government control of prices and levels of production—failed to work as well as the market-based systems of the West. The only significant remaining communist nation, China, has abandoned such policies and adopted Western-style market-based economics for much of its economy, if not democratic politics.

Since the 1970s, there has been a steady drumbeat of celebration of markets and market instruments, regularly combined with broad critiques of governmental incompetence or venality. In the wake of the oil crisis of 1973–1974 and the subsequent stagflation, critics in right-of-center think tanks such as the Heritage Foundation and the Cato Institute "blamed" governmental excess for the fiscal strains that emerged.

Markets do work well when well-informed consumers shop for products. Suppliers respond by trying to improve product quality and drive down costs. Over time, only high-value products in great demand tend to survive. In most product markets, we see value rising over time. Think about how computers have become smaller, cheaper, and more powerful. Surely these same market dynamics apply to health care goods and services as well, many commentators have assumed.

Yet we know there are many reasons to doubt they would. Most prices for most health care goods and services rise continuously. Provider incomes mostly rise. Many innovations, particularly in life-saving care, cost small fortunes and improve outcomes slightly. Somehow the medical marketplace produces a mix of effective and ineffective care that is misused, overused, and underused.

So why is health care so different? There are a number of reasons. First, consider the demand side of health care. Patients, renamed "consumers" for purposes of market analysis, tend not to shop for care. They may be ill, injured, or frightened, incapable of comparison shopping. Even if they can do some shopping around, how do they know what they want or need? They ask their health care providers—the sellers of health care goods and services—what they should do. The theoretical assumption of well-informed consumers does not apply to the purchase of most health care.

Moreover, even for those among us who try to be well-informed, there are other stumbling blocks. Whatever we learn, we typically don't know more than an educated medical professional. We can only speculate as to whether the recommended care is optimal. What economists call information asymmetry is surely the norm between consumer-patients and supplier-physicians. This is not a condition that leads to the idealized result of low prices and high quality.

Those of us who can afford health insurance buy it to protect ourselves against financial ruin. When fully insured, we are without financial worry about the cost of care; we have prepaid for our care and are in that respect liberated from fiscal concern. Most Americans, it appears, do not shop for better-priced care. On the other hand, when partly insured, we may well forgo necessary care entirely because we want to save our share of the costs. This is particularly true of lower-income patients. Decades of study show that patient cost sharing reduces the utilization of all medical care, not just unnecessary care.[32] Costs go down, as does health status. This is hardly evidence that patient cost consciousness leads to a sensible allocation of health care.

On the supply side, providers have financial and professional incentives to provide care that is high in cost even if modest in benefit. Why not do anything and everything to help a patient, regardless of the cost? If a test can offer even marginally valuable information, why not order it? The more a physician does, the more he or she earns in income. And who needs a lawsuit for failing to diagnose accurately? This is not to claim that physicians or other medical professionals are motivated solely by economic incentives. They have been trained to help sick people and often are prepared to try anything and everything that *might* make a positive difference.

There are yet more differences in how we should think about health care economics. We do not fret much if consumers in many other markets cannot afford the products they desire. Wanting a high-powered computer or a new car does not justify its social provision. But what if a tuberculosis victim is unable to afford a hospital stay? We all risk infection when such a person goes untreated, and that provides one basis for social provision. From a more altruistic perspective, what if a premature baby's parents cannot afford for their child to receive care for a month at the neonatal intensive care unit that charges $3,000 per day? No one wants to let that baby die. In the economics of health care, there is a community interest. Both enlightened self-interest and moral obligation lead most of us to want outcomes that normal market forces alone cannot reliably produce.

In health care, the "invisible hand" fails to drive down costs, improve quality, or ensure distributional outcomes that are regarded as fair. We can tinker with the rules, regulations, and payment schemes that govern medical care, but the forces that increase the demands for and supply of more care are relentless. Only powerful countervailing institutions can keep them under control. Only governments have the necessary authority, assuming they have the political will to use it.

America's fragmented system, with many payers and independent providers, has been very good at producing innovations in high-priced tertiary care. But it has not been good at matching quality—that is, significant improvements in the population's health—with cost. And, while the Affordable Care Act will insure more citizens have access to this system, the competition of health plans is unlikely to perform that task either. In enacting the ACA, the Congress and the president ignored the successful experience of almost every other developed nation.[33]

INTERNATIONAL EXPERIENCE

How can it be that other developed nations provide social insurance protection against the threat of ill health to all of their citizens at a cost 30–50% lower than the amount spent on health care in the United States? Do they skimp on effective care? If so, it is not obvious. Restrictions that

Figure 7.11 Life Expectancy, in Years, Total Population at Birth

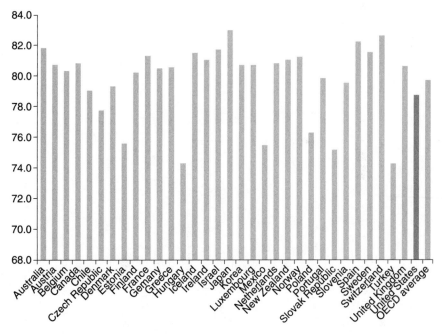

Source: Organisation for Economic Co-operation and Development, "OECD Health Data," OECD Health Statistics (database), 2012.

Note: All country data are from 2010, except those for Canada, which are from 2008.

Table 7.1 Health Care Comparison

	Australia	Canada	Germany	New Zealand	United Kingdom	United States
Continuity of Care *(bigger rates are better)*						
Have a regular doctor	92	92	97	94	96	84
With same doctor 5 years or more (among those with a regular doctor)	61	65	78	61	69	50
Access Problems *(lower rates are better)*						
Unmet need due to cost in past 2 years (prescription, doctor visit when sick or test or follow-up recommended by a doctor)	34	26	28	38	13	51
Very difficult to get care on nights, weekends, holidays without going to the ER (among those who sought care)	36	29	11	13	22	39
Waiting Time *(lower rates are better)*						
Waited 6 days or longer for a doctor appointment (last time sick or needed medical attention)	10	36	13	3	15	23
Waited 4 hours or longer to be seen in the emergency room (among those who visited an ER in the past 2 years)	17	24	4	12	14	12
Waited 4 weeks or longer to see a specialist (among those who needed to see a specialist in the past 2 years)	46	57	22	40	60	23
Waited 4 months or longer for elective surgery (among those who needed elective surgery in the past 2 years)	19	33	6	20	41	8

Key: Gray shading = best country performance. Box = worst country performance.

Source: Douglas McCarthy and Sheila Leatherman, Performance Snapshots, Commonwealth Fund, 2006, http://www.cmwf.org/snapshots. Data from 2005 Commonwealth Fund International Health Policy Survey. C. Schoen et al., *Health Affairs* Web Exclusive, W5-509-25.

Note: Sicker adults have a high incidence of chronic disease and recent intensive use of health care.

might exist within these systems do not, for example, appear to shorten life spans. In fact, American life spans are a little shorter on average than those of our Canadian, European, and Asian counterparts (see Figure 7.11). American infant mortality rates are higher. And while life expectancy hardly tells the whole story, there is little evidence showing that lower costs equal poor care.

Critics of government-run health systems frequently tell stories about long waiting lines for care. But there is almost no evidence of unusual queues for physician visits or emergency care in OECD nations. Anyone who visits an American hospital emergency room experiences the standard practice of a triage process where the urgent are seen immediately and the nonurgent tend to wait. Any American who wants to schedule a routine visit with a physician is likely to find that the next available appointment is weeks or even a month or more away. There is indeed evidence of waits for elective procedures in other countries, but such waits are also standard practice in America, especially for the uninsured. A 2007 Commonwealth Fund review of academic evidence suggests that the United States tends to lag, not lead, other countries in health system performance (see Table 7.1).[34] Compared to our Canadian neighbors and British cousins, Americans average fewer doctor consultations and shorter lengths of hospitalization, suggesting that access to care is often greater in other nations.[35]

Why are these nations able to produce health outcomes that are similar to those in the United States at comparatively bargain prices? It is not because they have all adopted the same model. In the United Kingdom there is true socialized medicine. The national government owns most of the hospitals and pays employed primary care practitioners (using a formula based on both patient load and fee-for-service elements). Nurses and hospital physicians are public employees, albeit well-paid ones. In most OECD countries, as in the United States, privately or self-employed physicians and privately sponsored not-for-profit hospitals provide care to citizens. The populations have insurance coverage from national, state, or provincial governments, or from a small number of government-authorized and regulated sickness funds that provide virtually identical coverage. This is socialized health insurance, not socialized medical care. In Japan, for example, citizens have health insurance from their employers or community not-for-profit plans. They get their care from physicians in private practice and from privately sponsored hospitals. Representatives of both types of providers negotiate rates for procedures and visits with the Ministry of Health. In Germany, Switzerland, and the Netherlands, the governments collect premium funds from workers and employers and redistribute them to hundreds of highly regulated sickness funds or health plans that negotiate with and pay private hospitals and self-employed physicians.

There are, in short, many models. What they share is that access to health insurance and health care is akin to access to kindergarten, highways, or national parks in the United States: everyone is welcome.[36] Citizens contribute funds to the system based on ability to pay, pick their own providers, and are covered against ruinous health care expenses. Everyone has continuous coverage and a large payer negotiating rates on their behalf.

This is a second important difference from the American system. Consumer buying power is typically absent in American arrangements. The uninsured have little influence and often face the highest prices for care. (Whether they can pay those bills is another story.) A small employer has less clout than a large employer who purchases health care on behalf of employees. A large employer has less clout than the state government that finances Medicaid coverage. The state has less clout than the federal government. Citizens pay different rates for the same care for no other reason than their places of employment or insurance statuses differ.

Medical care providers do benefit from arrangements in which the bargaining power of consumers is diffuse. They can command higher rates of pay. Fragmentation is economically advantageous for them, even if dealing with a multitude of payers makes their lives administratively complex. In other developed nations, providers negotiate on more even terms with the representatives of citizens. They tend to earn less than their American counterparts, but physicians still have incomes that are significantly higher than those of other professionals in the same countries.[37]

Insurance market fragmentation is the enemy of coordinated care and a recipe for continued inflation in health care costs. The American system of insurance generates the highest level of administrative costs of any such system in the world. These costs totaled an estimated $156 billion in 2007, and one pre–Affordable Care Act study estimated that administrative costs in the American health care system would increase to $315 billion by 2018.[38] This means less care provided for every dollar spent. It means dollars spent on advertising, billing, and marketing variations of products that cannot be understood until one has to use them. Even the Affordable Care

Figure 7.12 Health Expenditure as a Share of GDP, OECD Countries, 2010

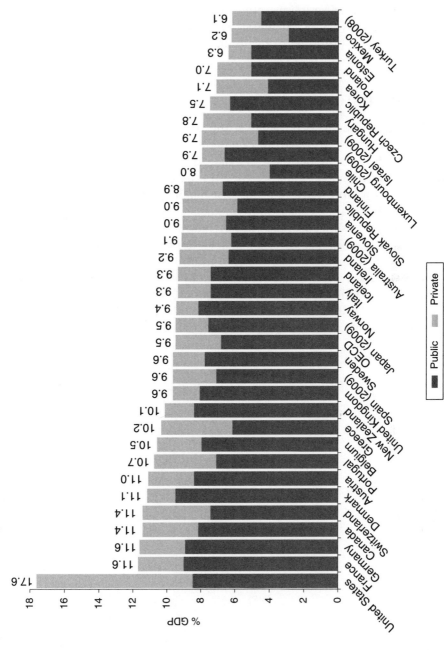

United States 17.6
France 11.6
Germany 11.6
Canada 11.4
Switzerland 11.4
Denmark 11.1
Austria 11.0
Portugal 10.7
Belgium 10.5
Greece 10.2
New Zealand 10.1
United Kingdom 9.6
Spain (2009) 9.6
Sweden 9.6
OECD 9.5
Japan (2009) 9.5
Norway 9.4
Italy 9.3
Iceland 9.3
Ireland 9.2
Australia (2009) 9.1
Slovenia 9.0
Slovak Republic 9.0
Finland 8.9
Chile 8.0
Luxembourg (2009) 7.9
Israel (2009) 7.9
Hungary 7.8
Czech Republic 7.5
Korea 7.1
Poland 7.0
Estonia 6.3
Mexico 6.2
Turkey (2008) 6.1

■ Public ▨ Private

% GDP

Source: Organisation for Economic Co-operation and Development, "OECD Health Data 2012: How Does the United States Compare," http://www.oecd.org/unitedstates/BriefingNoteUSA2012.pdf.

Act adds administrative costs to the system in the form of state health insurance exchanges. Private insurers complain that the ACA's provision limiting their administrative costs to 15% of premiums will drive some of them out of business. By comparison, Medicare, America's one single-payer model of health insurance, spends 1–2% of its funds on administrative costs.

CONCLUSION

The protections in place against the threat of ill health to American family incomes are far from complete. Becoming "medically needy" by spending down income and exhausting assets before qualifying for protection remains common. By 2014, assuming full implementation of the Affordable Care Act, the vast majority of Americans will have protections against catastrophic medical expenses. But this will occur at a high and rising cost that will weigh down the broader economy and empower the interest groups that seek to push the United States back to its pre-ACA position as world outlier. Providing health insurance protection for all is not, by comparative standards, unaffordable. But it could be in modern-day America, where a commitment to market-based solutions to rising health care costs may make unaffordability a self-fulfilling prophecy. The United States is likely to continue to lag the developed world in health care cost performance (see Figure 7.12) and health outcomes.

8

The Threat of Involuntary Unemployment

BETWEEN MARCH AND NOVEMBER OF 2008, one titan of American finance after another—Bear Stearns, Fannie Mae, Freddie Mac, AIG, Lehman Brothers, Merrill Lynch, Washington Mutual, Countrywide Financial, and Wachovia—collapsed outright, fell into government receivership, or was acquired by a competitor at a bargain-basement price. Panic reigned in financial markets. Stock prices swooned. Debt markets seized up. Lending for home mortgages slowed from a torrent to a trickle.

The ravaged firms were not alone in having made large, losing, often inscrutable bets on the American housing market. Other highly regarded financial firms—Morgan Stanley, Goldman Sachs, and Bank of America—gambled in similar ways. But for the Federal Reserve's role as lender of last resort and the Bush administration's efforts to prevent a worldwide economic Armageddon, they too would have faced extinction. Had someone a decade earlier produced a novel or movie depicting similar events, critics would have dismissed the work as the worst sort of fear-mongering fantasy.

But this was all too real. The aftershocks rocked the country. Economic activity, as measured by gross domestic product, fell 3.7% in the third quarter of 2008 and 8.9% in the fourth.[1] By Barack Obama's inauguration day in January 2009, 13 million Americans were unemployed (see Figure 8.1). Home prices dropped precipitously as sales slowed to a small fraction of prior levels. Many home borrowers found themselves "upside down" or "underwater," with what they owed on their mortgages now well in excess of their homes' values. It was a new world.

What went wrong? Bank of America chief executive officer Brian Moynihan located the blame for the debacle: "Over the course of the crisis, we, as an industry, caused a lot of damage. Never has it been clearer how poor business judgments we have made have affected Main Street."[2]

Figure 8.1 Unemployed Americans (in thousands)

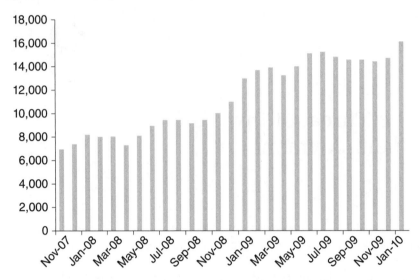

Source: Labor force statistics from U.S. Bureau of Labor Statistics, Current Population Survey, Series ID LNU03000000, downloaded http://data.bls.gov. These figures are not seasonally adjusted.

Amazingly, by June 2009, the economy—buoyed by the Bush administration's rescue effort and the Obama administration's Stimulus Act—began to grow again. The country emerged from the depths of recession. But, like a hungover reveler the morning after a bender, the American economy staggered—mostly sideways. It would be a shadow of its former self for years to come.

Official "unemployment" continued to grow, peaking at more than 16 million in January 2010. Other estimates suggested another 8.5 million Americans were working part-time instead of the desired full-time.[3] Edward Lazear, chairman of President George W. Bush's Council of Economic Advisers, explained the jobless recovery: "I think most of it had to do with investment. . . . tightness in financial markets that persisted through 2009 prevented firms from investing in the way that they otherwise would, and I think that slows the rehiring of workers."[4]

Unemployment insurance (UI)—the joint federal and state government program—took on added significance during the aftermath of the financial collapse. As part of the Stimulus Act, President Obama and the Democratic Congress extended the traditional period of UI benefits from 26 to 59 weeks (and ultimately 99 weeks) at a cost of $40 billion. (Total UI spending in FY 2010 would be $140 billion, almost triple that of 2008.)[5] The Stimulus Act changed the formula used to calculate the level of benefits, which were on average $300 per week.[6] The act put an extra $25 per week into the wallets of the struggling unemployed workers who qualified.[7]

Qualified? One might assume, even hope, that all the Americans who lost jobs during the Great Recession would receive support. But this is simply not true, or anywhere near true. Analysts at the nonpartisan U.S. Government Accountability Office concluded in 2010 that of "the 15 million workers who lost jobs from 2007 to 2009, half received Unemployment Insurance."[8]

POINT OF DEPARTURE

Since we are less inclined to use the detached language of the auditors and accountants at the GAO, we might well have added a descriptive "only" to modify "half received Unemployment Insurance." But to those who follow public policy in this area, it comes as no surprise that unemployment insurance would serve such a limited percentage of those who lost their jobs. The program's problems have been known for decades.[9] Unemployment insurance's original design—especially its delegation of broad authority to state governments—ensures that its protections will be uneven and, at times, inadequate to the threat citizens face of joblessness.

From a poverty alleviation perspective, the limited coverage of the program is unfortunate, because unemployment insurance can be helpful even if inadequate. A 2010 Congressional Budget Office report showed that in the aftermath of the 2008 financial crisis "the poverty rate was 14.3 percent. . . . without UI benefit . . . it would have been 15.4 percent."[10] Millions of families were spared impoverishment because of unemployment insurance. And, of course, the money that those families qualifying for benefits received and spent helped to prevent the economic downturn from becoming even worse.

In Chapter 2, we reviewed the available evidence on the incidence of involuntary unemployment. We reported that, on average, American workers endure four stints of joblessness during their lifetimes. And while it has long been the case that the better educated fare better than the less educated, the world economy is constantly churning. Companies are created and destroyed. They gain and lose competitive advantage, often in very short order. Even during the best of times, hundreds of thousands of Americans lose their jobs every month. Family incomes fall quickly as a matter of course, sometimes by 100%.

No insurance company offers a policy that protects breadwinners from involuntary unemployment. The major reason is the great likelihood—indeed, near certainty—of adverse selection. That, as noted earlier, is the tendency of insurers to attract as customers those who know they will need protection in the near future. While, theoretically, rules could be structured in a way to limit adverse selection, the "evidence of absence" suggests that no insurance company believes this would be a winning business proposition. Social insurance is the only unemployment game in town.

MEASURING UNEMPLOYMENT

We begin our analysis with a brief discussion of how unemployment is measured. Much as we saw with the measurement of poverty, there are competing views about the best way to measure the underlying rate of unemployment—and the choice of method has obvious implications for how the scale of the problem is defined and ultimately who, and how many, qualify for support.

The U.S. Department of Labor reports data monthly on employment and unemployment. The source of these data is a survey instrument called the Current Population Survey (CPS). Surveyors interview a sample of 60,000 households monthly. Statisticians design questions that elicit sufficient information about work or job search activity to allow them to estimate reliably the numbers of persons across the United States who are employed, unemployed, or not in the workforce.[11] The last group includes students, retirees, and homemakers, as well as people who have given up looking for work. The detailed survey data allow for even finer gradations within the categories: (1) those working part-time but desiring full-time employment, a group also known as the "underemployed"; (2) those "marginally attached" to the workforce, that is, available but not seriously looking for work for a variety of reasons; and (3) "discouraged workers," those who have given up looking for jobs after a long stretch of effort. The official government unemployment figure, known as "U-3," does not count these three latter groups as unemployed. Thus, during times of poor economic performance, the official figure understates the rate of joblessness.[12]

Figure 8.2 shows a recent decade's trend in the official U-3 rate and five other distinct ways the Department of Labor measures unemployment. The curves tend to run parallel to each other, but at a given time they may produce widely varying results. In 2011, the range of estimated unemployment rates ran from 5% (the "U-1" rate of those who have been unemployed more than 15 weeks) to 16% (the "U-6" rate, in which underemployed, marginal, and discouraged workers are included). Each "unemployment" number describes the "reality" in a different way. Saying that the unemployment rate is 8.5% (U-3), for example, does not tell the full story.

Figure 8.2 U.S. Measures of Unemployment (%)

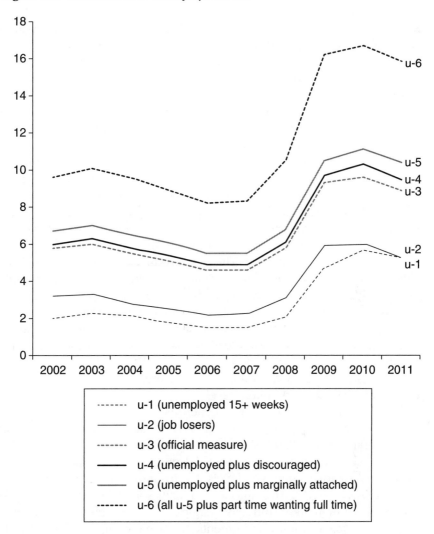

Source: Labor force statistics from U.S. Bureau of Labor Statistics, Current Population Survey, Table A-15, "Alternative Measures of Labor Underutilization for States," http://www.bls.gov/lau/stalt_archived.htm. A fuller description of each of the six categories is available with the statistics.

HOW UNEMPLOYMENT INSURANCE WORKS

As the GAO report makes startlingly clear, being counted as officially unemployed does not mean that one qualifies for unemployment insurance benefits. The possible reasons for this are related to the historical roots and range of current provisions of unemployment insurance.

In Chapter 3 we reviewed the program's history. At the height of the Great Depression, tens of millions of Americans lost their jobs. The Social Security Act of 1935 sought to strengthen the inadequate patchwork of existing state-run unemployment insurance programs through the use of financial carrots and one big stick. The stick was federal intervention—complete with a federal payroll tax on employers—where states were unwilling to put programs with minimal standards in place. The carrots were for the willing: federal payment of the state's cost of administration and a contingency fund that states could borrow from if their programs ran short of money.

The stick was large—a federal tax on employers that was considerably higher than needed to fund an unemployment insurance program meeting federal standards. Because states could institute state programs that met federal standards and spare their employers the high federal tax, every state developed a UI program.[13] States now set employer tax rates, benefit levels and duration, and eligibility guidelines, such as requirements of work history. This has produced what policy analysts call "programmatic heterogeneity." States differ in their political cultures and fiscal circumstances, but they all have this in common: employers can be counted on to remind governors and legislators constantly that high UI taxes hurt the "business climate," job creation, and interstate competition for new, job-creating businesses. Hard economic times remind those same politicians that generous UI benefits contribute to state budget deficits. Both of these familiar pressures tend to lead states to restrict coverage and benefit levels.

Massachusetts, a state with generous UI benefits, requires an employer-specific payroll tax of 1.26% to 12.27% on the first $14,000 each worker earns. Employers who lay off more workers and place more demands on the Massachusetts UI program pay higher taxes than those with steadier employee levels. (In insurance jargon, the program is "experience rated.") This amounts to taxes somewhere between $170 and $1,700 per worker annually. Virginia, a state with lower benefits and tighter qualification requirements, taxes between 0.77% and 6.87% on the first $8,000 of payroll expense per worker. That's between $60 and $550 per worker annually.[14] In total, state taxes for unemployment insurance amount to just under 0.8% of total wages.[15] See Figure 8.3 for the state variation around that average, which ranges from 0.4% to 1.94% of total payroll.

The maximum weekly payments, averaging $439, vary as much as fourfold from state to state. At the low end are the Gulf states of Mississippi, Alabama, Florida, and Louisiana. New Jersey and three New England states offer much more generous benefits (see Table 8.1).[16]

Figure 8.3 Employer Contribution Rates by State, 2011 (percentage of total payroll)

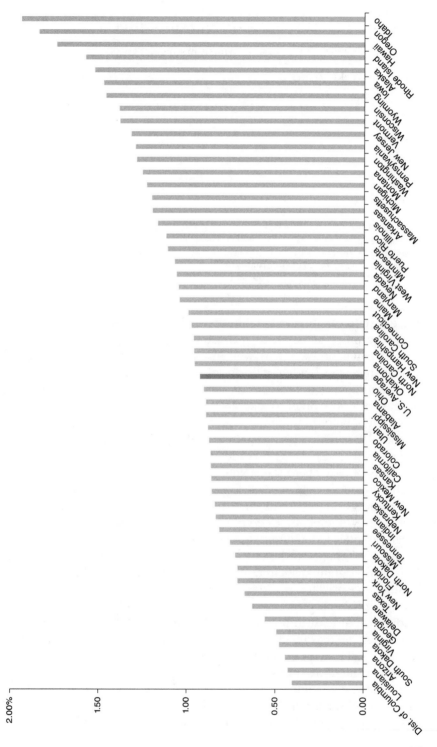

Source: U.S. Department of Labor, Employment and Training Administration, "Average Employer Contribution Rates by State," 2011, http://workforcesecurity.doleta.gov/unemploy/avg_employ.asp.

Table 8.1 State Variation in Unemployment Insurance Benefits

Maximum Weekly Benefit ($)	Number of States
Less than 250	3
251–300	2
301–350	7
351–400	8
401–450	13
451–500	5
501–550	6
551–600	3
More than 600	4

Source: Authors' analysis of data from U.S. Department of Labor, Employment and Training Administration, Office of Unemployment Insurance, *Significant Provisions of State Unemployment Insurance Laws, Effective January 2012* (Washington, DC: U.S. Department of Labor, January 2012), http://www.ows.doleta.gov/unemploy/content/sigpros/2010-2019/January2012.pdf.

Note: Figures include the District of Columbia.

There is state variation in the duration of benefits as well. During vibrant economic times, most states provide a maximum period of 26 weeks of cash payments, which is well in excess of the 15-week average of benefits received.[17] When jobs are plentiful, unemployment tends to be short-term. During times of economic trouble, however, it is typical for an unemployed worker to take 26 weeks to find a new job. The federal government helps fund benefits beyond the standard period through the Extended Benefits (EB) program. Passed in 1970 and signed into law by President Nixon,[18] EB provides federal matching funds for another 13 weeks of benefits to states with high unemployment rates.

The financial crisis of 2008 led both the Bush and Obama administrations and Congress to expand these arrangements. In 2008, Congress enacted the Emergency Unemployment Compensation (EUC) Program, which provides federal funding to states for 34 to 53 weeks of additional emergency benefits. If the emergency benefits are exhausted, the traditional EB program kicks in to provide further access to UI benefits. The Stimulus Act of 2009 provided for full federal funding of the extension through 2012. This act represents an expansion of the federal role in funding UI, at least in time of economic turmoil.[19] Together, these programs generated as much as 99 weeks of unemployment insurance payments in states with generous programs, somewhat less in states with more restrained programs.

When the economy operates at or near full production capacity, states tend to build up surpluses in their unemployment insurance trust funds. In troubled economic times, outflows rise, and trust fund balances fall. Figure 8.4 portrays this pattern of buildup and dispersal over time. But what is most striking is the powerful impact of the 2008 recession, which overwhelmed state funds. To make payments, states borrowed heavily from the federal government. They must ultimately repay the $30 billion they borrowed or face penalties in the form of higher federal payroll taxes and interest payments.

WHY UNEMPLOYMENT INSURANCE IS FAILING SO MANY

Neither the depletion of trust funds nor the variation in state benefit levels is compelling evidence of poor program design. One expects a terrible recession to deplete surpluses built up for that very purpose. State economies vary in character, so a one-size-fits-all program might not work everywhere. Nonetheless, there is ample evidence that the American unemployment insurance program suffers from fundamental design flaws.

Together, the variation in state programs and general UI trends over time reveal in different ways the program's problems. Two program measures—the rate of income replacement and the proportion of workers receiving benefits—show how and suggest why unemployment insurance fails to provide adequate protection.

Figure 8.4 Unemployment Insurance: Trust Fund Balance (in billions)

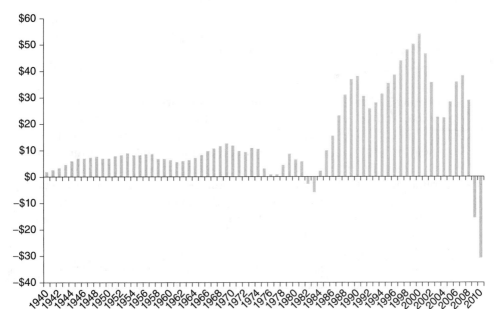

Source: U.S. Department of Labor, Employment and Training Administration, "Unemployment Insurance Chartbook," Section B.5, http://www.doleta.gov/unemploy/chartbook.cfm.

To attract businesses and create jobs, many states compete with one another by reducing employer levies and restricting both the qualifications for and level of unemployment insurance benefits. The replacement rate is the proportion of lost income unemployment insurance provides. Figure 8.5 shows the great variation among states around the national average replacement rate of 46%, from 33% to 56%. The level, far from generous anywhere, is clearly insufficient in certain states, especially for low-wage workers.

These differences partly reflect cost-of-living differences, but they also reveal an unhealthy competition among states vying to attract economic development. This explanation, moreover, does not make beggar-thy-neighbor competition good public policy. Indeed, in other arenas states are not permitted to engage in a "race to the bottom" to attract job-creating enterprise. There are many ways we do not allow companies or states to gain economic advantage over their neighbors or competitors. For example, we do not let states lure corporations to do business within their borders by allowing them to dump refuse into local rivers or expose workers to carcinogenic levels of chemical dusts. The federal government mandates baseline employee protections to create a uniform system in which all economic competition must occur. It is unclear what rationale, if any, exists at the federal level to allow states to provide inadequate, nonuniform social insurance protections as a technique to incentivize business creation.

The extent of unemployment insurance shows not only similar state variation but also degradation over time. The percentage of workers in covered employment peaked at close to 60% during the Eisenhower administration and has fallen to less than 30% in 2012 (see Figure 8.6).

Changes in the American labor market explain some of the decline in coverage. More citizens now pursue flexible arrangements, including part-time and contractual work, than in the recent past. This is especially true of homemakers, many of whom devote some but not all of their time to work outside the home and may quit jobs in times of family crisis. By not adjusting program eligibility criteria to take into account these changes, states have indirectly reduced program outlays. The result is what we saw during the financial crisis of 2008 and ensuing recession. Many workers fail to qualify for unemployment insurance when they are without jobs.

There are also other reasons state-dominated effort makes little economic sense. Recessions are often regional in nature. A downturn in the Texas oil industry leading to a pocket of unemployment can coexist with high economic growth, fueled by the same lower oil prices, in the industrial Midwest—or vice versa. One state's capacity to fund benefits

Figure 8.5 State Unemployment Insurance Replacement Rates, 2010 (percentage of prior income)

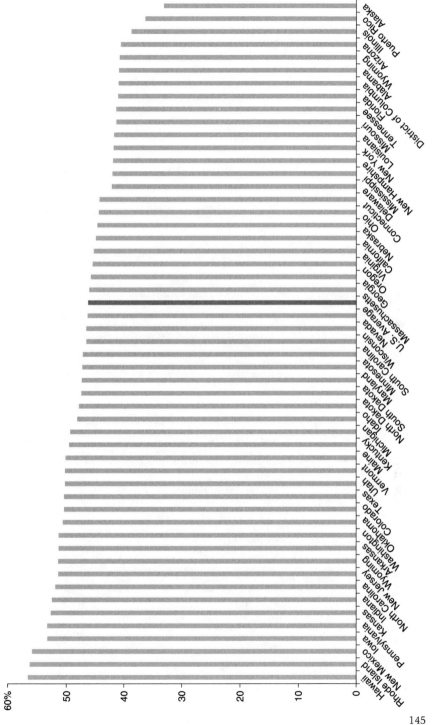

Source: U.S. Department of Labor, Employment and Training Administration, "Unemployment Insurance Chartbook," Section A.17, http://www.doleta.gov/unemploy/chartbook.cfm.

Figure 8.6 Regular Program Insured Unemployment as a Percentage of Total Unemployment

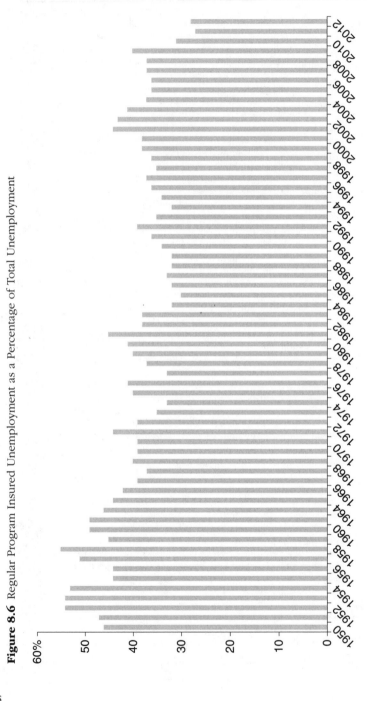

Source: U.S. Department of Labor, Employment and Training Administration, "Unemployment Insurance Chartbook," Section A.12, http://www.doleta.gov/unemploy/chartbook.cfm.

will be declining just as the need for those benefits increases. Meanwhile, a sister state profits from growing revenues and declining demand for benefits. The risk of regional unemployment could be better addressed with a national program, one that redistributes program funds from areas of low to high unemployment.

Workers in search of better jobs often move from state to state, especially if they live in border areas. A move to a new state erases a long track record of employment, and the task of establishing eligibility for unemployment insurance begins anew. For migrant or temporary workers, this pattern happens regularly. Here, once again, state-based insurance is poorly designed for a mobile workforce.

Other gaps in coverage result from more general design flaws. Self-employed contractors, for example, are outside the system. If work dries up, no unemployment compensation is forthcoming. In states with strict work or earnings requirements, lower-wage or part-time workers may not qualify for benefits when work ends even if they have worked at these jobs for many years. In fact, in 2007, the GAO found that "although low-wage workers were almost two-and-one-half times as likely to be out of work as higher-wage workers, they were about half as likely to receive UI benefits."[20] These workers and their families—near the poverty level in good times—face destitution during dark economic times.

DOES UNEMPLOYMENT INSURANCE ENCOURAGE UNEMPLOYMENT?

Limitations on UI coverage are not merely the result of interstate competition or historic design flaws. Policy analysts typically worry about the personal incentives implicit in any public policy; unintended consequences can make policies ineffective or even counterproductive. In unemployment insurance the fear is that the presence of the program itself—or aspects of its design—unwittingly encourage increases in the rate of unemployment. "While raising unemployment benefits or extending the duration of benefits beyond 26 weeks would help some individuals who might otherwise face financial hardship," Harvard economist Martin Feldstein lamented in 2007, "it would also create undesirable incentives for individuals to delay returning to work."[21]

Estimates of the magnitude of the effect differ, but it is well established in the economic literature that the program itself does increase unemployment some. This is not surprising. Someone receiving unemployment benefits—even if only the average 46% of prior income—is likely to use the available benefit duration to find the best job possible. Why grab the first job available, especially if it is a downgrade from the one lost?[22] Since unemployment insurance is an earned benefit, why not make full use of the advantages it offers? The program does give the displaced worker a bit of negotiating leverage.

The debate on this topic became particularly shrill when Congress and President Obama agreed on extensions to the benefit period in the aftermath of the financial crisis of 2008. Another Harvard economist, Robert Barro, argued in 2010 that the "jobless rate could be as low as 6.8%, instead of 9.5%, if jobless benefits hadn't been extended to 99 weeks."[23] Other economists found much smaller rates of increase, from nothing to 1%,[24] but they did not receive comparable attention in the *Wall Street Journal*'s op-ed pages.

The crux of Barro's argument is that even in times of great economic trouble, many employers hire workers. Without UI to rely upon, unemployed workers would presumably be taking those jobs in larger numbers. Barro cites data from the particularly bad month of March 2009, when "3.9 million people were hired and 4.7 million were separated from jobs." But what does this demonstrate? That many of the unemployed could have taken jobs but were refusing to do so? Or might it have been that 3.9 million represented the sum total of available jobs?

It turns out that during the period Barro describes, there were close to six unemployed persons for every job posting (see Figure 8.7). If someone turned down a job, someone else grabbed it. (While 2009 to 2012 showed great improvement, in 2012 there were still three unemployed persons for every posted job.) And we should also remember that remaining unemployed to search for a better job has some economic benefit as well. Forcing workers to take jobs for which they are overqualified, for example, is not self-evidently sensible policy.

But What about Moral Hazard?

Even if the incentive to avoid work is small, the fear that more generous unemployment insurance benefits will induce shirking may have significant effects on the political will to improve the system's protections. Might this be countered by giving workers what Wall Street types call "skin in the game"? Professors Graetz and Mashaw have suggested coupling unemployment insurance with a system of mandatory private accounts funded by worker contributions. An individual's account would build during employment, but it would be drawn down during periods when the worker receives UI benefits. The worker's contributions would be excluded from income for tax purposes, and any surplus would be converted to a retirement account upon retirement.

Source: Michael J. Graetz and Jerry L. Mashaw, *True Security: Rethinking American Social Insurance*, pp. 202–208 (Yale University Press, 1999).

Figure 8.7 Numbers of Unemployed Persons per Job Posting (seasonally adjusted)

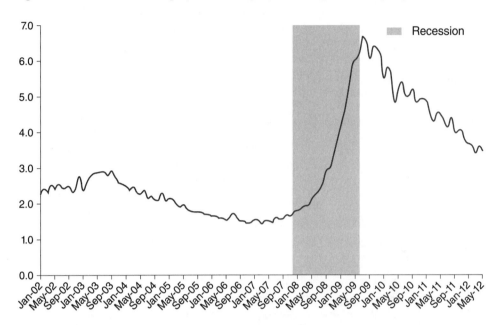

Source: U.S. Bureau of Labor Statistics, *Job Openings and Labor Turnover Survey Highlights* (Washington, DC: U.S. Department of Labor, May 2012), http://www.bls.gov/jlt/jlt_labstatgraphs_may2012.pdf.

RECENT REFORMS AND POSSIBLE MODELS

American unemployment insurance is in need of repair—but, we would argue, not of the sort recommended by critics in organizations such as the Cato Institute or even reforms put forward by the Obama administration.

The recent reform efforts of the Obama administration can best be characterized as positive but incremental changes to a broken system. The Stimulus Act of 2009 offered $7 billion in incentive payments for states that adopted some sensible policy reforms. One-third of the money came with an agreement to count the last quarter year of a person's work effort when determining eligibility rather than the standard four of five prior quarters. This helped many low-income workers, who frequently change jobs to make an extra dollar per hour. The remaining two-thirds of the federal money came if a state adopted two of four eminently sensible policies: providing extra money to beneficiaries with dependents or offering benefits to previously nonqualifying groups, including those participating in training programs, those searching for part-time work, and those who left jobs for "compelling" family reasons such as sickness of a child or domestic violence.[25] Thirty-six states ultimately changed their policies in order to capture the incentive funds.[26]

More recently, the president proposed and the Congress passed the American Jobs Act of 2012. It contained a similar but smaller—

Figure 8.8 Maximum Duration of Unemployment Insurance Benefits in Twenty-One OECD Countries, 2005

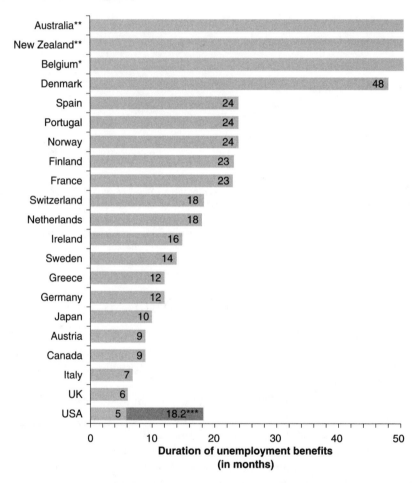

Duration of unemployment benefits (in months)

Source: Gary Burtless, "Unemployment Insurance for the Great Recession," testimony for the Committee on Finance, U.S. Senate (September15, 2009), 15, http://www.brookings.edu/~/media/research/files/testimony/2009/9/15%20regulation%20burtless/0915_regulation_burtless.pdf.

*Belgium essentially provides unemployment benefits of indefinite duration.

**Australia and New Zealand offer only means-tested benefits. If the eligibility test continues to be met, unemployment benefits can last indefinitely.

***Including maximum additional UI weeks temporarily made available in 2009 under the EUC and EB programs.

$100 million—incentive program encouraging states to adopt or expand "work-sharing" programs.[27] The idea is to pay workers unemployment insurance benefits not just when they are fired but also when their work hours are reduced, in prorated amounts. This encourages employers to reduce workers' hours rather than lay them off during a temporary downturn that is expected to improve. Work-sharing programs receive the major share of credit for Germany's lower rate of unemployment during the recent recession.[28]

These incremental reforms strike us as avoiding the fundamental design problems that lead states to run a race to the bottom. While the Obama administration takes a step forward, many states take two steps back. The Center for Budget and Policy Priorities reports that Arkansas, Missouri, South Carolina, Illinois, and Michigan reduced benefit duration in 2011 and 2012.[29] Florida cut the maximum duration of benefits and made it harder to qualify for ongoing benefits by requiring more proof of job-hunting activities—this at a time when the state unemployment rate was still over 10%.[30]

The way to avoid this state competition—which weakens social insurance protections—is for the United States to adopt national standards and national funding, as have many nations of the developed world. Figures 8.8 and 8.9 show the broader nature of protections in place for unemployed workers in other comparable societies. America

Figure 8.9 OECD Unemployment Insurance Recipiency Rate, 2005

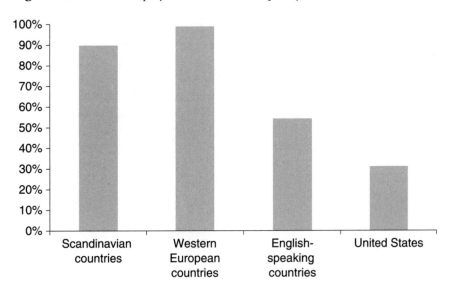

Source: Wayne Vroman and Vera Brusentsev, *Unemployment Compensation in a Worldwide Recession* (Washington, DC: Urban Institute, June 2009), 9.

need not adopt Western European replacement rates and benefit durations to produce a more adequate program, but surely states should not be competing in ways that reduce benefits to only the lucky few. And, as these data show, generous UI benefits do not necessarily produce high unemployment rates. Australia, New Zealand, and Norway, to mention only a few countries with generous UI provision, have some of the lowest rates of unemployment in the developed world.

Moreover, unemployment is an economic problem that states have few tools to address. The U.S. Constitution bars the states from stimulating their economies by printing money or protecting themselves by restricting the free movement of goods, people, or funds. Making states responsible for insuring the unemployed makes little sense in this constitutional context. Such a piecemeal system would not have been adopted had it not been for constitutional scruples held in the 1930s—and long since abandoned—concerning federal taxing and spending authority.

C h a p t e r

9

The Threat of Disability

DISABILITY ARISES IN MANY FORMS AND FOR MANY REASONS. A baby is starved of oxygen during childbirth. A construction worker slices off a finger with a power saw. Another loses partial lung function after spending a year cleaning up dusty debris at Ground Zero. A retired professional football player forgets instructions he was given moments earlier. A nurse suffers back strain from helping an obese patient into bed. A young adult develops schizophrenia. An oncologist diagnoses an energy-depleted 55-year-old salesman with multiple myeloma. A soldier in Iraq suffers a traumatic brain injury when an explosive device detonates underneath a transport vehicle. A Cornell student is paralyzed for life by a prescription drug–induced stroke. Another suffers the same fate as the result of an act of drunken horseplay.

Disability may be innate, as in the cases of those born with developmental deficiencies. It may be total, as in the case of the worst traumatic brain injuries, but more often it is partial. It may be temporary or permanent. It may lead to a shortened life span, but often it does not. It may occur on the job, but more often it happens away from work. Whatever its genesis and character, disability leaves the victim with a diminished capacity to work for a living. Through rehabilitation and retraining some can overcome the functional limitations engendered by their disabilities, but many cannot regain sufficient functioning to enter or reenter the workforce.

The incidence of personal disability increases with age. As the American population has aged over the past decades, collective rates of disability have risen as well (see Figure 9.1).[1] So it is perhaps unsurprising that the utilization and costs of the largest social insurance program that protects Americans from disability-induced impoverishment—Social Security—are on the rise.

Figure 9.1 Percentage of U.S. Civilians, Ages 16–64, with a "Severe" Work Disability, 1995–2008

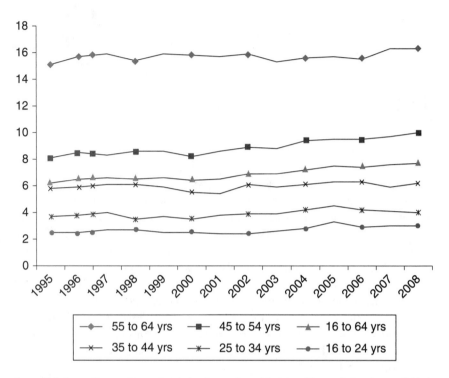

Source: U.S. Census Bureau, Current Population Survey, Annual Social and Economic Supplement, Table 1, http://www.census.gov/hhes/www/disability/disabcps.html.

Nonetheless, shouts of "crisis" pervade the mainstream and business media. *Businessweek* warns that "federal disability insurance nears collapse."[2] A *New York Times* business writer concludes that "disability insurance takes too many workers out of the job market prematurely. It reduces their lifetime income and, to top it off, slows economic growth."[3] The assumption, often unspoken, is that the program is unwise, ungovernable, and unaffordable.

Before plunging into this fray, let's step back and examine the range of private-sector commercial products and public programs that protect Americans against the real threat of disability. As we saw in Chapter 2, three in ten Americans will experience a disability significant enough to miss a work period of ninety days or more during their careers. The reductions in earned income during those periods will often be significant.

THE MARKET FOR COMMERCIAL DISABILITY INSURANCE

Unlike the case of involuntary unemployment, private insurance markets do play a role in protecting citizens against income loss due to disability. Some of the largest, oldest, and most trusted insurance companies in the world offer products in the individual and group short- and long-term disability markets: Aetna, The Hartford, Met Life, Prudential, and Lincoln Financial. A sales force numbering in the hundreds of thousands peddles their wares. While the individual market in particular runs the risk of adverse selection and moral hazard, rigorous underwriting standards ensure that the possibilities do not destroy the functioning of the market. A person cannot qualify for an individual disability plan without a physical, blood work, and background check, and the products available will replace only a percentage of income, so the incentive for a return to work is great.

The federal government encourages the writing of private group short- and long-term disability policies through the tax code. Workers who receive compensation in the form of noncash benefits pay no income taxes on the dollars used to pay the premiums for their insurance policies. In 2012, this policy cost the federal treasury $3.6 billion.[4] Workers without access to group disability benefits who desire such protection must pay for similar policies with after-tax income. They are sure to have higher premiums for the same products, since the insurers cannot spread administrative costs and risk over a large group of workers.

How well is the private market for disability insurance protecting the American public? In 2011, only 36% and 33% of workers had access to short- and long-term disability plans, respectively. Between 80% and 90% of those workers received the benefit without any cost-sharing requirement, so it is unsurprising that the vast majority—35% of the 36% and 31% of the 33% who had access—"took up" the short- and long-term policies.[5] In general, the larger the firm, the more likely the benefit was offered. At firms with more than five hundred employees, 50% of workers had at least the option of long-term disability coverage, but this was true of only 18% of workers at firms with fewer than fifty employees. Entrepreneurs and the operators of small businesses must often seek out the more expensive individual coverage for disability.

For insured workers who are deemed to be disabled by the administrative and medical staffs of the insurers, these policies pay out a fixed percentage of annual employee earnings, typically 60%, and rarely higher than 67%.[6] Most short-term policy benefits run out in 26 weeks.[7] Long-term policy benefits continue until retirement. However, most private policies require that long-term recipients apply for Social Security disability benefits, and any receipts from that source are then deducted from the private insurer's payments.

Setting the replacement rate at a fraction of prior income is neither an accident nor a sign of employer stinginess. The policy design guards against moral hazard. Employee income drops with disability status and rises significantly with a return to full-time work. (If that, indeed, is possible.) There is great incentive for workers to overcome that which ails them.

Information about the size of the market for private disability insurance is not available from public sources, but the market's size can nevertheless be estimated. In 2011, corporate members of the Council for Disability Awareness paid out $9.3 billion to 662,000 beneficiaries in claims for long-term policies.[8] These companies' collective share in the individual and group markets approached 75%. Taking into account their administrative costs and need for profitability, we can estimate that their annual business revenues are in the range of $20 billion.

While this might sound significant, it is in fact only a small fraction of the amount spent on long-term disability insurance through public programs. In a *New York Times* interview, Stephen Brobeck of the Consumer Federation of America correctly noted that private disability insurance merely "complements and supplements" other programs.[9] Private markets alone—even with preferred tax treatment of their products—have not provided adequate solutions to the threat of disability.

A CENTURY OF WORKERS' COMPENSATION

While disability insurance provides income protection for workers who become ill or get hurt outside the workplace, workers' compensation is the main recourse for those who are injured on the job or fall victim to occupational diseases caused by exposure to dangerous radiation, dusts, or chemicals. Recall from Chapter 4 that Progressive Era reformers pushed successfully to create state-based, employer-financed "workers' comp" programs. They replaced an expensive, slow, and uncertain tort system with what was presumed to be a low-cost, no-fault, guaranteed compensation system. How well is it working at present?

Coverage is vast. In 2010, 124 million workers, approximately 85% of the American workforce, received state-level mandated worker protection.[10] (Only Texas has a program that is optional for employers.) Coverage is wide but shallow. In most states, workers' comp benefits fail to replace even two-thirds of a worker's predisability income.[11] As in unemployment insurance, state efforts to protect workers have a race-to-the-bottom quality. States compete with one another in the market to attract economic development; social insurance protections are often a casualty of these strategies or bidding wars.

In 2010, employers providing workers' compensation benefits paid $73 billion in the forms of premiums to insurance companies or state funds, direct payments to employees for lost wages, and payments to health care providers for care of those harmed. Of the $73 billion, $28 billion went to workers for income replacement and $28 billion financed health care services. The equivalence in these figures is the culmination of a long-term trend of an increasing percentage of workers' comp funds spent on health care. Growth in U.S. health care costs explains much of this increase, but not all. It appears that workers' compensation patients often receive care of close to double the intensity of similarly afflicted non–workers' compensation patients.[12]

The balance, $17 billion, represents administrative costs and profits. (Private insurers play the largest role in this public program, as evidenced by their majority share of benefit payments to the disabled workers. See Figure 9.2.) Workers' compensation programs' ratio of benefits

Figure 9.2 Sources of Workers' Compensation Benefits Paid

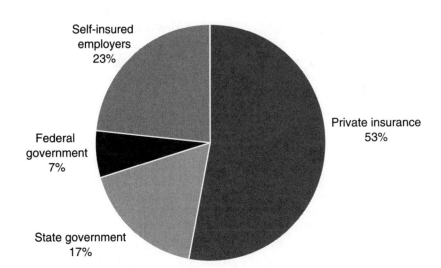

Source: Ishita Sengupta, Virginia Reno, John F. Burton Jr., and Marjorie Baldwin, *Workers' Compensation: Benefits, Coverage, and Costs, 2010* (Washington, DC: National Academy of Social Insurance, 2012), 15.

to administrative costs is better than that of the tort system, but the system is far from the cheap and prompt payment regime that its founders envisaged.[13] Disputed workers' comp cases often lead to the same sort of dilatory litigation that the programs were meant to avoid.

The trend in employer cost per employee over time suggests a well-managed fiscal endeavor, if not an overly generous one. Costs per $100 of covered wages fell from $2.18 in 1990 to $1.23 in 2010.[14] There are a variety of theoretical reasons this may have happened: a reduction in workplace injuries and accidents, a narrowing of what qualifies as a disabling injury, a reduction in the average length of disability engendered by improved rehabilitation therapy or vocational services, or an outright reduction in average benefit payments to disabled workers. As might be expected, all of these factors have played some role.

The good news is that the rate of workplace injury is, in fact, falling. In 1992, there were 3.0 cases of injuries requiring time off from work per 100 U.S. workers. In 2010, this number was 1.1, a reduction of almost two-thirds.[15] Total workers' compensation claims were down by 51.7% over that period.[16]

But there is also evidence of tightened eligibility standards and reduced payment levels by states. During the 1990s, incurred benefits fell by 40% in real terms. According to researchers, states "established more restrictive procedures and higher evidentiary standards in claim processing, and changed compensability rules for particular conditions, such as psychological injuries and cumulative trauma disorders."[17] An insurance industry product "innovation," the deductible, increased employers' costs and hence their scrutiny of claims. The trend toward increased employer cost sharing continued during the 2000s.

Workers who qualify as permanently disabled are prevented by federal statute from receiving more than 80% of their prior income from the sum of workers' comp and Social Security disability payments.[18] The fear again is moral hazard. Despite occasional anecdotes in the media about "disabled" workers continuing to work secretly in vocations requiring good health, it appears from program data that administration has been quite effective over time. Fraud surely occurs, but it is not widespread. Although fraud is difficult to measure, academic researchers estimate that between 1% and 2% of workers' compensation claims are outright fraudulent.[19] The vast majority of workers' comp claims, 76%, lead only to payment of medical bills.[20] For the remainder, only 0.3% lead to a finding of permanent total disability (see Figure 9.3). Nevertheless, there

Figure 9.3 Types of Disability in Workers' Compensation Cases with Cash Benefits, 2007

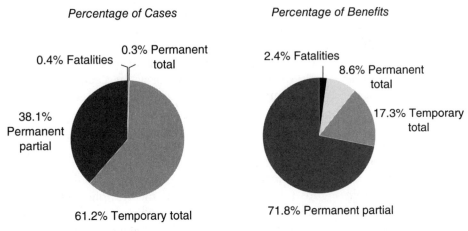

Percentage of Cases

0.4% Fatalities   0.3% Permanent total

38.1% Permanent partial

61.2% Temporary total

Percentage of Benefits

2.4% Fatalities   8.6% Permanent total

17.3% Temporary total

71.8% Permanent partial

Source: Ishita Sengupta, Virginia Reno, John F. Burton Jr., and Marjorie Baldwin, *Workers' Compensation: Benefits, Coverage, and Costs, 2010* (Washington, DC: National Academy of Social Insurance, 2012), 12, Figure 3.

have been at least 4,500 workplace fatalities annually over the past decade.[21] Permanent total disability due to work injuries, while infrequent, is clearly a real phenomenon.

SOCIAL SECURITY DISABILITY INSURANCE

What happens to persons who become disabled outside of work but are not covered by private disability insurance? There are two possibilities in the United States. Workers who have contributed over time to Social Security and qualify can receive long-term disability benefits under the Eisenhower-era Social Security Disability Insurance (SSDI) program. For those who fail to meet contribution requirements, there is the possibility of benefits under the means-tested Supplemental Security Income (SSI) program. Some, by virtue of their disability and impoverished status, qualify for both programs. We begin by looking at the workings of SSDI.

As you will recall, workers and employers each pay 7.65% FICA payroll taxes that fund the Social Security (OASDI) and Medicare programs. A portion of these taxes—0.9% for employees and 0.9% for employers—funds SSDI. A disability insurance trust fund is the relevant accounting convention: payroll taxes go in, and program payments go out.

Almost all American workers contribute to this fund across their working lives. Workers who believe they have become disabled can apply to the program for benefits. To qualify, they must be benefit-eligible, severely impaired for at least five months, and unable to perform substantial work. To be benefit-eligible, a person must have worked and contributed FICA taxes in at least five of the past ten years. "Severely impaired" is defined as having a "medically determinable physical or mental impairment which can be expected to result in death" or that exists "for a continuous period of not less than 12 months."[22] The "inability to engage in substantial gainful activity" is defined as being unable to meet the mental or physical requirements of jobs paying at least $1,040 per month.[23] An applicant cannot qualify until at least five months have passed from the onset of the disability. From Figure 9.4, one can see that most applicants fail to meet these strict criteria. Less than a quarter qualify upon initial application. After appeals, approximately 40% of applicants are ultimately successful.

Figure 9.4 Final Outcome of SSDI Disabled-Worker Applications, 2001–2010

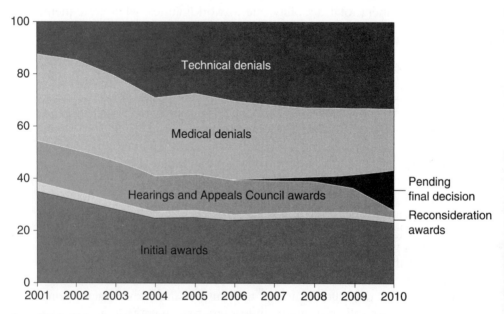

Source: U.S. Social Security Administration, *Annual Statistical Report on the Social Security Disability Insurance Program, 2011* (Washington, DC: Social Security Administration, July 2012), 141.

POTENTIAL BENEFITS AND APPLICATION PROCESS

The benefits to a qualified applicant come in three forms. First, monthly cash payments replace a portion of the worker's lost income. As with Social Security pensions (SSDI work disability is in essence early retirement), the payment formula is progressive. While high-income earners receive more, low-income workers have a higher percentage of their former earnings replaced. Second, after a two-year waiting period, the disabled worker qualifies for health insurance through the Medicare program. (If income is low enough or out-of-pocket medical expenses are high enough, the individual may qualify for Medicaid, too.) Finally, some disabled workers receive vocational rehabilitation vouchers, which help pay for them to train for new jobs.

The application process might best be characterized as rigorous. A high bar is set. The five-month waiting period clarifies that the program is not for the temporarily disabled. (In fact, no federal program exists to assist the temporarily disabled.) One in four applicants fails to clear the first hurdle of technical qualification, having insufficient work history to qualify. (For those in this cohort, the only alternative is application to the means-tested SSI program, which has the same criteria as SSDI for determining work disability.) Of those still in consideration, only one in three will receive approval on the first judgment.

Although SSDI is a federal program, these first judgments are rendered by each state's Disability Determination Service, which works with the federal government to administer SSDI. The wide variation in rates of rejection by state agencies suggests the somewhat subjective nature of these determinations (see Figure 9.5). This variation is somewhat surprising, given that the substantive criteria and application process are the same in all states. A reviewer checks an applicant's disability against a list of medical conditions considered "severe enough to prevent an individual from doing any gainful activity."[24] For those who have severe impairments that fail to make the list, the reviewer asks two more questions: (1) Can the individual do the work he or she previously did? (2) Can the individual do any other type of work? If, after consideration of the applicant's age, education, and work experience, the reviewer concludes that work opportunities exist for that person in the "national economy," the application is rejected. Note that the criterion is the ability to do some jobs somewhere in the national economy, not whether the applicant is likely to be hired for such jobs. Disability program requirements seek to distinguish disability sharply from unemployment.

Figure 9.5 Variations in State Agency Initial Allowance Rates, Fiscal Years 1980–2010

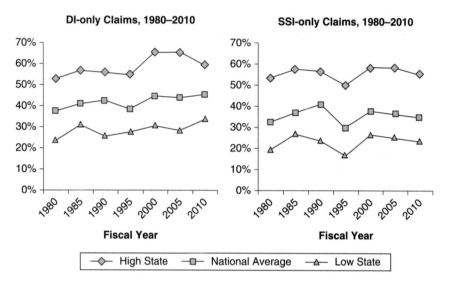

Source: Social Security Advisory Board, *Aspects of Disability Decision Making: Data and Materials* (Washington, DC: Social Security Advisory Board, February 2012), http://www.ssab.gov/Publications/ Disability/GPO_Chartbook_FINAL_06122012.pdf.

The successful applicant receives a monthly benefit that is related to the level of his or her prior payroll tax contributions to the program. The average monthly benefit received in 2011 was $1,110, but there is substantial variation across the more than 8 million SSDI beneficiaries.[25] (See Figure 9.6 for the distribution of benefits.)

For the initially unsuccessful applicant, there are four levels of appeal. The first, reconsideration, is essentially the same as the initial application process, but with a different, more experienced reviewer. The second, appeal to a federal administrative law judge (ALJ), leads in a majority of cases to the applicant's hiring an attorney, who usually works "on contingency"—that is, the lawyer collects a fee (conventionally one-quarter of past-due benefits) only if the appeal is successful. In such an appeal, no one represents the government. ALJs, like state agency examiners, are charged with the independent responsibility to develop the evidence they need to render their decisions. At the third level of appeal, which may occur following a negative decision by an ALJ, the application is reviewed by an appeals council within the Social Security Administration, and the fourth level, if necessary, involves appeal to a federal district court. While benefits ultimately won

Figure 9.6 SSDI Monthly Benefit Level Distribution

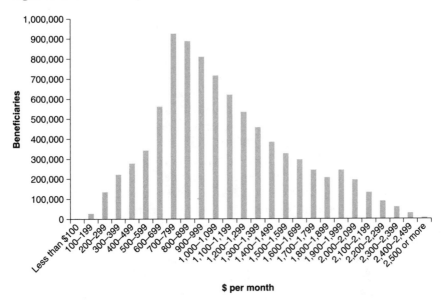

$ per month

Source: U.S. Social Security Administration, "Disabled Worker Beneficiaries in Current Payment Status at the End of June 2012, Distributed by Benefit Level, Sex, and Age Group," http://www.ssa.gov/OACT/progdata/benefits/da_mbc201206.html.

are retroactive to the date of the disability, one can imagine the strains on household income brought about by a process that lasts more than a year on average if the claimant succeeds only after an appeal to an ALJ.[26] About one in five initial applicants will succeed only after a trip down this long and winding road.

CONTINUING DISABILITY REVIEWS AND RETURNS TO WORK

An award is not the end of the story for the successful applicant. Social Security law requires that all cases be reviewed on a regular basis, with the frequency dependent on the severity of the disability. Some cases are reviewed biannually. Others, where medical improvement is not expected, may go five years without review. In 2011, program officials terminated the benefits of 134,770 persons who had previously qualified.[27] (Another 268,245 beneficiaries died.)

The process—known as a Continuing Disability Review (CDR)—that leads to the termination of benefits produces significant returns to taxpayers. In 2012, the Social Security Administration estimated those savings at $9 for every $1 invested in CDRs.[28] A related fraud-prevention effort by the SSA's Office of the Inspector General—Cooperative Disability Investigations—saved SSDI $228 million, a return of $17 for every $1 in resources invested.[29] Somewhat surprisingly, Congress has appropriated funding for such efforts in only twenty-two states.

Disabled workers leave the SSDI rolls for other reasons as well. For example, when beneficiaries reach full retirement age, they "transfer over" to the old-age pension program of Social Security. Some—a small fraction—return to gainful employment. Just under 40,000 did so in 2011.[30]

Policy makers added a variety of work incentives to SSDI through the bipartisan Ticket to Work and Work Incentives Improvement Act of 1999. The act encourages disabled workers to experiment with returning to work without loss of benefits during a 9-month trial period. After a successful transition to work, Medicare benefits are maintained for up to 93 months. And, in the event that such a worker becomes unable to work again within the first five years, he or she can simply request SSDI reinstatement, without having to go through the lengthy application process again. These programs reduce the economic and psychological barriers that discourage disabled workers from attempting reentry into the workforce.

THE SSDI TRUST FUND

There is much confusion about one particular technical aspect of Social Security, the accounting convention called a trust fund. A trust fund is for all intents and purposes a bank account. The U.S. Treasury receives FICA payroll taxes from employers and employees (as well as Self-Employment Contributions Act, or SECA, taxes from the self-employed) and deposits them in three separate trust fund accounts: Old-Age and Survivors Insurance (OASI), Disability Insurance (SSDI), and Medicare. These funds are immediately available for program administrative expenses and benefits payments. To the extent program receipts exceed program expenditures, a surplus builds up in the trust fund. This has been the historical pattern, as large numbers of workers contributed more than sufficient payroll taxes to cover current program expenses. This can be seen in Figure 9.7, which depicts SSDI trust fund receipts, expenditures, and asset balances over time. The trust fund balance stood at more than $153 billion as of the end of 2011. As the figure shows, the balance grew every year from 1993 until 2007, when it peaked at more than $200 billion. Since that time, program expenditures have exceeded receipts by $61 billion. The Great Recession reduced employment and program receipts, while expenditures increased as more people filed for and received disability benefits.

Figure 9.7 Social Security Disability Insurance Trust Fund, 1957–2011 (in billions of $)

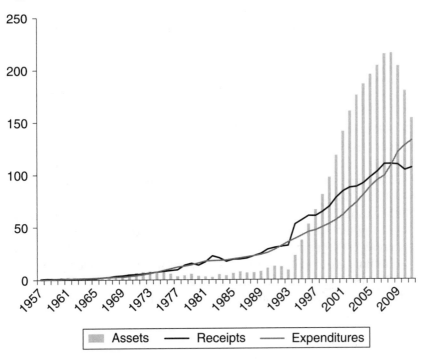

Source: U.S. Social Security Administration, "DI Trust Fund, a Social Security Fund," summary table, http://www.ssa.gov/oact/STATS/table4a2.html.

This recent trend is cause for concern and thoughtful action, but not panic. If the pattern of decline continues, eventually the surplus will be drawn down entirely, and a buildup of debt will begin. Existing revenues would cover only 80–90% of program expenditures. Policy makers will need to make difficult choices: raise payroll taxes or reduce expenditures slightly, or transfer money from other government sources to cover program deficits. However politically distasteful any of these options might be, the need to take such actions is in no way an indication of the "bankruptcy" of the system, despite claims to the contrary.

The federal government has known since 1983—when a commission chaired by future chairman of the Federal Reserve Alan Greenspan examined Social Security financing—that Social Security, including the Disability Insurance program, had a long-run (seventy-five-year) imbalance between expected receipts and expenditures. This is driven by demographic change, as the populous Baby Boomers retire and the ratio of beneficiaries to current workers increases. In Chapter 10 we will examine the range of policy changes necessary to shore up all of the Social Security trust funds, including the SSDI fund. Here we will say only that the growth in utilization of the disability insurance program is both predictable and manageable. There is no crisis, only a declining trust fund surplus engendered by a combination of recession and demographic shifts.

UNDERSTANDING THE GROWTH IN SSDI BENEFICIARIES AND EXPENDITURES

The annual percentage of the "disability-insured" population applying for and receiving benefits has doubled over the past decade. The rise has been particularly steep since the beginning of the Great Recession of 2008 (see Figure 9.8). In 2011, Social Security paid benefits to just over 9.8 million disabled workers, dependent spouses, and children.[31]

It has long been understood by those who study disability insurance that during times of economic distress, the incidence of claimed disability increases.[32] Impairments that might have been overcome during times of economic growth and high rates of employment become the basis for claims of disability. It is not hard to see why. When a layoff occurs and few jobs are available, a stint on unemployment insurance is prolonged.

Figure 9.8 SSDI Applications, 1975–2010

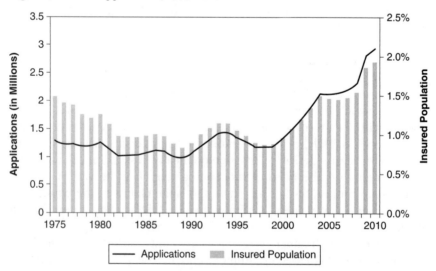

Source: Social Security Advisory Board, *Aspects of Disability Decision Making: Data and Materials* (Washington, DC: Social Security Advisory Board, February 2012), http://www.ssab.gov/Publications/ Disability/GPO_Chartbook_FINAL_06122012.pdf.

When those benefits ultimately end, still-unemployed workers face a world in which disability payments, even at a fraction of their old wages, look appealing. Employers who might have made accommodations for workers' impairments in a booming economy can no longer afford to do so. If retirement is close, retraining for a new career may seem overly burdensome. As a recession drags on and jobs are not plentiful, many no doubt make the choice to see if a musculoskeletal malady or a mood disorder qualifies them for disability insurance benefits. As we have seen, a majority of applicants do not qualify on their first try (and no one without a significant work record ever will).

It is thus unsurprising that the rate of SSDI applications—and the rate of rejections—increased from 2008 to 2012. The rise in program demand is predictable and could lead, absent a rigorous application assessment process, to unsustainable program fiscal imbalances.

The recent growth in program expenditures is a function of much more than economic troubles. Over the past three decades, the work-force grew as women began working outside the home at increasing rates. The labor force grew not only in size but also as a percentage of the adult population. Women became much more likely to be insured against disability, and their rates of program utilization now approach those of men (see Figure 9.9).

Figure 9.9 Percentage of Working-Age Population, Ages 20–64, Receiving Disability Insurance Benefits

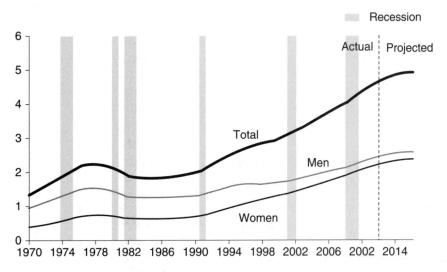

Source: Congressional Budget Office; U.S. Social Security Administration.

During the same period, the American workforce aged. Members of the larger-than-average Baby Boomer generation entered the workforce, built careers, and now are beginning to retire. As we saw in Figure 9.1, rates of disability increase with age. As the mix of workers has gotten older, over-all rates of disability have climbed. According to researchers, this shift has produced 16% of the increase in SSDI program growth for male insureds.[33]

Policy changes within and outside the program, however, appear to be the most important factors.[34] The 1983 Greenspan Commission rec-ommendations led Congress to phase in a change of the Social Security retirement age from 65 to 67. Disabled beneficiaries now spend an extra two years on the disability rolls before claiming their old-age pensions. In 1984, Congress unanimously rolled back the Reagan administration's tighter standards for continuing eligibility for SSDI payments, which had set off a political firestorm and a flood of appeals to federal courts by beneficiaries whose benefits had been terminated.[35] The new standards led to the growth of claims based on musculoskeletal maladies and mood disorders; 40% of beneficiaries' disabilities fall into these classifi-cations.[36] This is nearly double the pre-1984 rate.

Absent policy change, the Congressional Budget Office projects that an increase in the SSDI payroll tax from 1.8% to 2.2% of covered wages is necessary to shore up the program's finances over the next seventy-five years.[37] This increase could be reduced if the wage base on which the tax is levied were increased above the current $113,400 cap. Doing so would cause the top 5% of earners to pay more in payroll taxes.

Of course, Congress could make incremental policy changes as well. Benefit formulas could be adjusted. Pension indexing formulas might be adjusted to better reflect actual economy-wide inflation. The presi-dent could request and the Congress fund higher levels of Continuing Disability Reviews. Some combination of revenue enhancements and expense reductions would almost certainly ensure that the social insur-ance protection from disability available to American workers will be in place for generations to come. The projected shortfall is, after all, a modest 0.4% of covered wages. There is no crisis.

SUPPLEMENTAL SECURITY INCOME

In Chapters 4 and 5, we provided brief discussion of the Supplemental Security Income program. SSI is an alternative residualist model to SSDI's social insurance approach to support for the disabled. SSI is a Nixon-era federal means-tested program that provides income support to the needy aged, blind, and disabled. It replaced three joint federal and state categorical assistance programs: Old-Age Assistance, Aid to the Blind, and Aid to the Totally and Permanently Disabled. The federal government sets the rules for SSI and provides the vast majority of the funding, which states can choose to supplement.

In 2011, SSI served 8.1 million beneficiaries, two-thirds of whom qualified on the basis of disability. Of these, 1.2 million beneficiaries were blind or disabled children. The SSI standards for determining disability are the same as in the SSDI program. Total program expenditures in 2011 were $51 billion, and the average benefit was $502 per month.[38] Most SSI beneficiaries qualify for Medicaid health insurance benefits and food assistance as well.[39]

SSI is a program of last resort for the destitute. Most recipients have limited work histories. Few qualify for Social Security benefits, and those who do have incomes well beneath the federal poverty level. In 2011, 1.4 million beneficiaries received both SSI and SSDI. This number had increased only slightly between 2005 and 2011.[40] That the Great Recession did not swell the ranks suggests that program qualification criteria are quite rigorous. This is not unemployment insurance. Figure 9.10 illustrates the tight control over this means-tested program over time.

Figure 9.10 SSI Recipients as Percentage of the Total Population by Age, 1979–2009

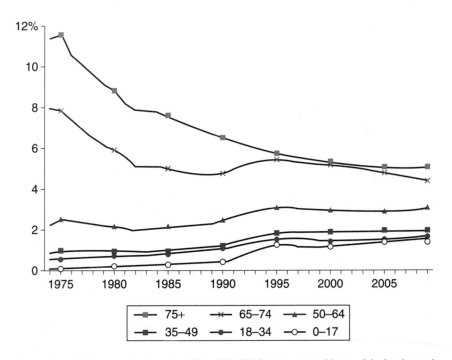

Source: U.S. Social Security Administration, Office of the Chief Actuary, *Annual Report of the Supplemental Security Income Program* (Washington, DC: Social Security Administration, 2010), Table IV.B7.

To qualify for SSI benefits, an individual must have less than $2,000 in assets; for a married couple, the amount is $3,000. Exceptions are made for a residence and an automobile. Rules prevent applicants from qualifying by transferring assets to others in the prior five years. A recipient is allowed $65 dollars per month of income before benefits are reduced by a dollar for every dollar of earned income. (Program administrators terminated the benefits of 805,000 recipients in 2011; more than half had exceeded either income or asset limits.)[41]

Work incentives similar to those in the SSDI program are built into SSI. Beneficiaries qualify for vocational rehabilitation at state agencies or through private providers. They may deduct "impairment-related" work expenses from any earned income. Medicaid benefits may be continued, even if new earnings disqualify ongoing cash benefits. And, finally, a former SSI beneficiary whose income falls back below program thresholds can file for expedited reinstatement to the program.

This is crucial because, unlike in the SSDI program, SSI benefits are not retroactive to the time of the disability. The application process is similarly rigorous, and only one in three applicants ultimately qualifies. In 2010, program administrators rejected nearly 1.7 million applications for SSI.[42]

While program benefits are modest and fail to lift more than half of beneficiaries' incomes above the federal poverty level, SSI is a godsend to those who do qualify. It alleviates the poverty of an unfortunate class of citizens, raising many Americans up from "extreme poverty" (income less than half the official FPL) to a standard of living just below the FPL.[43]

ADDITIONAL PROTECTIONS

The major federal programs for disabled workers, SSDI and SSI, are targeted at persons who are out of the workforce. It is possible to receive these benefits while having some earnings, but the earnings levels that are sufficient to disqualify a beneficiary are quite low. Just as few beneficiaries ever return to full-time work, few SSDI or SSI beneficiaries work while receiving benefits. Hence it is reasonable to conclude that these federal programs do not provide replacement income for either temporary disability or partial disability.

For workers injured on the job, workers' compensation may provide benefits for those with temporary and partial disabilities as well as for those with total permanent disabilities. And the special scheme of compensation for veterans who are disabled during active service or whose conditions are exacerbated by military service may receive compensation for total disability and for partial disabilities that may be as slight as conditions that impair only 10% of a veteran's prior functioning. And, as we noted earlier, more than 30% of workers are covered by private group disability insurance that provides a partial salary or a wage replacement on either a permanent or a temporary basis.

While there are many ways for a worker to fall into the gaps between these various programs, the largest such pitfall may be with respect to partial or temporary disabilities that are not work or service connected. A worker who is ill or injured and who cannot work for some period of time is ineligible for unemployment insurance. In order to be eligible for the unemployment insurance program, a worker must not only be covered and lose his or her job for an acceptable reason but also be "available for work." Ill or injured workers are, of course, unable to meet this standard.

Ill or injured workers whose impairments arise from circumstances occurring outside of work will have temporary disability coverage only through an employer's group disability insurance plan, unless they live in one of the five states (and Puerto Rico) that have temporary disability insurance programs. (There is also a special federal program for railroad workers.) We will not here attempt to plumb the depths of the variations among these programs. Suffice it to say that none of these programs lasts longer than 52 weeks and most last for only 26. In the states that have them, temporary disability insurance is designed to be an alternative to unemployment insurance for workers who are temporarily unemployed because of illness or injury and cannot satisfy the unemployment insurance "available for work" requirement. Indeed, these programs are generally administered by the states' unemployment insurance commissions. As with unemployment insurance itself and private disability insurance, eligibility for these state programs is based on inability to do a worker's regular work, not inability to hold any job available in the national economy. Because New York and California are among the states providing temporary disability insurance, coverage is broader than a mere five participating states might suggest. Even so, considerably less than half of American workers have access to any of these state-run programs.[44]

As our review of the protections in place against income losses due to disability shows, the vast majority are for long-term, not short-term, disability. Coverage for short-term disability is limited to employer-provided benefits for about one-third of workers and state workers' compensation. Federal government programs cover only federal employees. Broader coverage for long-term disability makes sense because the threat to family income is much greater and of longer duration in cases of such disability.

Long-term disability of many causes and forms—blindness, deafness, paraplegia, quadriplegia, developmental disorders, mental illness, musculoskeletal maladies—threatens all of us. While it is possible to live and work with a disability, the physical, emotional, and intellectual challenges presented by long-term disability place the disabled person at an economic disadvantage. Family incomes rarely, if ever, rise as the result of disability. Medical expenses jump, sometimes to permanently high levels, while human capabilities fall.

Long-term disability may be partial or total. Only workers' compensation provides benefits for partial disability, such as the loss of a limb, and then only when the disabling event occurs on the job. The bulk of long-term disability arises from causes unrelated to the workplace. All other commercial insurance and public programs protect against total and permanent disability. Figure 9.11 illustrates the sum total of protections available in the United States. The public sector provides or mandates the vast majority of protections against income loss due to long-term disability. Only a small percentage of Americans can count on commercial insurance during times when they are disabled and unable to work.

Figure 9.11 $228 Billion of U.S. Disability Protection, 2011

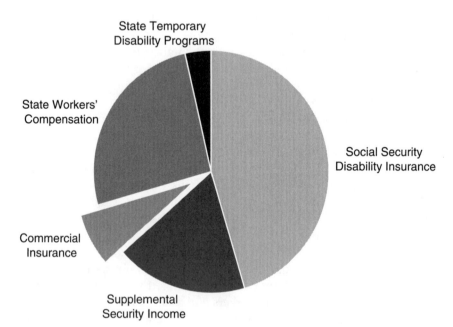

Source: Authors' calculations from various sources cited elsewhere in this chapter. Workers' comp and SSDI figures include payments for medical services.

Note: Collective state temporary disability program data are unavailable. Our estimate is based on data from California and New Jersey, two of the five states with programs.

The contemporary debate about SSDI and SSI coverage in the United States—which is dominated by the ideological opponents of public provision and financing of protections—focuses on the growth in expenditures and caseloads for these programs. A progressive critique would begin in a much different place. The disabled who do qualify receive rather meager benefits, and only in cases of total and permanent disability. Applicants must demonstrate almost a half year of little or no work income, and even if approved for benefits they must wait up to two years to qualify for needed health insurance benefits in the Medicare or Medicaid program. The fear of moral hazard–induced program growth does not fully explain these gaps in coverage; they are also the residue of ideological opposition. Americans generally learn of the gaps only once they are in need.

INTERNATIONAL EXPERIENCE AND REFORM POSSIBILITIES

Like the United States, all developed nations struggle to design disability protection programs that avoid moral hazard while providing beneficiaries with sufficient benefits and incentives for a return to work. Over recent decades, caseloads have grown as working populations have aged and the world economy has faltered. U.S. system performance might best be described as on par with that of its international competitors. Figure 9.12 shows U.S. disability caseloads exactly at the average of twenty-eight OECD nations.

While U.S. rates of disability are average, U.S. spending as a percentage of income is lower. In 2009, the United States spent 1.7% while OECD nations spent 2.6% of gross domestic product (GDP) on "incapacity-related" public and mandatory private disability insurance programs.[45] The difference is explained in part by other nations being more likely to have publicly funded short-term disability programs and schemes to address partial disability.

Short-term disability programs cover individuals for up to a year before long-term disability coverage is necessary. Many countries (and employers) monitor the use of short-term disability closely, as it is often a precursor to long-term disability and movement out of the workforce. Early intervention is possible. Other nations spend a greater fraction of overall funding on vocational rehabilitation programs in a collective attempt to retrain disabled workers. As Figure 9.13 shows, the United States lags most developed nations in both the percentage of program funding and the percentage of national income spent on rehabilitation and employment programs. We are more likely to pay cash benefits to disabled workers than to commit the resources required to attempt to rehabilitate and retrain them.

Figure 9.12 Disability Benefit Recipients in Percentage of the Population Ages 20–64 in Twenty-Eight OECD Countries, Mid-1990s and Latest Year Available

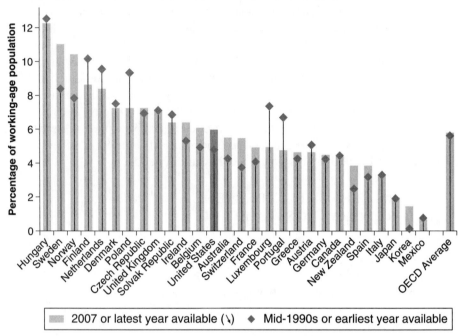

Source: Organisation for Economic Co-operation and Development, Directorate for Employment, Labour and Social Affairs, *Sickness, Disability and Work: Keeping on Track in the Economic Downturn,* background paper (Paris: OECD, 2009), 14, Figure 2, http://www.oecd.org/els/employmentpoliciesanddata/42699911 .pdf. Data provided by national authorities to OECD.

From the standpoint of human development, these training and rehabilitation programs demonstrate the commitment of a country to its impaired citizens. But economically, these are challenging enterprises, heavy on administrative costs and uncertain in effects on employment. Program expenditures finance public employees or private contractors charged with helping the disabled regain abilities or retrain for new work. Medical and vocational rehabilitation providers must be paid to assess levels of partial disability. Jobs, as during the current recession, may be in short supply even for those rehabilitated and qualified. Governments continue to fund some level of financial subsidy to the partially disabled person.

The reality is that the American approach is certainly cheaper in the short run, and possibly over the long run as well. Even in countries that take an intensive approach to rehabilitation, the vast majority of disabled

Figure 9.13 Active Labor Market Spending on Employment Programs and Vocational Rehabilitation, 2007

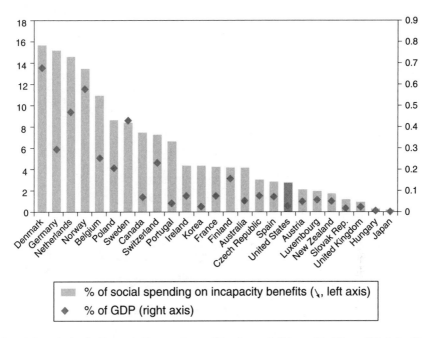

Source: Organisation for Economic Co-operation and Development, *Sickness, Disability and Work: Breaking the Barriers* (Paris: OECD, 2010), 59, http://ec.europa.eu/health/mental_health/eu_compass/reports_ studies/disability_synthesis_2010_en.pdf. Data from OECD ALMP database, OECD SOCX database, and data provided by national authorities to OECD.

workers do not return to work. In the Netherlands, a frequently cited best-practice model,[46] 3% of the disabled leave the long-term disability rolls annually, a slim two percentage points more than in the United States.[47] Those who do leave the rolls tend to have incomes much lower than those without disability.

By comparison with other Western democracies, the United States has both a high application rate for SSDI and SSI and a correspondingly high rejection rate of applicants. This probably reflects the limited alternatives available to impaired, unemployed workers (high application rate) and the stringency of the disability standard applied in these two programs (high rejection rate). Contemporary gaps in medical insurance coverage may also motivate high application rates in the United States, because eligibility carries with it access to Medicaid or Medicare (after a two-year wait). If this is true, full implementation of the Affordable Care Act may reduce application rates for SSDI and SSI benefits.

Figure 9.14 New Disability Benefit Claims per Thousands of the Working-Age Population, 2000 and 2008, and Share of Rejected Benefit Applicants, 2008

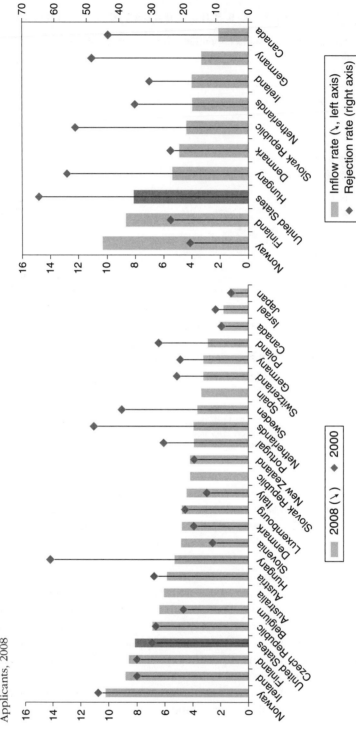

Source: Organisation for Economic Co-operation and Development, *Sickness, Disability and Work: Breaking the Barriers* (Paris: OECD, 2010), 66, http://ec.europa.eu/health/ mental_health/eu_compass/reports_studies/disability_synthesis_2010_en.pdf.

A search of campaign websites failed to locate a mention of the issue of disability protections from either candidate for U.S. president in 2012. Nor does the most prominent recent plan to reform Social Security, that of the Bowles-Simpson "supercommittee," address disability insurance.[48] The supercommittee cochairs propose a reform in the old-age insurance program that would gradually increase the retirement age from 67 to 69. If enacted, this plan, as we have seen from the prior rise in age from 65 to 67, will further stress the finances of SSDI over time. Program caseloads will grow as more who would have retired claim disability instead.

Crisis-mongering is the only certainty in the absence of a forthright discussion of coverage, benefits and costs. We believe widespread awareness on the part of the American public of the threat of disability and the state of protections available would shift the debate in a direction likely to buttress rather than limit social insurance protections. Fiscal pressures push us in the opposite direction.

10

The Threat of Outliving
One's Savings

THE FINAL STAGE OF A LONG LIFE BRINGS INTO STARK RELIEF BOTH A significant threat and a different dimension of social insurance. Recall the Enron retirees described in Chapter 1: the unexpected collapse of the leading Fortune 500 company they had worked for blew away a lifetime of work-generated savings and investment returns. Millions of dollars of retirement savings evaporated into the ether almost overnight, and instead of living comfortable retirements, seniors found themselves dependent on Social Security checks for subsistence incomes.

Recall as well the history in Chapter 4 of the Great Depression of the 1930s. An economic collapse pushed a quarter of Americans out of work. The stock market cascaded downward; one-half of American stock market wealth disappeared in a month's time in late 1929, 90% would be gone by 1932. Others who avoided the risks of equity markets lost their savings when banks collapsed. (Deposit insurance was a policy innovation that came too late to protect citizens of the time.) Four out of five American senior citizens rode out their golden years in poverty, dependent on government assistance programs and the charity of family and friends.

Do you think such events could not happen again? Ask the current generation of retirees, who watched in horror during 2008 as their vast retirement portfolios fell in value by 40–50% during the financial crisis. Many had thought that diversification strategies would prevent the heavy losses suffered by the Enron retirees, who made the mistake of putting all their financial eggs in one basket, but almost all stocks— domestic and international, small cap and large, value or growth—fell by high double-digit percentages. Bond funds performed only slightly better. Only those few who had the knowledge and capacity to bet against mortgage bonds saw positive returns. And who knew one could bet against mortgage bonds? Even with all the ex post analysis available, most Americans still have a tough time understanding such strategies or finding investment vehicles that offer greater diversification protection.

THE DIFFICULTY OF RETIREMENT PLANNING

The challenges of planning for retirement are many. Consider the following questions from the perspective of a young adult: How long will I live? Am I saving for the average lifespan of 70–80 years? Or will I die at 100? (Maybe I will die at 65 and need not have saved for retirement at all!) If I do live a long life, how will my health hold up? How many years will I be able to continue with gainful employment? How will my career go? Will I be among the few who rise to the top of the corporate pyramid or the many whose rise tails off or is abruptly ended by downsizing or outsourcing? Will I require care in a nursing home? If so, how many years at an average of more than $50,000 a pop? How will my investments perform? Or the economy more broadly? Will my house appreciate in value? Will inflation eat away at any gains I have made?

It all reminds us of the old joke: Want to make God laugh? Tell him your plans! There are large numbers of uncontrollable variables that make successful retirement planning difficult indeed.

Of course, all of the aforementioned questions assume one has the capacity and the will to save. Most American families struggle to pay their current bills and save what they can for their kids' six-digit college educations. As we have seen, the vast majority of American families have little in the way of assets beyond small retirement accounts, the family car, and home equity, which isn't what it used to be.

Tough times accentuate the value but also the inadequacy of rational planning for retirement. Who could argue with the commonsense dictums: Study and work hard. Exercise thrift. Avoid behaviors known to lead to poor health. Don't put all your financial eggs in one basket. Build networks of friends and work colleagues. Do everything possible to reach your human potential. Many who carry out all facets of such planning still fail to provide adequately for their own retirements. Bad luck of various sorts can bring you down, and, with regard to retirement planning, so can the good luck of longevity. What are we to do as individuals and as a national community? How has our nation balanced individual and collective responsibility for retirement?

THE THREE- (OR FOUR-)LEGGED STOOL

In the wake of the 1929 market collapse and Great Depression that followed, President Roosevelt's Committee on Economic Security adopted a model for retirement security that consisted of three components: employer-based pensions, private savings, and public pensions. The imagery conveyed was that of a well-constructed three-legged stool. The aim of public policy was to ensure that citizens would avoid impoverishment in old age through a mix of personal and employer-subsidized savings, encouraged by various tax incentives, and a program of social insurance—Social Security's old-age protections. Over time, as we have seen, the model has led to the reduction of old-age impoverishment from 35% in 1960, when most retiring workers began to have had substantial attachment to the Social Security system, to less than 10% in 2011.[1] This is surely the greatest evidence of the success of the program of American social insurance envisioned by Theodore Roosevelt, signed into law by Franklin Roosevelt, and improved by many other presidents over the past eight decades. (Oddly, one will look in vain for any evidence of this triumph at the FDR Memorial in Washington, D.C., yet another sign of our nation's contemporary inattention to the accomplishments of American social insurance.)

Let's examine the individual legs of the stool to understand their evolution over time and how, and at what cost, each protects American retirees. A fourth leg—work during retirement—has altered the imagery in recent years and will surely continue to be a feature of the program's design in the future. This strikes us as a sensible addition, given the improvements in both life span and health over the decades, but it also can be taken too far as a solution. Natural aging and physical work take a toll across the decades of a working life.

Leg 1: Employment-Based Pensions

Almost 150 years ago, American railroad companies began to provide employees with retirement pensions. The payments rewarded long tenures, typically three decades, of loyal company service. Because the promise of retirement support was contingent upon lifetime service, these pensions tended to lock in employees to the companies that provided them. (Shorter "vesting" periods—that is, the periods of employment after which benefits were assured—would be a wise policy development that came 100 years later.) Large American companies occasionally followed the railroads' lead, but as late as the 1920s, pensions in private-sector employment were the exception, not the rule.

Congress passed the first broad government pension program in 1862 to promote military enlistment and to honor the service of disabled Union Civil War veterans.[2] These pensions covered only disability and death, but over the next century, retirement pensions became standard features of compensation packages for government employees across occupations (beginning with police and firefighters) and at all levels of government.

Companies and governments offered what came to be known as "defined-benefit pensions." The "benefit" was a fixed monthly payment beginning at the age of retirement and continuing until death. The level of benefit was "defined" by formulas that factored in the length of employee service and average income over a certain period of time.[3] The employer bore the risk of the commitment. If an employee (or often his surviving wife) lived to be 100, the payments kept flowing. What made this model work financially was that life spans were shorter in the earlier twentieth century. The average person died at 47 in 1900 and at 60 in 1930.[4] Thus the average person did not live very long into retirement. For every 100-year-old retiree, large numbers died in their 60s. Moneys paid into a pool by or on behalf of the dead were available to fund the sustenance of those who lived longer than average.

In 1921, Congress changed the tax code in ways that encouraged the substitution of pensions for cash compensation.[5] Employers could deduct contributions to pension funds before taxes. The federal government would not levy taxes on pension fund investment gains. Only at the time of disbursement of the actual pension funds would payouts be taxable. This tax deferral is valuable in part because it allows investment gains to accrue for decades on principal amounts that would otherwise have been paid to the government. Additionally, under progressive taxation the tax rates paid by those in retirement are likely to be lower than the rates they paid when working.

Large American companies, including those in the auto and steel industries, negotiated generous pension provisions with their unionized workforces. By 1960, 40% of American workers had gained access to employment-based pensions.[6] The changes in tax law ushered in the growth of defined-benefit pensions, but they failed to ensure that benefits would be guaranteed or that workers of all income levels could participate.

Two days after Christmas 1963, the 100-year-old and struggling Studebaker Automobile Company announced it was shutting down its American plants; 7,000 workers lost their jobs. Studebaker guaranteed pensions for the retired and those nearing retirement but broke its pension promise to employees under age 60 no matter how long they had worked for the company.[7]

The Studebaker collapse was no aberration; more than 1,800 pension plans had failed in the prior four years.[8] While normal business venture risk tended to explain the failures, the absence of any federal regulatory standards for pensions ensured the damages would be great and somewhat randomly distributed. Congress spent the better part of the next decade considering and debating pension policy reform.

In 1974, President Nixon signed into law the Employee Retirement Income Security Act. ERISA required five-year vesting schedules and broad worker participation in order for pensions to qualify for favorable tax treatment.[9] The law created a new quasi-governmental entity, the Pension Benefit Guaranty Corporation (PBGC), to ensure that workers would receive promised pension benefits. The PBGC levied premiums on corporations to build up a fund sufficient to guarantee pensions up to $45,000 per year per worker. Executive pensions at higher salaries remained uncovered by insurance.

The ERISA framework removed much uncertainty from individual retirement planning but created a new problem for taxpayers. Corporations (and unions) now had an incentive to push off into the future considerations that would have been more important in the present in a world without insurance. The classic moral hazard problem took the form of large promises for future benefits as a way of solving today's contested contract issues.

Such decisions, coupled with the predictable failure of a percentage of companies, led to public assumption of large unfunded pension liabilities. Taxpayers picked up the pension obligations of such once-esteemed American companies as Delta and Northwest Airlines, Kaiser Aluminum, Bethlehem Steel, and Delphi, once General Motors' parts division. In 2011, the PBGC estimated a gap of $26 billion between its assets and expected obligations.[10] Shortfalls in public employee pensions—not guaranteed by the PBGC, but rather by state and local government taxpayers—are estimated by Moody's Investor Service at an astronomical $2 trillion.[11]

Given changes in the economy and the inherent challenges in managing and regulating pension funds, it is perhaps unsurprising that the defined-benefit version would become less common over time. Workers now tend to change employers more frequently, sometimes before they can accrue sufficient time to be vested in pension plans. For their part, companies competing in global markets tend to have less stable workforces, and the companies themselves average shorter life spans. Delphi CEO Robert Miller's view is probably reflective of that of his peers: "A [defined-benefit] pension plan makes no sense in today's world. It's not wise for a company to make financial promises 40 or 50 years down the road."[12] Were it not for an evolution in retirement products over the past three decades, policy and insurance industry entrepreneurs might need to invent a replacement.

In 1978, however, President Carter signed into law another set of tax code changes, the Revenue Act of 1978, which led to the creation of an employment-based pension option, now known as the "401(k)." Section 401(k) of the Internal Revenue Service (IRS) Code established that employees would not be taxed on income they elected to receive as deferred compensation.[13] In 1981, the IRS issued regulations that codified the use of deferred compensation as a source of retirement plan contributions. In the 401(k) model, workers can contribute a certain percentage of their pretax income to retirement savings accounts of their own. Companies often choose to match part or even all of employee contributions. Employees select investment options for the funds (not always wisely, as we saw in the case of Enron) and can "roll over" their plans to new employers' plans or individual plans when they change jobs. The 401(k) model is an example of a "defined-contribution plan."

While defined-contribution plans recognize, and may indeed promote, worker mobility, defined-contribution plans shift the many risks inherent in retirement planning from companies to workers.[14] Further, there is no government-sponsored insurance program to backstop defined-contribution pension programs.[15] Nevertheless, as Figure 10.1 shows, defined-contribution plans have slowly but surely replaced defined-benefit plans as the standard U.S. employment benefit for employees who have pension plans from their employers (most private workers have no plans at all). In the private sector, defined-benefit plans are going the way of the dodo bird. To a lesser degree, public-sector employers are also participating in this shift. Where defined-benefit plans continue to exist, they are under pressure from political groups that object to what they see as special treatment in guaranteed retirement income for public-sector employees.

Preferential tax treatment for employment-based pensions continues. In the FY 2012 budget year, the projected tax expenditure for "net exclusion of pension contributions and earnings" was a whopping $123.4 billion.[16] The distribution of benefits from this tax treatment can be inferred from Figure 10.2. Participation in employment-based retirement plans increases with the income levels of workers. Since marginal income tax rates increase as well, from 10% to 39.6%, the bulk of the tax benefits from the ability to exclude retirement plan contributions from current income fall to high-income workers. Researchers estimate that two-thirds of federal tax expenditures for retirement saving go to those in the top fifth of the income distribution.[17]

In the second quarter of 2012, the Investment Company Institute calculated the asset value of private defined-benefit plans at $2.4 trillion,

Figure 10.1 Shifting U.S. Retirement Plan Composition, 1979–2009

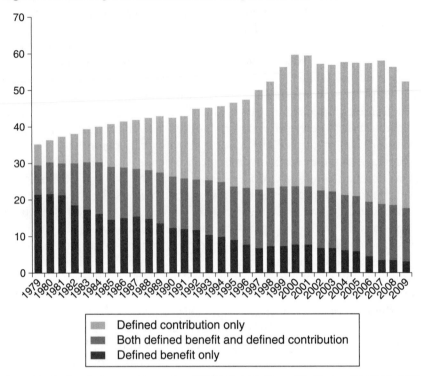

Source: Pension Benefit Guaranty Corporation, *2011 PBGC Annual Report* (Washington, DC: PBGC, 2011), iii, http://www.pbgc.gov/documents/2011-annual-report.pdf.

that of defined-contribution plans at $4.7 trillion, and that of government plans of all stripes at $4.6 trillion.[18] This total of $11.7 trillion would be more than $100,000 for every American household,[19] but averages do not reflect the actual allocation of these assets. The Employee Benefit Research Institute has reported that in 2010, 75 million of the 152.6 million American workers had access to pension plans through their employers or unions. Of those 75 million, 60.7 million participated.[20] Thus only 39.8% of workers were building this leg of the retirement stool. Even among those with employment-based pensions, participation is not normally distributed around the average earner but skewed toward the better-off.

Leg 2: Private Savings—Individual Retirement Accounts

Over recent decades, Americans have gained international repute for their low rates of personal saving and high rates of consumption. The

Figure 10.2 Percentages of Wage and Salary Workers Ages 21–64 Who Participated in an Employment-Based Retirement Plan, by Annual Earnings and Gender, 2010

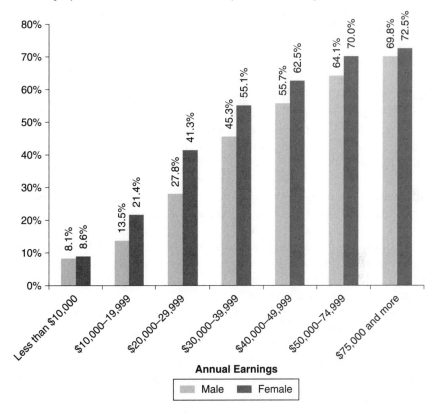

Annual Earnings

Male ▪ Female

Source: Craig Copeland, *Employment-Based Retirement Plan Participation: Geographic Differences and Trends, 2010*, EBRI Issue Brief 363 (Washington, DC: Employment Benefit Research Institute, October 2011), 14.

federal government, too, has spent well in excess of revenues during the past decade, reversing Clintonian budget surpluses with large and growing deficits during both the Bush and Obama administrations. As you will see in the next section, the Social Security program has been the exception to this rule, even as deficit hawks and "entitlements" skeptics have made much of the program's fiscal challenges engendered by the retiring Baby Boom generation.

For purposes of this discussion, when we consider the state of private saving for retirement we will count only resources pledged for that purpose. Americans save for many reasons, especially college education. (A private university education now costs in excess of $50,000 annually.)

Saving goals are often for the near future—the rainy day, the big vacation, or the down payment on a house. Saving for retirement is a special case; since 1974, the U.S. government has provided special incentives for citizens to save for this purpose.

In 1974, ERISA created the individual retirement account (IRA).[21] The law allowed anyone not having access to an employer retirement plan to set up an individual account at a financial institution and deposit into the account $1,500 per year of income on a pretax basis.[22] In 1981, Congress increased the contribution limit to $2,000 and broadened the rules to allow any taxpayer to contribute.[23] A series of changes have since pushed the annual limit up as high as $5,500 per individual and allowed for $1,000 catch-up contributions by those 50 and older.[24]

How successful has the IRA been in helping Americans save adequately for retirement? Measured by rates of participation and the nest eggs developed by those willing and able to save, quite successful. In 2011, 46.1 million households, 38.8% of all American households, held IRAs.[25] As of the second quarter of 2012, the total value of IRA assets was $5.1 trillion.[26] Researchers estimate the average value of these IRAs at $122,100; for those who have contributed for twenty years or more, that average rises to $167,700.[27]

Unfortunately, however, the actual distribution of IRA assets among American households means that IRAs provide security to fewer families than these numbers might suggest. As Figure 10.3 shows, the story with IRAs is similar to the story with employer pensions: relatively few Americans, primarily the well-off, own a large share of the assets. The median IRA value, $42,500, is much lower than the average value. (It rises to $80,000 for those contributing for twenty or more years.) Only those in the top third of the distribution have savings in excess of $100,000.

This distribution would not be especially troubling if the tax expenditures required to encourage contributions were not so large. The projected tax expenditure for IRAs in 2012 was $20.2 billion.[28] Judging from how IRA ownership rates rise with income (see Figure 10.4), the lion's share of the benefits of these tax expenditures go to those who are most well-off. The median household income of those owning an IRA is $75,000, compared to $35,000 for those who do not.[29]

In fact, there is a great deal of overlap in the households that benefit from the employer and individual retirement tax breaks. Three out of four households that own IRAs also participate in employer-sponsored plans.[30] Those in this group—almost a third of U.S. households—use federal tax policy to help craft a retirement stool with three (relatively) strong legs. Almost all of them will supplement their private efforts with public pensions. Most will live quite comfortably, especially since they

Figure 10.3 Percentages of Households with IRA Assets in Specified Ranges, 2011

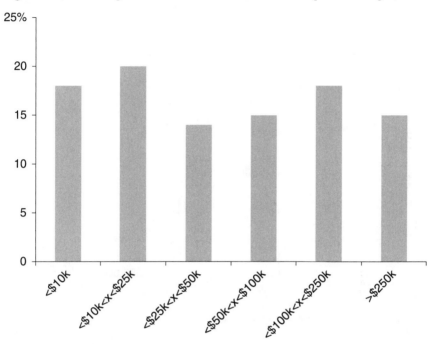

Source: "Appendix: Additional Data on IRA Ownership in 2011," *ICI Research Perspective* 17, no. 8A (November 2011): 7.

also have earned Medicare benefits, which will cover many of their health care costs in retirement.

However, 31% of households, have neither IRAs nor employer pension plans.[31] Within this group, those with steady work histories will qualify for and be wholly dependent on Social Security to finance their golden years. For those without work records sufficient for qualification, there is the residualist means-tested safety net program, Supplemental Security Income.

Leg 3a: Public Pensions—Social Security's Old-Age Program

We reviewed the history of the Social Security program in Chapter 4 and the workings of Social Security survivors and disability insurance components in Chapters 7 and 9. The old-age pension component dwarfs the other two in terms of public awareness, budget size, and constituents served. This component is considered the "third rail" of American politics. Because of its wide base of participation and popular support, only courageous politicians dare approach the issue of its reform. It has been adjusted only at the remote margins since the 1983 Greenspan Commission reforms.

Figure 10.4 Percentage of U.S. Households Owning Traditional IRAs by Household Income, 2011

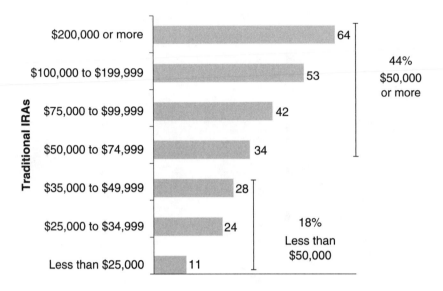

Source: "Appendix: Additional Data on IRA Ownership in 2011," *ICI Research Perspective* 17, no. 8A (November 2011): 4.

In 2010, 156.7 million workers—94% of the American workforce—and their employers contributed FICA payroll taxes to fund the program.[32] For the first $106,800 earned, workers paid 3.6% (this figure returned to 5.3% in 2011) and employers 5.3%.[33] Self-employed workers paid in SECA payroll taxes of the same cumulative percentage. These contributions added $545 billion to the Old-Age and Survivors Insurance trust fund. The trust fund, as we have discussed, is essentially a large bank account used to pay out claims and hold reserve funds. Interest earned on the beginning-of-year reserve balance of $2.3 trillion (yes, trillion) of reserves produced another $108 billion, and taxes on higher-income senior benefits produced $22 billion.[34] (The projected 2012 tax expenditure for those Social Security benefits on which no tax would be collected—the "exclusion of untaxed social security and railroad retirement benefits"—was $35.3 billion.)[35] In 2010, total trust fund payouts were $585 billion, $92 billion less than revenues. The trust fund reserve grew to $2.43 trillion.[36]

In 2010, 37.5 million beneficiaries received an average of $1,129 per month.[37] One can see from Figure 10.5—a depiction of the distribution of monthly payments to beneficiaries—that the amounts received vary by the size of household and the lifetime earnings record of the worker.

Figure 10.5 Percentage Distribution of Monthly Old-Age Pensions in Social Security Program

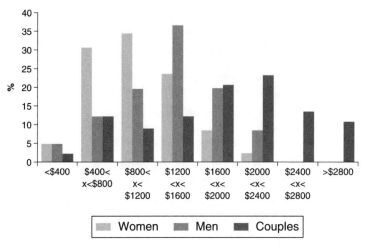

Source: U.S. Social Security Administration, *Annual Statistical Supplement to the Social Security Bulletin, 2011* (Washington, DC: Government Printing Office, 2011), Table 5.B6.

The current generation of female retirees, mostly born in the 1930s and 1940s, tended not to work as much as their male counterparts, or to work in professions that were not as lucrative. Hence they earned smaller pensions. Many in that group are widows, too. One can see that the monthly benefits of households are cut proportionately when the size of a household falls to one.

To assist in retirement planning, the Social Security Administration provides each worker with an annual assessment of the projected future benefits he or she has earned. The sample in Figure 10.6 shows estimates of the Social Security benefits earned in each program component: old age, survivors, and disability. (The assessment also details the worker's status with regard to Medicare, which is run by a separate agency.) These estimates are adjusted annually for inflation.[38]

Note in particular the way the monthly amount varies with retirement timing. Full retirement age (FRA) is somewhere between 65 and 67 (for those born after 1960), but benefits can begin as early as the month after one's 62nd birthday. There is nearly a $1,000 monthly difference if one delays retirement from 62 to 70, and a $500 difference if one waits until the FRA of 67. The SSA reduces (or increases) the size of the monthly check that the beneficiary would have collected at FRA commensurately with the duration of early (or later) retirement. Approximately three out of four Americans begin to receive benefits at some point between 62 and FRA.[39] Actuarially speaking, the expected long-term payout falls, so

Figure 10.6 Segment of a Sample Social Security Statement

Your Estimated Benefits

*Retirement You have earned credits to qualify for benefits. At your current
earnings rate, if you continue working until . . .
your full retirement age (67 years), your payment
would be about ....$ 1,590 a month
age 70, your payment would be about...................$ 1,983 a month
age 62, your payment would be about...................$ 1,096 a month

*Disability You have earned enough credits to qualify
for benefits. If you became disabled right now,
your payment would be about ....$ 1,450 a month

*Family If you get retirement or disability benefits, your spouse and children
also may qualify for benefits.

*Survivors You have earned enough credits for your family to receive survivors
benefits. If you die this year, certain members of your family may
qualify for the following benefits:
your child.. $ 1,133 a month
your spouse who is caring for your child .... $ 1,511 a month
your spouse, if benefits start at full
retirement age .... $ 1,477 a month
Total family benefits cannot be more than .... $ 2,782 a month
Your spouse or minor child may be eligible for
a special one-time death benefit of $ 255.

Medicare You have enough credits to qualify for Medicare at age 65. Even if
you do not retire at age 65, be sure to contact Social Security three
months before your 65th birthday to enroll in Medicare.

*Your estimated benefits are based on current law. Congress has made changes to
the law in the past and can do so at any time. The law governing benefit amounts
may change because, by 2033, the payroll taxes collected will be enough to pay
only about 75 percent of scheduled benefits.

Source: U.S. Social Security Administration, "Get Your Social Security Statement Online," last revised
November 23, 2012, https://www.socialsecurity.gov/mystatement.

this pattern of retirement prior to FRA works to the advantage of long-
term program financing.

No American product would be complete without a warning label, and
Social Security is no exception. At the bottom of the benefit schedule, the
SSA warns that long-term program financing must be shored up in order
to ensure payment of full benefits. This introduces some uncertainty
in retirement planning and highlights the importance of making small
policy adjustments well in advance. It also belies the nonsensical notion
that Social Security is going "bankrupt" and won't be around for today's

**"Just what exactly is your generation going to
do about my generation's social security?"**

Source: The Cartoon Bank

young adults. Even if no changes are made, an estimated 75% of benefits
are assured.[40]

To qualify for the benefits of old-age insurance, a retired worker (or
surviving spouse or child under 18) must have earned forty "credits"
over a working life. In 2012, one credit was earned for each $4,500 of
income, up to four credits. Even ten years of typical full-time, or decades
of part-time, work experience qualifies one for a pension.

As we have seen, the sizes of these pensions vary as much as eightfold
across households, depending on the size of the unit and the earnings
history of the workers. Much is often made of how Social Security is a
bad deal for the well-off, who, it is claimed, end up getting much less on
average than they contributed. Leaving aside for a moment the confused
assumptions of such a claim, let us explain the nuts and bolts of the
formula.

The SSA first calculates a beneficiary-specific output called the average
indexed monthly earnings (AIME). The AIME is essentially the average
of a worker's monthly earnings over time brought forward into current,
inflation-adjusted dollars. From this value, the SSA calculates a primary
insurance amount (PIA) using the following formula:

90% of up to first $791 of AIME + 32% of AIME
between $750 and $4,768 + 15% of AIME above $4,768[41]

Two examples will demonstrate how this works and the implications for workers. A qualifying worker with AIME of $1,500 per month, or annual average salary of $18,000—essentially a full-time minimum wage job—receives (0.90 × $791) + [0.32 × ($1,500 − $791)] = $712 + $227 = $939 per month. Almost two-thirds of the worker's income is replaced. A higher-income qualifying worker with AIME of $8,350 per month—close to $100,000 per year—receives (0.90 × $791) + [0.32 × ($4,768 − $791)] + [0.15 × ($8,350 − $4,768)] = $712 + $1,273 + $537 = $2,522. While this pension is substantially higher than that of the minimum wage worker, only 30% of the higher-income worker's prior income is replaced.

What is important to remember when assessing the fairness of a scheme producing such results is that Social Security is a multidimensional insurance program, not a retirement savings program. As we have seen, Social Security provides protection against the threats of long-term disability, early death of a family breadwinner, and outliving one's savings. Ex post, it is always easy to calculate whether an insurance product was a "good deal." If your house burns down, thirty years of annual $1,000 premium payments look like a good deal when compared to the hundreds of thousands of dollars required to rebuild. But if your house never burns down, you do not claim the insurance contract was unfair. Ex ante, you were pleased to buy protection and hoped your house would not go up in flames.

Should you be pleased to buy the protections offered by Social Security, even if it means you might look back and see a record of contributions in excess of benefits received? Just as in the case of homeowners' insurance, from the vantage point of early adulthood, workers cannot know whether they will be high or low lifetime earners. While there is surely room for debate about payroll tax rates, the amount of income subjected to that tax, and the distribution and level of benefits, we would argue that the current approach is fundamentally sound. Private markets function poorly for this insurance protection. U.S. payroll tax burdens, as you will see, are small when considered relative to our international economic competitors. The Social Security old-age program's administrative expenses, $3.5 billion in 2011, or 0.6% of benefits paid, are dramatically lower than those of commercial insurance plans and most mutual funds.[42] The benefits of the program, while not overly generous to anyone, provide sustenance to the permanently disabled, to orphans, and to senior citizens.

On average, seniors obtain almost $3 of every $5 of their income from Social Security (see Figure 10.7). It is indeed disconcerting to imagine life before Social Security rounded out this pie. After we conclude our review of the state of the four legs of the stool individually and

Figure 10.7 Income Sources, Americans Age 65 and Older, 2010

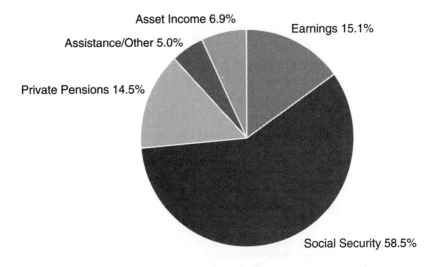

Source: U.S. Social Security Administration, Office of Retirement and Disability Policy, *Income of the Population 55 or Older, 2010* (Washington, DC: Social Security Administration, 2012), 234–37, Table 8.A1.

collectively, we will take up the issue of program reform generally and what would be required to shore up the seventy-five-year imbalance in Social Security finances in particular.

Leg 3b: Public Means-Tested Assistance for the Poor Aged— Supplemental Security Income

Social Security does not lift all American seniors out of poverty. Some fail to qualify for program insurance. Others qualify, but their benefits are not sufficient to lift them out of poverty. Almost 1.2 million of these poor seniors received Supplemental Security Income program benefits in 2011.[43] Of these, 56.3% also received Social Security benefits.[44]

We discussed SSI in the chapters on the threats of birth into a poor family and disability. This Nixon administration federal program provides means-tested benefits only to those who are aged, blind, or disabled and poor. SSI supplements the incomes of those qualifying up to $698 per month.[45] Payments to poor seniors in 2010 totaled $4.8 billion.[46] This is less than 1% of the $577 billion in benefit payments in the old-age and survivors insurance component of the Social Security program during the same time frame. SSI is a small-scale supplement, as its moniker indicates.

Figure 10.8 Labor Force Participation Rates of Workers 65 and Older, 1948–2007

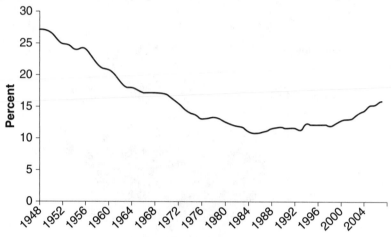

Source: U.S. Bureau of Labor Statistics, "Labor Force Participation of Seniors, 1948–2007," July 29, 2008, http://www.bls.gov/opub/ted/2008/jul/wk4/art02.html.

Leg 4: Working beyond Traditional Retirement

In 2007, only about 15% of American seniors worked.[47] But as one can see from Figure 10.8, this is actually a 50% increase (from 10% to 15%) from two decades earlier, when senior employment hit its lowest level in decades. More recent data are unavailable, but we know from recent surveys of those approaching retirement that this trend is likely to continue. In 2011, according to the nonprofit Transamerica Foundation, "39 percent of American workers plan to retire after age 70 or not at all, and over half (54 percent) of workers plan to work in retirement."[48]

Of those planning to work, almost half cite "necessity" as the reason. The tumult of the "Great Recession" upset the retirement plans of many, as both stock portfolios and home equity plunged in value while unemployment increased. High levels of personal debt—much of it related to the tapping of what looked like home equity—contribute to that necessity.

For those seniors who plan on working, current data might temper their expectations concerning their earnings. Seniors, on average, earn about 10% less per week than younger workers.[49] Higher rates of part-time work undoubtedly play a role. Of those seniors working, 44% work part-time.[50] As we have seen, rates of disability increase as the population ages; so do medical expenses and energy levels. What one intends may not be what one is capable of doing.

We believe modest expectations for work in retirement are in order. One ought not to think for a moment, however, that work is a reasonable substitute for the combination of private and public pensions that provide the lion's share of sustenance for seniors. It is a nice, but uncertain, complement to a well-constructed three-legged stool.

Summary: State of the Four-Legged Stool

Now that we have examined the four legs of the stool individually, what might we say about the state of retirement protection generally? How are seniors doing? Only one in ten lives in poverty. This is indeed a triumph of American public policy over the past eight decades, and it is too often ignored or glossed over in contemporary discussions about Social Security. According to the nonpartisan Center for Budget and Policy Priorities, absent Social Security benefits, 43.6% of American seniors (14.5 million citizens) would live in poverty.[51]

Our analysis and the summary data show there are three segments of American retirees. The first, the top quintile of American seniors, built a very durable four-legged stool. From Figure 10.9, we can see that the seniors in this segment own a mix of private pension and investment

Figure 10.9 Sources of Income by Quintile for Americans Age 65 and Older

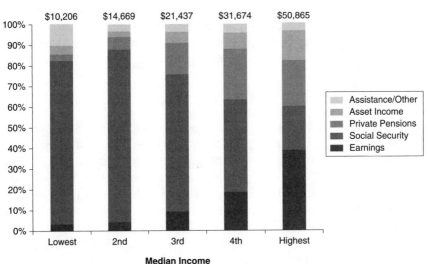

Source: U.S. Social Security Administration, *Income of the Population 55 or Older, 2010* (Washington, DC: Social Security Administration, 2012), 94, Table 3.A6, and 250, Table 8.A5.

assets, contributed the most to and receive the highest pensions from Social Security, and continue to work gainfully in their retirements. While there is, of course, much variation in this top slice of income earners, all are well-off in comparison to those occupying lower floors of the income pyramid.

Hence some proposals to balance Social Security's long-term book would slice about 20% from the average high-income earner's pension. But how many of us could accommodate that sort of reduction in our current income? As we move downward through the next two quintiles, public pensions provide 40–60% of seniors' income. The roles of ongoing earnings from work and payments from private pensions dwindle commensurately. Public pensions determine the life prospects for this middle and upper-middle class of seniors.

Finally, those in the lowest two income quintiles depend almost entirely on Social Security and assistance programs for their subsistence. We might call this segment the poor aged. At the extreme low end, means-tested social assistance programs provide an additional boost, if not out of poverty, then out of hunger or homelessness. While SSI is the primary source of assistance for poor seniors in the lowest quintile, state and local governments as well as private charity play complementary roles in combatting destitution among this group.

Our system ensures a minimum level of subsistence for all who have earned through their labor the status of insured. It provides ample tax incentives and rewards for hard work and saving across one's lifetime for retirement. That the well-off receive great tax benefits for employment-based and individual pensions is balanced to some considerable degree by the progressive nature of public pensions. There is something for all Americans in this crazy quilt of retirement policy. Our strong and durable protections are worth protecting or, dare we say, improving.

THE INTERNATIONAL CONTEXT

We have attempted throughout this book to place the U.S. experience in an international context. While we believe the United States is exceptional in many ways, we know that there is much that can be learned from others on both personal and national levels. Our country ought to be secure enough in its collective state of mind to continue to borrow from other great cultures. The beauty of our nation's capital owes much to Greek and Roman architectural forms and French urban design. Presidents Theodore and Franklin Roosevelt drew American social insurance designs primarily from Germany and England.

All European, Asian, and Middle Eastern nations—with the exception of Burma—provide old-age insurance programs to their citizens.[52] The standard vehicle, as in the United States, is the public pension funded by a combination of employee and employer payroll taxes. The programs differ along many dimensions, especially in the extent to which the benefit payment is flat (one size for all) or varies more proportionally with lifetime earnings. A not insignificant number of nations mandate or encourage private pensions to supplement public pensions.

Citizens retire with old-age pension benefits at a range of ages across nations. Figure 10.10 suggests that the age of 65 is still the most typical. Only three countries match the current U.S. age of 67: Israel, Iceland, and Norway. The United States is one of the outliers. A surprising number of Persian Gulf states, as well as three of the world's most populous states— China, India, and Indonesia—have statutory retirement ages between 55 and 60. These policies undoubtedly reflect cultural differences and a desire to free up jobs for younger workers.

Payroll tax rates vary a great deal as well, as illustrated in Figure 10.11. Here the United States is closer to the outliers on the left-hand side of the distribution, especially when compared to our European allies. (Europeans typically bear additional payroll taxes over what is pictured here in order to cover the cost of financing their health systems.) What is not evident from the data is any income limit on which the tax is levied. Again, European nations are less likely to draw a line at an upper income level as we do ($113,700 in 2013).

As might be predicted once one understands the lower payroll tax story, compared with most nations the United States pays lower public

Figure 10.10 Percentage Distribution of Statutory Male Retirement Age

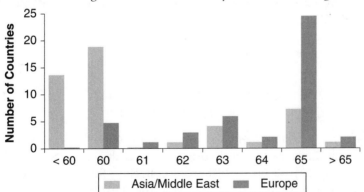

Sources: U.S. Social Security Administration, *Social Security Programs throughout the World: Asia and the Pacific, 2010* (Washington, DC: Government Printing Office, 2010), 21–22, Table 3; U.S. Social Security Administration, *Social Security Programs throughout the World: Europe, 2012* (Washington, DC: Government Printing Office, 2012), 21–22, Table 3.

Figure 10.11 Contribution Rates for Social Security Programs (OASDI)

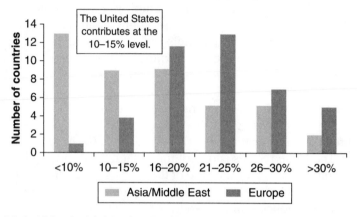

Sources: U.S. Social Security Administration, *Social Security Programs throughout the World: Asia and the Pacific, 2010* (Washington, DC: Government Printing Office, 2010), 23–24, Table 4; U.S. Social Security Administration, *Social Security Programs throughout the World: Europe, 2012* (Washington, DC: Government Printing Office, 2012), 23–24, Table 4.

pension benefits in relation to prior earnings (see Figure 10.12). The average OECD nation replaces almost three-quarters of preretirement income; the United States replaces on the order of half.[53] (We leave aside here the uncertainties concerning whether some countries will actually be able to keep their pension promises.) Our largest and most formidable economic competitors' policies run the gamut from high replacement (China at 91%) to comparable replacement (Germany at 58%) to lower replacement (Japan at 41%).

Thus, seen in the international context, U.S. protections are neither particularly expensive nor generous. Compared with workers around the world, Americans work longer, retire for shorter periods, and rely to a much greater extent on savings accumulated through personal saving and contributions to employer plans.

SOLUTIONS TO THE SOCIAL SECURITY TRUST FUND SEVENTY-FIVE-YEAR IMBALANCE

In the United States, members of the post–World War II Baby Boom generation have begun to retire. As a result, the ratio of workers contributing payroll taxes to retirees collecting Social Security benefits will likely fall from 3:1 to 2:1 over the next two decades before stabilizing.[54] In time, Social Security's annual revenues will no longer be in excess of its annual expenses. Instead of continuing to build a trust fund surplus, we will draw it down over time to ensure full benefits are paid to the Baby Boomers. When the OASI trust fund is drained—now

Figure 10.12 Net Pension Replacement Rates: Average Earners

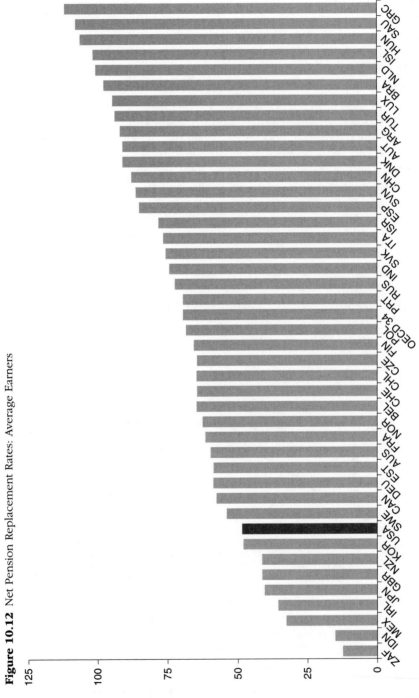

Source: Organisation for Economic Co-operation and Development, *Pensions at a Glance 2011: Retirement-Income Systems in OECD and G20 Countries* (Paris: OECD, 2011), 125.

projected to occur in 2035—existing payroll taxes will cover only 75% of the projected bill.[55] While this is a far cry from "bankruptcy," few seniors could withstand a 25% cut in benefits without serious consequences for their livelihoods.

Figure 10.13 depicts the projected future gap between payroll tax revenues and outlays. The 1983 Greenspan Commission, while it solved the then near-term fiscal problem, failed to agree on program reforms to solve this well-understood long-term issue. Three decades of political leaders since have done nothing to meet the challenge. In fact, President Obama and the Congress added to the problem by reducing payroll taxes as part of the stimulus plan in 2009 and again in 2011.

What policy reform options exist for preserving the insurance protections of Social Security in full for future generations? Absent program changes, the trustees estimate that a 2.6% increase in the payroll tax, from 12.4% to 15%, is required.[56] Of course, this increase would not need to be so large if the amount of income on which the payroll tax is levied were increased from its current level of $106,500. The Congressional Budget Office estimates that increasing the ceiling on the income subject to payroll taxes to $250,000 would solve half

Figure 10.13 Social Security Income, Cost, and Expenditures as Percentage of Taxable Payroll

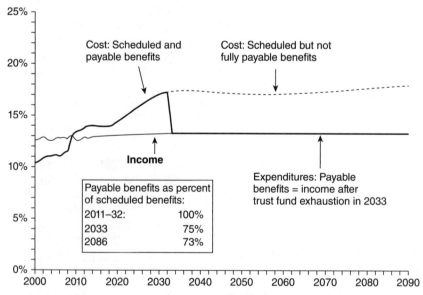

Source: Board of Trustees, Federal Old-Age and Survivors Insurance and Federal Disability Insurance Trust Funds, *2012 Annual Report of the Board of Trustees of the Federal Old-Age and Survivors Insurance and Federal Disability Insurance Trust Funds* (Washington, DC: Government Printing Office, 2012), 11, Figure II.D2.

the problem. Collecting FICA taxes on all income would eliminate the problem entirely.[57] Either change would hit upper-income families hard; a worker making $250,000 annually would pay more than $15,000 extra per year in taxes without any improvement in the public pension benefit he or she could expect. On the other hand, wage growth over the past two decades has strongly favored upper-income workers, so fairness suggests that some increase in their contributions might be reasonable. Alternatively, some portion of workers' "fringe" or "in-kind" benefits might be subjected to FICA taxes. Over time, compensation has shifted from cash to employment-based benefits such that a lower percentage of total payroll is now subject to the FICA tax than in the early decades of the program.

Absent any tax increase or base broadening, the trustees report that an "immediate and permanent reduction of 16.2%" in program expenses is required to solve the long-term projected shortfall.[58] Cutting the benefits of current retirees by this level—or, frankly, by much at all—seems unfair since those in this group have no time to make adjustments in saving or work efforts, and across-the-board cuts would be devastating for lower-income retirees. One possibility that would reduce payments somewhat less for current and more for future retirees is to change the way annual cost-of-living increases in program benefits are calculated, substituting for the consumer price index (CPI) a "chained CPI" more indicative of actual inflation. This would solve 30% of the long-run shortfall,[59] and it seems, on its face, both equitable and efficient. However, more information is needed before it will be possible to assess whether this index of inflation for the whole population holds true of retirees, whose "consumption basket" tends to diverge from that of younger consumers, particularly with respect to out-of-pocket medical expenses.

A gradual increase in the FRA from 67 to 70 would produce another 50% reduction in the shortfall.[60] The argument in favor of this change is one of generational fairness. Life spans (and retirement durations) have increased by five years since 1935. Shaving some time off average retirement merely eliminates a windfall policy makers never intended. Workers who wish to retire earlier would still have the option to do so with the current penalty of lower monthly benefits. (It is likely that disability claims would increase in such a scheme. The burdens of an increased retirement age fall disproportionately on physical laborers.)

And, finally, benefit formula tinkering can solve a portion of the problem as well. Recall the formula used to calculate benefits:

90% of up to first $791 of AIME + 32% of AIME
between $750 and $4,768 + 15% of AIME above $4,768

Why Have Cost-of-Living Increases for Social Security Pensions?

At one level the answer to this question is obvious. Inflation is a form of compound interest that seriously erodes pensions' real value over the expected period of retirement. Even before the consumer price index (CPI) was used to adjust Social Security pensions automatically, Congress routinely adjusted payments to keep pace roughly with inflation. But at a deeper level this process is problematic. Workers' wages or salaries do not automatically adjust for inflation. Why should pensions be different? This is particularly an issue given the "pay-as-you-go" nature of Social Security—that is, pensions are funded primarily by current workers' FICA taxes. Why not use the health of the overall economy, measured by gross domestic product (GDP), as a basis for adjusting pension payments? That would align the interests of current pensioners with those of current workers—a situation much more consistent with the "all in the same boat" philosophy of social insurance. To be sure, this would mean that pensions could go down as well as up. But why not? Fair is fair. (And pensioners may well benefit. Over the past two decades—including the Great Recession—GDP has increased 1.2% faster than the CPI.)

The percentages might be reduced somewhat across the board or at the higher income levels. Reducing all by 15% would solve 80% of the shortfall. Reducing just the top bracket from 15% to 10% solves 10% of the problem.[61]

There are a large number of possible solutions, none of them particularly painful if done thoughtfully and in a timely manner. Modest incremental changes will ensure that Social Security will protect our children and their children over the next century.

Not all possible reforms, however, are wise ones. In the final section of this book, Part III, we will review the state of our protections more generally and critique what we consider to be species-altering proposed reforms that would address the challenges facing Social Security and Medicare by dismantling the programs' protections. Adopting such changes—which are in no sense necessary responses to projected further fiscal difficulties—would be tantamount to turning our backs on eight decades of success.

I I I

Thinking about the Design of Income Security Programs and Their Reform

C h a p t e r

11

Accomplishments and Limitations

THE UNITED STATES HAS A RELATIVELY COMPREHENSIVE SYSTEM OF SOCIAL insurance. Our programs of social provision begin with a bedrock assumption: family income will generally come from work wages or salaries, deferred compensation in the form of pensions, or investments in financial markets (roughly speaking, invested savings, although inheritance plays a small part for many families). We live and work in a vibrant market economy.

Second, we recognize, however, that over the life cycle of any individual there are risks to adequate income from temporary or long-term inability to work and inadequate reserves to withstand major shocks, such as catastrophic medical expenses. American programs of public provision protect against all of these common risks. While we have been at pains to highlight some of the gaps and shortcomings in various American social welfare programs, we should not forget the many successes. Social Security pensions and Medicare have assisted the vast majority of Americans to maintain an above-poverty lifestyle in retirement. At one time old age and poverty, or near poverty, seemed virtual synonyms. That is no longer the case.

At the other end of the life cycle our patchwork quilt of programs for families with children reduces the incidence of childhood poverty by roughly 50%, and very few children remain uncovered by some form of health insurance. During our working lives virtually all of us are covered, at least nominally, by the unemployment compensation system. A combination of Social Security disability benefits, Supplemental Security Income for the disabled, workers' compensation, state-provided temporary disability insurance, and subsidized private disability insurance cushions loss of income resulting from illness or accident. Social Security's Old-Age, Survivors, and Disability Insurance provides more total life and disability insurance for working families than all private insurance combined. And while Americans have long lamented the high cost of medical coverage and lack of universal health insurance, since the enactment of Medicare and Medicaid, those programs combined with subsidized employment-based insurance have meant that the vast majority of Americans have had access to health insurance. If the implementation of the Affordable Care Act is successful, health insurance will become more nearly universal.

Looking at more broadly based and programmatically less complex systems of social insurance in other industrialized nations provides fertile ground for criticizing American arrangements. The United States is often regarded as a social insurance laggard—and there is surely some truth to that charge. But we should not forget that American social provisions against the major risks of inadequate family income are substantial. We have done a lot, and we spend a lot, to ensure family economic security. How then should we think about where we are and what our goals should be for future improvement of Americans' income security?

VARIATIONS IN PROGRAM DESIGN

Only the Social Security programs of retirement and disability pensions, survivors benefits, and Medicare Part A health insurance exemplify the traditional model of social insurance. All workers and families with substantial connection to the workforce are covered. Contributions produce the entitlement, which in turn is linked to earnings (or, in the case of hospital insurance, to a common benefit). The entitlement to benefits depends on the occurrence of a defined risk, combined with prior contributions to the system, not on a demonstration of impoverishment, as in means-tested welfare programs. Social insurance programs are national in scope, managed by the federal government (but with some functions contracted out).

Nevertheless, as the discussions of various programs in Part II reveal, American social programs exhibit remarkable variation, or heterogeneity. It is worth pausing for a moment to consider our complex set of program arrangements, which, while not uniquely American, distinguish our range of social policies and our mix of social insurance programs from those found elsewhere in the developed world.

First, where social insurance is concerned, we have the standard worker-contributor model of participation, not one based on citizenship. Universality of coverage for us typically means all workers and their families, not all citizens. Social insurance coverage is earned through contributions, although in some programs "earned" has special meanings. For example, workers' compensation recipients earn those benefits by giving up rights to tort recoveries; veterans' benefits are earned through service in the military.[1] This much is familiar, the basic contributory principle of social insurance.

Second, however, as a country we do a substantial amount of broad social policy through our income tax code. This is especially noticeable in thinking about the relief of childhood poverty, or cushioning the effects of being born into a poor family. Other than public education, our largest expenditures to ensure against childhood poverty are the Earned Income Tax Credit and other tax exemptions and deductions for families with children. And, as mentioned earlier, the majority of Americans obtain health insurance through their places of employment. Income tax subsidies for that insurance represent the largest single tax expenditure in the federal budget. Our largest housing program is the tax expenditure represented by the home mortgage interest deduction.[2] We also regulate the availability of employment-based pensions, life insurance, and disability insurance through conditions in the tax code on employer deductibility of those costs. These tax expenditures are largely invisible in public budget debates, but they go some way toward closing the gap between what the United States spends on family income security and the expenditures of other developed nations with which American efforts are often compared.[3]

Another important feature of American program design is disaggregated implementation. The administrative implementation of American income security programs often takes place at the state and local level or through the use of private entities, both profit and nonprofit. The variations on this theme are impressive. The federal unemployment insurance program simply prompts state action by imposing a tax that everyone wants to avoid. And, as we have seen, there are limited federal conditions on the design of state unemployment insurance systems that will make the states' employers immune from most of the federal levy. The result, in practice, is an extremely wide dispersion in the availability of unemployment benefits from state to state. Other programs, such as Medicaid and TANF, help finance state programs through direct transfers from the national treasury. Those transfers may come with detailed conditions for the structure of the supported state programs, as in Medicaid, or as block grants with very substantial state discretion for program design, as in TANF.

Some programs financed exclusively with federal funds nonetheless use state implementation. Remember that SNAP benefits are administered by state welfare departments and the nearly 4 million initial disability decisions made annually under the federal SSDI and SSI programs are made by state agency personnel under contracts between the Social Security Administration and state governments.

Finally, some federal social insurance programs contract out implementation in part to private for-profit or nonprofit entities. While we have suggested that Medicare conforms closely to the core social insurance model of national coverage and administration, the federal Centers for Medicare & Medicaid Services contracts with private insurers to make all the initial decisions concerning the coverage of particular Medicare expenses and to offer an array of private plan coverage options for beneficiaries through Medicare Part C. What is more, by subsidizing coverage through employment the federal government implicitly delegates the provision of health insurance for the majority of American workers to private companies. And until the passage of the Affordable Care Act there was virtually no federal regulation of the content of those policies.

America's economic security programs also use virtually every funding approach imaginable. Consider just health insurance: Medicare Part A is financed by earmarked payroll taxes or "contributions"; Medicare Part B is paid for by voluntary premiums combined with general taxation; employment-based health insurance is funded by both employer and employee contributions combined with federal tax subsidies; federal and state taxes finance Medicaid; and many preventive and specialized health services are funded through tax-subsidized charitable contributions, untaxed fees paid to charitable and nonprofit providers by those utilizing their services, and federal and state grants and contracts funded largely through general taxation. Similar heterogeneity is evident in children's and retirement programs as well. Perhaps the strangest funding vehicle is the unemployment insurance program's technique of imposing a federal tax that was never meant to be collected to induce state requirements of employer, experienced-rated contributions.

Finally, note that the design of America's income security programs responds to virtually every vision of the goals of social provision sketched in Chapter 3. TANF was our poster child for the behaviorist approach, but other programs have behaviorist elements. The disability insurance program requires that many beneficiaries be referred to state vocational rehabilitation programs for possible assistance in getting back to work. The unemployment insurance program demands evidence of job search by beneficiaries. Its experience rating of employers was meant to force them to do a better job of managing their businesses and avoiding layoffs of personnel. Means-tested programs such as SSI, Medicaid, and SNAP are obviously residualist in their requirement that families demonstrate current impoverishment to qualify for assistance. These programs also tend to be administered at the state or local level, along with housing assistance for the poor.

Most programs include crosscutting philosophical elements. We have suggested that universal public education may be America's most egalitarian social welfare program, but in its concrete incarnations no student will miss the behaviorist orientation of his or her public school. And, of course, most people would consider universal public education as primarily directed at opportunity enhancement and training for citizenship—not as an income security program. Public education—like most social welfare programs—combines purposes and philosophical visions. Even a relatively straightforward transfer program like the Earned Income Tax Credit has multiple aims—it has a clear residualist antipoverty goal, but it has egalitarian features as well. By relieving lower-middle-class families of income tax and FICA tax burdens, the EITC makes both taxes more strongly progressive. It also shifts the burden of funding both general government budgets and Social Security programs to higher-income families. And because it operates as a wage subsidy, it is opportunity enhancing, making work pay for those with lower-valued skills. It has behaviorist overtones as well—only those who do work and earn some income need apply.

The overall lesson is clear: America's social welfare programs directed at family economic security are complex compromises. They represent balances among visions of social welfare goals and understandings of the proper location of public responsibility. They also reflect compromises among conceptions of governmental and individual and private responsibilities and governmental and market allocation of goods and services. The complex nature of American social programs is hardly an accident. It is the outcome of the forces—political, economic, social, and philosophical—that shaped policy judgments at critical junctures in American history, that is, the points at which these programs were enacted, amended, or reformed.

That we can understand how these programs got to be the programs they are does not mean they must or will remain in their present form. Public policy reform, we suggest, is much like a perpetual-motion machine.

What can we learn by looking back at these programs about how design affects performance and what reform proposals might make sense— whether or not they are enactable in the current political context? Several things stand out rather starkly. First, our practice of doing social policy through the tax code often has perverse distributional consequences. Neither tax credits nor deductions reach those with no income tax liabilities—the potentially worst-off populations are excluded from benefits. And deductions benefit those in higher income brackets more than those in lower brackets. If income security is the goal, this is poor program design.

Second, state and local financing of income security programs produces major differences in the availability of income support across the nation. And because many lower-income Americans live in states or localities with more limited fiscal capacities, geographic divergence is not random. Again, the least well-off may receive the least assistance. Federal formula grants to the states often reduce, but do not erase, these effects. There is surely an argument for making programs fit local political cultures. But to the extent low levels of assistance result from fiscal incapacity, or interstate or intrastate competition to "improve the local business climate," matching programs to underlying preferences is not what is happening. And in a national, indeed global, economy with a mobile population, the argument for local preferences in income security matters is not very strong.

Third, means-tested programs typically produce less effective protections than do more universal social insurance programs. These effects are difficult to disentangle from state and local financing because many means-tested programs have that feature as well. But some do not, and, however financed, means-tested programs have inevitable shortcomings. The demeaning nature of many eligibility investigations dissuades substantial numbers of eligible recipients from seeking assistance. The "us-versus-them" politics of targeting the poor creates political resistance to adequate funding. "Benefit cliffs"—situations in which extra income or a better job makes a person worse off because of the loss of means-tested supports—are almost inevitable.

We will not rehearse here the difficulties and design defects of the many social welfare programs described in prior chapters. Instead, in the remainder of this chapter we will take a closer look at the reform opportunities in our programs designed to alleviate childhood poverty and to protect Americans against the risks of high health care costs and unemployment. Then in the final chapter we will examine reform proposals for Social Security pensions and Medicare that seem to us to move in precisely the wrong direction. These two analyses have this in common: both emphasize the need to preserve and improve on the basic model of income security that we have referred to throughout as "social insurance."

POLITICAL COMPROMISE
AND PROGRAMMATIC DYSFUNCTION

All social welfare programs—indeed, all legislative programs—are at least partly compromises. Not only do public programs have multiple goals, but their proponents also have different reasons for supporting them.[4]

Sometimes compromise produces effective and sturdy program design. Social Security pensions are a good example. Coverage initially excluded agricultural and domestic workers, a necessary concession to Democrats representing southern and rural constituencies.[5] Supporters believed—properly, it turned out—that these populations could be added later. The desire to provide guaranteed immediate and permanent relief to all low-income or impoverished elderly was resisted in favor of a contributory program that would enjoy durable middle-class support. Immediate relief was relegated to a separate means-tested program that was designed to, and did, decline in importance as Social Security benefits became available to the vast majority of elderly retired workers. Benefits were made progressive, but those who contributed more were always meant to receive more. Progressivity was traded off in both benefits and taxes against the desire to reinforce a sense of earned entitlement. Pensions for the disabled were forgone in 1935 to avoid a holy war with the medical profession over "socialized medicine." But twenty-five years later, that program was added.

The overall design was of a sturdy core that could be refined and amended as opportunities arose or circumstances dictated. Social Security's architects understood that America's economic and demographic future remained uncertain. While surpluses in Social Security accounts permitted the addition of survivors insurance in 1939, looming deficits required adjustment of the full retirement age in 1983—several decades after the 1935 Committee on Economic Security had believed that adjustments would be necessary to maintain the program's soundness. Further adjustments have been the stuff of popular and political debate for the past two decades—a topic we take up in Chapter 12.

The compromises in enacting Social Security pensions did not weaken the program's basic social insurance characteristics: uniform national coverage, broad participation, contributory financing, and benefits tied loosely to contributions. Other legislative compromises have not been so successful.

Medicare might well have gone the way of Social Security pensions, with additions of both populations and covered treatments to produce universal comprehensive coverage. To some degree, as we saw in Chapter 7, that has been Medicare's fate. Part B, physician treatments outside hospitals, is voluntary but subsidized, and it is taken up by the vast majority of Medicare beneficiaries. And prescription drug coverage was added during the George W. Bush administration, but on a quite different model—one that, as we explain in the next chapter, carried with it the threat of unraveling the basic structure of the Medicare program.

Moreover, as some of its proponents had anticipated, Medicaid's coverage of the poor for many years relieved pressure to cover the nonpoor working population. To be sure, Medicaid itself has been expanded, particularly its coverage of children, but gaps in Medicare and Medicaid's own structure have produced significant stresses. The absence of long-term care from Medicare coverage has shifted that burden to Medicaid. Nursing home care of the poor elderly has placed enormous burdens on state budgets and limited the willingness of states to extend coverage to other populations. Leaving significant policy decision making to state governments, which have not only different political cultures but also different fiscal capacities, has produced significant variation in Medicaid coverage across the states. Finally, Medicaid, as we have noted, is a lumpy benefit based on the recipients' having low levels of income and resources. As a consequence, the eligibility rules create benefits cliffs—earning a bit more can cause beneficiaries to fall off the program, leaving them with no access to health insurance. Indeed, there is considerable "churning"; beneficiaries move on and off the program year by year with only limited ability to predict whether they will retain coverage or not.

Meanwhile, much of the health insurance provided to nonpoor workers and their families has remained tied to employment with employers who provide or offer coverage. So long as they retain coverage, many middle-class and upper-middle-class Americans are perfectly happy with these arrangements. That, combined with the political muscle of the private health insurance industry (not to mention the skepticism of some of the medical community), made universal access to health insurance both a consensus goal and an impossible dream until the Affordable Care Act of 2010. Moreover, the politics of the ACA's enactment, in particular the necessity to buy off the private health insurance industry, resulted in a wonderfully complex set of arrangements that is misunderstood and disliked by a substantial percentage of Americans. Finally, the ACA is as challenging a program administratively as perhaps has ever been enacted by the U.S. Congress.

Heterogeneity and complexity are not necessarily bad things in themselves. They may be the results of differing political preferences, differing local conditions, or the differing needs of various populations. Heterogeneous arrangements may also provide opportunities for experimentation and learning that are beneficial in the long run. But looking at the now so-called universal access to health insurance in the United States, it is difficult to perceive whether any of these values are being served. Moreover, the heterogeneity and complexity in these arrangements provide quite different levels of access to health insurance for different populations, a situation that is almost certain to lead to serious administrative difficulties and public misunderstandings. Whereas the relatively simple structure of Medicare, both in its coverage and financing, has led to immense popularity and very substantial improvements in the economic security of American seniors, both Medicare's "modernization" in the Medicare Modernization Act of 2003 and the complex and administratively challenging provisions of the Affordable Care Act of 2010 raise all-too-obvious possibilities for health system cost inflation, citizen and provider dissatisfaction, and continued political struggle. "Universal coverage" is to be applauded from the perspective of increasing Americans' economic security, but program design matters.

The multiplicity of programs benefiting children born into poor families, as described in Chapter 5, also suggests suboptimal program design. But here there are some better policy, not just political, reasons for the compromises built into these programs. First, there is an unavoidable trade-off between universality and targeting. A universal "demogrant" for all families with children to be taxed back from those not in need has much to recommend it in its simplicity and "everyone in the same boat" political structure. But if this demogrant were to be large enough to support families with virtually no other income, the overall budgetary numbers would be truly frightening. Hence, even in those advanced industrial economies that have demogrant programs, the benefit levels are quite low when compared with the needs of an otherwise impecunious family with children. Targeting expenditures on the poor is thus a necessary aspect of an overall set of family-friendly income-support policies.

Moreover, if the general public is to be convinced to provide substantial assistance to less well-off families with children, it is highly likely that they will want to provide assistance in ways that assure that those families and children are reasonably well nourished, well housed, and well cared for when ill or injured. Providing these so-called merit goods has broad political support, and if their provision is not to be assured by close regulatory supervision of family spending, they are likely to be provided in kind rather than in cash. Finally, the needs of families with children are diverse, and wise or prudent intervention often needs to be combined with various social services. The goal is not just to relieve poverty in the short run, but to reduce dependency in the long run, if at all possible.

The mix of targeting, income provision, and combining assistance with social services almost necessarily produces heterogeneity and complexity. And because combining supports with services almost demands local administration, programs are likely to be joint among national, state, and local jurisdictions. From this perspective it is not surprising that we find the fragmented efforts previously described. To be sure, means-testing programs of food, housing, and health insurance supports fail to tap into the "common threat, all in the same boat" politics that is the happy fate of more universal social insurance programs. But at least the SNAP food and nutrition program and Section 8 housing vouchers do not produce the means-testing cliffs associated with Medicaid. The level of support is adjusted as incomes rise or fall. The same is true of the largest cash-transfer program, the Earned Income Tax Credit. Moreover, because eligibility for the EITC is determined by the filing of a tax return, the common and despised task of all American families, means testing here does not carry the same sort of "welfare" stigma that attends many means-tested programs.

As we saw in our earlier discussion of programs for families at or near the poverty level, much more might be done to attack the persistent problem of childhood poverty in the United States. But much of that additional effort involves simply summoning the political will to better fund the programs already in place. If there is a glaring design flaw in the programs to assist families with children, it is in their extensive use of exemptions, deductions, and nonrefundable credits through the tax code. To be sure, this universalizes access, at least nominally. But exemptions, deductions, and nonrefundable credits do not benefit poor families who do not owe any taxes. And in a progressive tax system, these same provisions afford greater support, in absolute terms, the higher the family's income and hence its marginal tax rate. There seems no reason to think that these provisions would not remain generally popular, because generally available to all families with children, if they were converted into refundable tax credits. Economic supports targeted at families with children need not be designed so that they miss the neediest targets.

The political compromises in the unemployment insurance scheme have, as we saw in Chapter 4, turned out to be quite dysfunctional despite the scheme's nominal universality. This is a badly designed program. Now-anachronistic concerns about constitutional limitations produced strong federal tax incentives for state unemployment insurance programs rather than a national program. And, although workers surely bear some of the unemployment insurance tax indirectly, the only formal payers of this tax are employers. The behaviorist desire of Progressive reformers to punish "poor management" that resulted in worker layoffs produced a perverse system of experience rating. The rating policy increases employers' tax liabilities precisely when they encounter economic difficulties. The results have been disappointing.

Although there is nominally broad unemployment insurance for the American population, the percentage of workers who are in fact eligible for unemployment benefits during a spell of unemployment varies dramatically, as we have seen, from state to state. The number of workers eligible for benefits has also declined steadily over time. The increased restrictiveness on eligibility largely results from two sources: employer hostility to the program and the understandable concern of state legislatures to improve the business climates in their states in competition with their neighbors. That total unemployment benefits payments go up sharply at times when other state sources of revenue are declining hardly increases the political popularity of unemployment insurance in state legislatures. Most state legislatures face constitutional requirements for balanced budgets. In short, the responsibility for unemployment insurance is lodged at the wrong level of government. While state policies certainly matter, the large public policy drivers of economic performance involve national power. For example, trade policy, immigration policy, and overall fiscal and monetary policy have dramatic effects on employment prospects, but they are the exclusive domain of the national government. Unemployment insurance should follow that same model.

We are not aware of any other industrialized nation that saddles regions or localities with financing unemployment insurance. And while experience rating is used to some degree in most systems, it is done by industry, not by individual employer. This makes the fiscal responsibilities of employers much more predictable, reducing employer hostility and virtually eliminating employer incentives to contest awards to employees who have lost their jobs. As has become true in many of America's workers' compensation systems, unemployment insurance is now the site of adversarial contest concerning worker eligibility. This situation both increases administrative costs and lessens the reliability of benefits for workers who become unemployed. American unemployment insurance clearly needs an overhaul—a modernization, if you will. It should look more like a national social insurance program, and we offered some suggestions for reforms in Chapter 8 that might move us in the right direction. These reforms would make the program conform more closely to the social insurance models that have proved so durable and effective.

Despite the current program's obvious defects, unemployment insurance rarely makes its way onto the national legislative agenda. The occasions when it does occur typically in times of severe economic downturns, when the federal government needs to rescue state systems and/or provide for extensions of benefits beyond the standard twenty-six weeks. By contrast, modernization is already on the agenda of American politics with respect to our largest social insurance programs: Social Security pensions and Medicare. Because these are our largest domestic programs, and because the debates about them are so continuous and so heated, Social Security and Medicare warrant their own separate discussion, which we take up in Chapter 12.

C h a p t e r

1 2

Social Insurance, Markets, and "Modernization"

Social Security and Medicare are constant topics of American political conversation. For decades conservative commentators and activists have tried to convince the American public that these major social insurance programs are financially unsustainable and therefore require fundamental reform.[1] These programs, critics claim, unfairly deny Americans their freedom of choice and undermine their personal responsibility for coping with economic risks. Supporters of social insurance, by contrast, have often been defensive, arguing that these programs are in their current form politically protected. Any tinkering with their structures, many defenders fear, might unravel these two fundamental pillars of the American social contract.[2]

Whatever the truth of either of these common rhetorical positions, the public policy results of the past decade attest—at the very least— to the firm durability of our major social insurance programs for the aged and disabled. In 2003, instead of trimming back Medicare, a Republican-dominated Congress added a wonderfully complex and expensive prescription drug benefit.[3] And, despite one of the more extensive personal campaigns on a domestic issue ever launched by an American president, George W. Bush was unable to convince the American people that some portion of Social Security should be "privatized."[4] The fate of Social Security and Medicare, in our view, should be neither stasis because of political gridlock nor transformative change because of anxieties about the future. Both programs are crucial parts of the American social contract and respond to profound and deep-seated notions of fairness and collective responsibility.[5] They should not, however, be immune to modest adjustments in response to changed circumstances. To see why, we need to understand how basic social insurance arrangements became so remarkably durable both in the United States and elsewhere.

The short explanation is that the core features of social insurance programs are economically sensible and socially legitimate and thus politically acceptable. Social insurance is part of the essential social glue that holds an individualistic polity together and that makes the economic risks of a market economy tolerable. However fundamental to the social fabric of the nation, American social insurance programs have been and can be adjusted over time to meet fiscal, demographic, and technological challenges. They are not dinosaurs from another age, but evolving programs whose core social insurance principles can be expressed through a number of prudent adaptations.

Some mutations, however, are species altering. Much of the current enthusiasm for "modernizing" Social Security and Medicare, for example, has precisely that species-altering ambition. These reforms emphasize not protection against common economic risks in a changing world but individualized risk bearing. They extol increased responsibility and rewards for personal choice and celebrate the "marketization" of social provision. We do not deny for a moment the value of personal choice, individual responsibility, and market competition. Indeed, supporting a society based on a viable vision of those values is the fundamental function of social insurance. But social insurance programs designed to maximize personal choice and promote market competition will simply not deliver adequate social insurance protections. To see why, we need to explore the basic structure of social insurance and its capacity to face contemporary challenges—that is, its capacity to modernize while continuing to play its fundamental social role.

THE DURABILITY AND DESIRABILITY OF SOCIAL INSURANCE

Social insurance, as we have emphasized in earlier chapters, rests on the widespread acceptance of the proposition that protecting workers and their families from dramatic losses of economic status brought on by common risks to labor market participation is what a decent society should do. Across virtually all advanced industrial societies, these risks are taken to include those we have laid out in Part II of this book: birth into a poor family, the early death of a family breadwinner, ill health, involuntary unemployment, disability, and outliving one's savings. Indeed, there is a strong historical case that, beginning with Otto von Bismarck's social insurance initiatives in the late nineteenth century, the social provision of income protection against these risks has been a fundamental precondition for the flourishing of industrial capitalism. Looked at historically, social insurance is a deeply conservative idea, the major viable alternative to state socialism.

That social insurance programs have maintained their attractiveness as the appeal of socialism has waned testifies to their economic good sense and their social respectability. And that latter feature is due in substantial part to a complex ethic of fairness that is built into social insurance arrangements and has widespread appeal. Let us explain.

Economically, social insurance is a political precondition for the maintenance of market capitalism. It plays that role precisely because social insurance programs insure against risks that are dealt with poorly or not at all in private insurance markets. As we have described, two well-known difficulties beset private, voluntary insurance: adverse selection (the highest-risk people tend to be the biggest demanders of insurance) and moral hazard (the tendency of the insured to incur more than their fair share of losses). When both of these problems are characteristic of an insurance market, insurance rapidly becomes unaffordable. Indeed, this is a generally recognized description of markets that insure against risks such as illness, accident, disability, and unemployment.[6] If anyone is to be insured at reasonable cost, it is typically necessary that everyone, or nearly everyone, be compelled to be insured through a publicly mandated program.

Other risks, such as premature death and extended old age, have more modest adverse selection and moral hazard problems, but they encounter other difficulties. One is overoptimism, wishful thinking. (We did our best in Chapter 2 to dampen this human tendency with a hard look at the data on incidence of the six threats.) Another is the inherent difficulty of planning for stages like retirement, given the massive uncertainty of individual life expectancies, inflation rates in the distant future, and the short-run performance of investments near or during retirement. The myopia of Americans in planning for retirement has been demonstrated over multiple generations. Mandatory and near-universal programs of life, survivors, and old-age insurance solve these problems and two additional ones as well. Because we are unlikely to allow the aged to die in the streets, or their survivors to languish in abject poverty, compulsory participation in programs like Social Security makes everyone a contributor to a common pool. This eliminates free riders and simultaneously restrains the demand for overly generous benefits.[7]

That programs make economic sense does not necessarily make them durable. They must also be understood to be fair and socially respectable. Social insurance programs satisfy these conditions through several elements of their common design. First, the risks covered are generally not the fault of the beneficiaries. Think of the nightclub fire victims, parents with autistic toddlers, and the Enron retirees. Providing assistance where the victim has not caused the misfortune taps into one basic strain of our common understanding of fair arrangements. Covering most people at risk and treating everyone equally as risk bearers increases the sense of social insurance's fairness. The financing of most social insurance, unlike commercial insurance premiums, does not vary with individual risk. Finally, because benefits are funded (wholly or in substantial part) by contributions from covered workers, most insured workers sensibly regard those benefits as "earned" and therefore "deserved."[8]

Who Is Afraid of "Entitlements"?

For the past two decades, critics of social insurance have complained about "entitlements spending," not "social insurance budgets." The idea seems to be to disparage the legal guarantee of pensions or health care reimbursements by linking them with the common, and perhaps justified, complaint about people (often young people from upper-middle-class families) who are said to view themselves as "entitled" to a good life without having done anything to earn it. We are not sure who should be credited with this devious rhetorical ploy, but anyone who understands the social, economic, and political logic of social insurance should see it for what it is—an attempt to problematize justifiably popular programs without naming them. There is a further irony here. In law, the term *entitlement* is a synonym for a "property right." Why property rights should be viewed with alarm in a market economy, which could not function without them, is a mystery—explicable perhaps only if one views property rights as suspect whenever created by a government program.

This pedigree of cultural respectability is enhanced by the administrative arrangements social insurance programs use. The receipt of benefits does not require questions about morally freighted matters such as family income and assets, household composition, or individual work effort. Instead, it involves relatively innocent details about work history, objective facts like age, and, for survivors insurance, the number of dependent children.

These characteristic features of social insurance regimes largely explain why relative political stability has been their predictable fate. Social insurance programs engage most of the electorate precisely because they cover common risks and insure most of the population. And because practically everyone is both a contributor and a potential beneficiary, the politics of social insurance tends to be of the "us-us" rather than "us-them" form. Each individual's sense of earned entitlement or deservingness makes reneging on promises in social insurance programs politically costly.[9] Each individual's responsibility to contribute to the common pool makes extravagant promises of "something-for-nothing" future benefits less politically attractive.

CLOUDS OVER CAMELOT

The social, economic, and political "logic" of social insurance, we believe, helps to explain why these programs represent the largest category of federal nondefense spending and why they have persisted over such a long period in the United States and elsewhere. But sound general principles don't necessarily produce well-designed programs. And, with social and economic change, arrangements that fit well in one era can become outdated in another. A society's underlying sense of "fairness" or "appropriateness" in guarding against risks to loss of income from work can change as well.

Critics of America's social insurance arrangements claim that this is precisely what has happened to our largest social insurance programs—Social Security and Medicare. Demographic shifts, changes in financial markets, and hyperinflation in medical care have merged with a post-1970s "pro-market" ideological shift to produce severe criticisms of these programs of American social insurance. The fundamental claim is that Social Security and Medicare have become both financially unaffordable and socially unfair. Reducing collective responsibility for both pensions and health insurance in old age, the critics allege, would be both more equitable and more financially viable. While the techniques proposed for the two domains are somewhat different, virtually all "reform" proposals for Social Security and Medicare in recent years have emphasized more individual responsibility, increased consumer choice, and greater reliance on market competition.[10]

This is not the place to engage the details of the many reform proposals that have been put forward. We focus instead on the broad conceptual claims of unfairness and unaffordability. Unpacking the meaning of these terms provides an important, and often missing, perspective on what is really at stake in contemporary debates.

SOCIAL SECURITY: FAIRNESS, AFFORDABILITY, AND MODERNIZATION

The Fairness Debate

Fairness critiques take several forms, but two focus on the levels of benefits available to workers of different incomes and from different generations. On benefit levels there are two very different fairness complaints. For some the problem is that workers who make more and pay more into Social Security's FICA do not get the same "rate of return" as lower-paid workers who contribute less. Others make the opposite argument: that American social insurance redistributes too little to the poor while paying benefits to millionaires who don't need them.[11]

What these critics fail to understand is that social insurance successfully blends these two different visions of fairness. American workers can rightly expect that any increases in their Social Security contributions will lead to higher retirement benefits. Larger "contributions" (the common term for payroll taxes) mean that higher-wage workers receive larger pensions than lower-wage workers. This is the fairness vision of the "earned benefit": those contributing more should get something more in return. But the *degree* of financial hierarchy in Social Security benefits is reduced by another of its purposes—the commitment to a minimally adequate income for all workers. The ratio of benefits to former wages is higher the lower a worker's average wages. In short, America has constructed a worker-contributor, not a saver-investor or donor-beneficiary, vision of fairness. The "every boat on its own bottom" ethos of the market economy is tempered by the "everybody in the same boat" ethos of social insurance. Charitable ideals of redistribution from rich to poor are mediated by a vision of deservingness that depends on the contributory role of workers.

A somewhat broader fairness criticism is that *no one* is getting a "fair return" on his or her Social Security contributions. This version of the fairness argument usually features a thought experiment, one that imagines all workers putting their Social Security contributions into the stock market. Then, looking at average returns on common stock over long periods of American history, the analyst demonstrates that the return on these investments would substantially exceed the "returns" from Social Security contributions. Social Security thus fails to give a fair return on investment.[12]

This argument involves a category mistake. Social Security is a complex blend of public insurance against premature death, permanent disability, and unexpectedly long life. It is not an investment in a mutual fund. The illusion that all Americans can be better off by being investors ignores that each individual's lifetime returns will not be average. Individual investors will not only die at different ages, but they will also have widely varying returns on their portfolios. The stock market thought experiment conveniently forgets that individuals will bear their longevity and investment risks. This is not reforming social insurance; it is abolishing it.

This "investor-based" thought experiment also trades on the implicit notions of fairness that attend voluntary saving and prudent investment. But shifting Social Security to a mandatory savings and investment scheme actually eliminates any fairness claim for the returns voluntary investment produces in financial markets. As a matter of deservingness, the "investor" notion of fairness rewards prudence and self-denial. It depends on individuals' giving up current consumption as a hedge against an uncertain future. But compelling workers to save a fixed percentage of their wages rewards neither prudence nor self-sacrifice. The saver, after all, did not choose to save. And the amount of current consumption sacrificed is inversely related to affluence. Moreover, no proponent of this form of "modernization" imagines that "investors" would be permitted to invest in anything they choose. Prudence would almost certainly require the regulation of investment choices.

The clash between individualistic and collectivist visions of fairness does, to some considerable degree, frame the debate about risk bearing in the right terms. We believe that the social, political, and economic arguments that have accounted for the durability of social insurance remain persuasive. Opinion polling suggests that most Americans approve of social insurance's pragmatic blend of deservingness and equality. They have little taste for running the risks that "privatizers" of various stripes believe they should prefer. They overwhelmingly reject an every-family-for-itself vision of an "ownership society" mitigated only by charity-based notions of a social obligation to help the worst-off.[13]

Who Favors Social Security and Medicare?

Public support for both Social Security and Medicare is deep. Nearly twice as many Americans (60% to 32%) believe it is more important to maintain current levels of Social Security and Medicare benefits than it is to cut those benefits to reduce the deficit or reduce taxes, and nearly 80% of Americans believe the programs have benefited the country. While a majority of Americans (53%) are in favor of raising taxes on high earners to maintain Social Security, 42% favor spreading the tax increases among all taxpayers, showing a preference for the blend of "deservingness" and "equality" we mention.

Sources: Pew Research Center Poll, "GOP Divided over Benefit Reductions: Public Wants Changes in Entitlements, Not Changes in Benefits," June 2011, http://www.people-press.org/files/legacy-pdf/7-7-11%20Entitlements%20Release.pdf; CNN/ORC Poll, September 2011, http://i2.cdn.turner.com/cnn/2011/images/09/29/rel16f.pdf.

The fairness of shifting yet more financial risk to average American families is even more doubtful when considered in the context of America's overall retirement policy. Tax policy already offers greater subsidies to the retirement savings of higher earners than lower earners. The home mortgage interest deduction and the nontaxability of IRA, Keough, 401(k), and defined-contribution plans all provide much more assistance for wealth accumulation to highly paid Americans. The current structure of Social Security pensions somewhat reduces this imbalance. A shift to private accounts would almost certainly eliminate this important equalizing feature of the overall retirement system. Since the "personal circumstances" influencing lifetime earnings include being born black or white, male or female, able-bodied or impaired, and into a rich or poor family, the unfairness of this approach seems clear to most Americans.

Privatization schemes would also trade a portion of Social Security's protections—survivors benefits—for ownership of private accounts that would pass to the holders' heirs at death. Security for younger workers and lower-wage workers' families would again be traded for increased benefits to higher-wage workers, and particularly to the survivors of those who do not outlive the value of their individual accounts. This is not a trivial trade. Social Security survivors benefits provide monthly income to 7.5 million Americans; an average worker has protection roughly equivalent to a private life insurance policy worth between $400,000 and $475,000.[14] In short, the personal accounts approach to Social Security's retirement program would increase the stock market and other risks to families who are poorly positioned to bear them, while eliminating protections that are crucial for that same population.

The other major fairness claim that some "reformers" make has to do with intergenerational fairness. These critics of Social Security make much of the supposed unfair burden that retirees will in the future place on the working young. The poster child for this contention is a showing that in the absence of major changes in immigration or fertility, the ratio of workers to retirees will fall over the next several decades from the current 3:1 to 2:1. The image here is of an affluent older cohort enjoying a secure retirement on the backs of increasingly hard-pressed wage earners. But the real picture is quite different, as Figure 10.9 reveals.

First, most Americans over 65 have very modest income, and Social Security provides a huge proportion of that income for all but the most affluent.[15] Second, the real question of intergenerational fairness for tomorrow's workers is how many *dependents* they will be supporting, not how many old-age pensioners. Here, the data are clear. As elderly Americans have increased in number, this shift has been more than offset by a decrease in the number of children Americans are raising. American workers were supporting many more dependents—that is, nonworkers— in the 1960s than do the workers of today, a trend expected to continue into the foreseeable future. And while much is rightly made of the stagnation of the wages of middle-income Americans in recent years, working families are considerably better off than their counterparts fifty years ago (see Figure 12.1).

Figure 12.1 Total Dependency Ratio, Actual and Projected, 1950–2060 (children and elderly per 100 persons of working age)

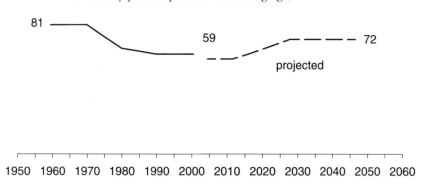

Source: Pew Research Center, 2008.

Note: Children are ages 17 or younger. Working ages are 18 to 64. Elderly are ages 65 and older. Projections for 2005–2050 are indicated by the broken line.

If one looks only at public expenditures, supporting oldsters certainly appears more expensive than supporting youngsters. But most financial support for children goes through family, not public, budgets. The central question about intergenerational fairness is this: Are future generations going to pay more for the support of their parents than they received from their parents for their support? The answer to that question seems to be no. A serious attempt to estimate these transfers over the next generation finds that, on average, parents will still transfer more to their children than will the children to their parents, even in the unlikely event that all future Social Security and Medicare deficits are closed by increasing taxes on workers.[16]

Although it has become almost a cliché, this issue of intergenerational equity in retirement pensions is really mostly a distraction. The first generation of pensioners eligible for Social Security retirement benefits indeed enjoyed a windfall. But that is history, not to be repeated. The simple economic logic of retirement finance is just this: either generation X can prefund its own retirement or it can fund the retirement of X – 1 and have its retirement funded by X + 1. Without going into pages of argument about risk-adjusted returns, possible changes in savings and growth rates, and other questions that are both arcane and speculative, we are prepared simply to assert the obvious. The best guess is that the burdens on current and future generations under the two schemes will be equivalent.

In short, criticisms of Social Security because it is "unfair" seem either confused or misinformed. But what about affordability?

The Question of Affordability

Debates over Social Security pensions typically arise in response to present or anticipated fiscal crises. These are often occasions for replaying in differing chords the profound opposition that social insurance has always generated among economic conservatives. The past several decades provide ample illustration of this pattern.

In the early 1980s, when public officials announced that Social Security accounts would be "bankrupt" without adjustment, Americans accepted without commotion the changes made by the 1983 Greenspan Commission. These changes bolstered rather than revamped Social Security; they combined modest reductions of benefits with small increases in social insurance taxes.[17]

Then, as a result of the early 1980s reforms, surpluses grew in Social Security's accounts during the 1990s. Oddly enough, this too awakened critics. Some fiscal gurus then complained that growing surpluses constituted a crisis in "slow motion."[18] The point is straightforward: when both deficits and surpluses bring cries of alarm, the evidence points toward ideological opposition, not episodes of programmatic crisis.[19] In the mid-1990s, long-term projections revealed the possible exhaustion of these surpluses, and the rhetoric of imminent disaster reemerged. What is the fiscal truth of the matter?

There is, of course, no "fiscal truth" of the matter. While Social Security's trustees are required by statute to make seventy-five-year projections of the system's finances, the uncertainties of such long-term projections are manifest. Imagine predicting the economic position of the United States in 2013 from the vantage point of 1938. Indeed, serious students of the actuarial assumptions upon which "crisis" talk is now based question whether, with more realistic assumptions, particularly concerning long-term economic growth rates, there is likely to be a fiscal shortfall in Social Security.[20] But it has become conventional to use the Social

Security actuaries' midpoint projections as the "true" state of the future world. If we do that, is there a crisis demanding major transformation?

Clearly not. According to most informed commentators, Social Security's fiscal future can be stabilized through quite moderate program adjustments. As the late Robert M. Ball, former commissioner of Social Security in both Democratic and Republican administrations, repeatedly argued, the system has for years had substantial surpluses, and total income will exceed outlays until about the year 2021. Thereafter, Social Security reserves must be retired to pay current benefits that exceed the level of current taxes. The reserves are projected to be depleted by 2033.[21] So, if we believe these projections represent future realities, unless some adjustments are made in benefit levels, taxation levels, or trust fund earnings, Social Security's retirement program will be able to pay only 77% of its bills in 2033.

From this perspective, critics are technically correct: the precise promises of the current system could not be maintained on present assumptions. On the other hand, the pessimistic assertion that something very like the current system cannot be financed is nonsense.

Indeed, there are many ways to close projected gaps in future funding with modest changes in current contributions and benefit levels. As discussed in Chapter 10, a rise in the cap on FICA contributions, including all state and local employees in the program, accelerating the phase-in of the increase in the normal retirement age, and inflating benefits by a more accurate consumer price index are but a few of the sensible proposals that serious students of Social Security's fiscal health have proposed as a balanced means of restoring confidence that the program is on a sound financial footing. This is not the place to discuss further the details of these and other proposals.[22] Our point here is simply to illustrate the silliness of the sky-is-falling, we-have-to-do-something-drastic rhetoric that has surrounded the debates over Social Security's future.

More important, "privatizing" and "personal accounts" have nothing to do with solving any projected fiscal imbalance in Social Security's revenue and payments. Existing retirees and those nearing retirement would have to be protected. They could not possibly build up sufficient income in private accounts. That in turn means younger workers would have to finance the pensions of current and near-term retirees at the same time they are contributing to their own private accounts. Since no one believes these workers could or should bear this double burden, massive borrowing would be needed to make good on the promises to retirees and older workers. Thus these proposals would make the fiscal situation much worse and would probably require large benefit reductions to balance Social Security's books.

There is, in short, nothing that can responsibly be called a fiscal crisis in Social Security pensions. The problems that exist are easily manageable, and the remedies are so affordable that in a less contentious political climate they probably could have been implemented without many noticing the changes. In sharp contrast, privatization would make the fiscal situation worse while violating the crucial values of fairness and security that support the existing system of Social Security pensions. Privatizing Social Security is a contradiction in terms. The principle of every boat on its own bottom is simply inconsistent with that of everyone in the same boat. Markets can supply a marvelous array of investment vehicles, but they cannot supply social insurance.

MEDICARE: FAIRNESS, AFFORDABILITY, AND MODERNIZATION

Medicare, largely ignored in the battle over health care reform in the early 1990s, returned to center stage in American politics following the Republican congressional victories of 2010. Given bipartisan calls for reductions in the nation's budget deficits and hostility among some Republicans to Medicare's social insurance roots, it was almost certain that the Medicare program would again generate intense and very public debate and conflict. Moreover, as with Social Security pensions, long-term projections for Medicare expenditures prompt worries about unsustainable budget outlays.[23] The public commentary about Medicare, then and now, reveals claims similar to those made about social insurance itself, claims of unaffordability and unfairness, as well as somewhat masked ideological objections operating under the banner of "modernization."[24]

The Question of Affordability

Fearful projections of Medicare's fiscal future mistakenly focus concern about a real and general problem on a single health insurance program. Medical care inflation is a problem of American medicine, but it is not a crisis caused by Medicare's structure. For most of Medicare's history, program expenditures have grown about as rapidly as outlays in the private medical economy. There have been a number of temporal shifts (as Figure 7.9 reveals), but the important reality in the period after 1997 has been rapid inflation in American medical care generally, not just, or even particularly, in Medicare.

Over the very long run—from, for example, 1970 to 2001—Medicare costs per enrollee grew less rapidly (9.6% per year) than did costs for the privately insured (11% per year).[25] And over the period 2006–2010, costs per enrollee rose at very similar rates for both Medicare (4.2%) and private insurance (4.5%).[26] These data give no reason for complacency about the costs of American medical care, but neither do they support any claim of a distinctive problem in Medicare's capacity to restrain medical inflation.

Yet whenever there is a more rapid rate of increase in Medicare expenditures in combination with projected deficits in the Medicare trust fund, critics use projections of Medicare's future outlays to suggest the program is in need of fundamental reform. Suggestions for reform are often fabulously complex, but they typically have these common features: the explicit or implicit claim that the "common pool" social insurance features of Medicare are the cost-control culprit and the assertion that adding choice, competition, and individual responsibility (the contemporary mantra is "consumer-driven health care") will solve the problem. There is almost no evidence to support these beliefs.

The common pool feature of Medicare cannot plausibly be a cause for fiscal concern. As detailed in Chapter 7, the experience of other industrial democracies has repeatedly demonstrated the superior capacity of more universal social insurance programs to restrain growth in overall medical expenditures. Any comparison of growth in health expenditures of the United States and social insurance nations such as Germany, the Netherlands, and France would show American expenditures to have grown more rapidly in recent decades. And these are countries with both older populations and more widespread and intensive use of health care than in the United States.[27] (The simple facts in the previous sentence are so little appreciated that we suggest you read the sentence again.) Countries with older populations, greater use of medical care, and, in addition, equal or better health results do a better job of restraining medical inflation than the United States. None of them rely on competition or individual responsibility as a major cost-control device.

One might more plausibly argue that fiscal restraint is difficult because Medicare does not cover everyone. Medicare has been given few instruments to control capital expenditures, but its powerful constraints on payments to hospitals and doctors spill over into pressures on private payers. The latter fight back by adopting some of Medicare's cost-control techniques, which then increases political pressures from providers to ease up on cost control. What the experience of the past forty years demonstrates is that fragmented American arrangements for financing medical care are comparatively weak instruments for controlling expenditure growth. That does not indict Medicare's social insurance character, but it does highlight a serious problem that Medicare (and the rest of the medical economy) will have to confront.

Once again, however, critics tout individual responsibility, choice, and competition as the "solution" to both the problems of American medicine generally and Medicare's fiscal problems in particular.[28] One response is a broad proposal for medical savings accounts (MSAs) or health savings accounts (HSAs). Instead of participating in group insurance at the place of employment or paying the health insurance portion of FICA taxes, Americans are urged to make pretax contributions to HSAs to cover their medical needs. A version of such accounts was included in the 2003 Medicare Modernization Act (MMA).[29] Presumably the buildup in an HSA, along with an inexpensive "high-deductible" or "catastrophic" insurance policy, would provide a person with sufficient reserves for medical care both during working years and in old age.

There are major transitional problems with this scheme, but those need not distract us from the main line of argument. For the young, the healthy, and the affluent an HSA approach is individually sensible— particularly so if, as is virtually certain, the tax-free savings could be tapped for other purposes once a sufficient cushion is achieved. The "good risks"—that is, those individuals who pose little actuarial risk of developing expensive health problems—will be better off by opting out of Medicare into HSAs. What happens to the rest of the population is only slightly less clear, but broadly predictable. With good risks now not contributing to the insurance pool, "bad risks" must be "insured" by general taxation. In short, instead of medical care being a part of social insurance, the system would move rapidly toward segmentation: private insurance for the young, healthy, and relatively well-off; welfare medicine for everyone else. Moreover, according to estimates by the American Academy of Actuaries, the flight of the healthy to HSAs could more than double the premiums for those left in both the basic Medicare program and more comprehensive private policies. Medicare would then appear to be hopelessly unaffordable, making it yet more politically vulnerable.[30]

An alternative "privatization" approach retains social insurance coverage for the elderly but attempts to save public funds by having private managed care plans compete for Medicare's patients. This alternative poses no direct threat to social insurance. Rather, the worrisome issue is whether managed care can both save money and deliver decent medical care at the same time to the elderly—or anyone else. These are crucial questions for the whole of American medicine, not just Medicare. Recent experience is not very promising. Medicare Advantage plans have attracted beneficiaries, but their increased benefits have been possible only because of federal subsidies to the private plans. Moreover, even with Affordable Care Act changes that reduced the difference, Medicare

Advantage costs the public more per enrollee than traditional Medicare, a disparity that is likely to increase over time.[31]

Still another approach to "reforming" Medicare would change its character by converting it into a voucher program. That proposal is a familiar suggestion from conservative think tanks such as the Heritage Foundation. In 2012, the selection of Congressman Paul Ryan as the Republican vice presidential candidate prompted a flurry of attention to Ryan's version of a voucher system for Medicare. The idea of offering cohorts of Medicare beneficiaries choices among private insurance firms to which to give their vouchers—and the picture of these firms competing for such customers by vigorously forcing hospitals and physicians to accept lower rates of increase in their income—is mostly a fantasy. But it is a cost-control fantasy with a clear objective: namely, reducing the claims of Medicare beneficiaries on public budgets. Such voucher schemes—sometimes called "premium support"—are essentially ways to reduce the risks to public budgets of persistently high rates of medical inflation. If the budgeted vouchers rise, for example, with the consumer price index and not the medical price index, Medicare's protection will necessarily be reduced.

"Not tonight, honey, but here's a voucher."

Source: The Cartoon Bank

In simple terms, this is a scheme for reducing health insurance protections for the elderly and pushing more of their health care costs back onto them. The claim that these elderly sick "consumers" will then themselves drive down costs by shopping for health insurance bargains is based on no evidence. In our view it is simply a mistake, a product of the erroneous belief that the health care market functions like the market for most consumer goods. As we explained in Chapter 7, this is simply untrue. Voucher forms of reform are part of efforts both to reduce federal deficits and to transform the role that Medicare plays in American public life.[32]

What Is the Difference between Health Care Economics and Health Care Budgets?

The voucher proposal for cost savings is a splendid example of the conflation of budget reduction and cost savings. The medical expenses not covered by the value of health care vouchers would not go away. They would just be borne by patients, providers who went unpaid, and other public budgets. Of course, some savings might occur when patients forgo care they cannot afford, but that is hardly a public policy improvement. And the notion that shopping and competition will do the trick seems to be a product of the triumph of hope over experience. The United States has the most competitive health care system in the developed world and the least success in controlling health care costs.

The basic point is just this: much of the criticism of Medicare as unaffordable misdiagnoses the problem. If medical care is lurching toward "unaffordability"—whatever that means—it is doing so generally, not just for those with Medicare insurance. If the same problem plagues private insurance markets—and it does—privatizing Medicare cannot plausibly be the solution.

The Fairness Debate

Indeed, the current controversies over Medicare's financing divert us from the more fundamental issue of whether the insurance risks of ill health should be dealt with in a universal, contributory, "social insurance" program or left to a patchwork system of private payment, private insurance, and diverse public subsidies for veterans, the aged, the poor, participants in employment-based health insurance, and so on. For while we think of Medicare as the socialization of the costs of health risks—which it is—we often forget that it is an unfinished program of social insurance. Medicare was meant to be the first step toward a much broader social insurance approach to sickness expenses. To make sense of claims that Medicare is unfair—because it spends too much on the elderly and the disabled, shifts undue burdens to working-age adults, or undermines cost-conscious utilization—one needs to remember Medicare's origins, why it did not expand as its framers expected, and what that has meant for debates about its supposed failings.

Medicare's original advocates took for granted that the rhetoric of enactment should emphasize the expansion of access, not the regulation and overhaul of American medicine. Decades of controversy about universal government health insurance had prompted reformers to concentrate on Social Security retirees as a promising step toward broader social insurance coverage of sickness expenses. The clear aim of the original Medicare bills in the early 1960s was to reduce the risks of financial disaster from hospital expenses for the elderly and their families—expenses that would undermine the economic security that Social Security pensions were meant to provide. And the understanding then was that Congress would demand a largely hands-off posture toward the hospitals providing the care that Medicare would finance.[33]

The reform strategy of the 1950s and early 1960s was incremental, proceeding from the accurate assumption that social insurance programs enjoyed vastly greater public acceptance than did means-tested assistance programs. Leaders within the Social Security Administration made sure that Medicare fell firmly within the social insurance tradition of benefits "earned," not given as charity. The aged were targeted as the first group for coverage because they had lower earning capacity and higher medical expenses than any other age group, and they had already "paid" their Social Security dues. The original Medicare bill avoided a means test by restricting eligibility to persons over age 65 (and their spouses) who had contributed to Social Security during their working lives. The initial plan in fact limited benefits to sixty days of hospital care. Physician services were originally excluded in the hope of softening the medical profession's hostility to the program.[34]

The form adopted—Social Security financing for hospital care and premiums, plus general revenues for physician expenses—had a political explanation, not a consistent social insurance rationale. Part A of the legislation, hospital insurance, was clearly based on social insurance principles of funding, eligibility, and common benefits. Physician insurance (Part B) was an unexpected afterthought, financed by a combination of general revenues and individual, flat-rate premiums that were voluntary but highly subsidized.[35] So, from the beginning, there was some confusion over Medicare's social insurance structure. However, the key assumption in 1965 was that the program would expand in coverage and adopt a more unified structure of finance. The future was to be universalistic, and the benefits were to expand to protect against the major costs of illness.

As a result, the original legislation was not tightly linked to the special circumstances of the elderly. Left out were provisions that specifically addressed the problems of the chronically sick elderly—those whose medical conditions would not dramatically improve and who needed to maintain independent function more than to triumph over discrete illness and injury. Viewed as a first step of reform, of course, the Medicare strategy made sense to its promoters. But from the perspective of 2003, the year Congress last undertook serious efforts to reform Medicare, with essentially no serious restructuring of its benefits, Medicare was open to the charge that it needed expansion, especially insurance protection against the costs of pharmaceuticals.

From the standpoint of universal protection, moreover, Medicare was and remains somewhat conceptually divided. It separates retired workers from those still on the job, thus breaching one version of social solidarity and giving rise to concerns about unfair special treatment for one segment of society. And because Medicare covers only two groups of the population, those "retired" because of age or disability, it can all too easily take on the coloration of interest group politics. These politics are not the vitriolic struggles of us-versus-them welfare policy, but it is quite easy to claim as "unfair" the relatively generous treatment of Medicare beneficiaries in comparison with the circumstances of ordinary American families flailing in the sea of either uncertain insurance coverage or added constraints on their choices within insurance coverage. The question is whether the rest of the population shares this vision of unfairness as opposed to wanting Medicare's security and choices in their own coverage.

Precisely this charge of perceived unfairness arose in the mid-1990s, and from sources otherwise friendly to social insurance. As a matter of principle, according to Aaron and Reischauer, "Medicare beneficiaries should have a degree of choice among health plans similar to that enjoyed by the rest of the population."[36] The grounds for this assertion, which essentially called for reducing the doctor and hospital choices Medicare could make, were never stated explicitly. But the critical argument was that Medicare beneficiaries had more choices than the rest of the population. Described as the "last remnant of relatively unmanaged fee-for-service care," Medicare was, on this view, unfair to those with less choice.[37] There was and is no empirical evidence for the implication that the non-Medicare population regarded Medicare beneficiaries' greater choices as "unfair." On the other hand, it is the case that Medicare beneficiaries are more satisfied with their medical insurance coverage than other insured Americans are with theirs.[38] Indeed, academic support for a voucher system has largely eroded. Even Henry Aaron, once a strong proponent for adopting a voucher system as part of Medicare reform, has largely repudiated his previous position, now preferring the development of health care exchanges as a method of controlling health care costs.[39]

Changes in private medical insurance have also made Medicare appear to be an outlier—a form of insurance now perceived by critics as too generous. When adopted, Medicare's Part A duplicated the structure of Blue Cross's regulated form of private social insurance. The addition of Part B, modeled on the federal employees' plan for high-paid civil servants, was, as noted, unexpected. It did not strictly follow the classic form of compulsory social insurance financing, but its combination of generous tax subsidies from general revenues and modest monthly premiums meant that all but a tiny minority joined the Part B common pool. So what we had at the outset was a Medicare program that looked a lot like the community-rated Blue Cross and Blue Shield plans.

Developments over the past decades have undermined this common experience of health insurance coverage. Traditional Blue Cross and Blue Shield plans have largely disappeared and, where they exist, are exceedingly expensive. In that respect, we have no argument with the claim that Medicare has become a structural outlier. So there is a parallel with Social Security and private investment developments. The diffusion of shareholding and defined-contribution forms of tax-free saving for retirement gives support to critics of Social Security who argue that it too should "modernize" itself in line with these developments in private financial markets that emphasize individual risk bearing. This would have seemed ludicrous in the early years of Social Security, just as it would have seemed absurd to celebrate insurance firm competition and managed care in the context of the 1960s, or to suggest that Medicare's older form and more comprehensive coverage were out of step with what was available to the rest of the population. But that argument can now be made. And it carries with it an implicit claim of unfair special treatment and wasted resources—resources that could be put into more "modern," "competitive" health insurance markets.

As we have noted, there is no evidence that any substantial number of Americans accept this "unfairness" claim or favor moves to align Medicare's coverage with what has emerged in the private market. Nor, as the discussion of affordability reveals, is there any reason to believe that competition yields cost savings that will permit a "fairer" distribution of coverage. Indeed, the only "modernization" movement that has gained traction is the complaint about Medicare's failure to respond to changes in the nature of medical care, not changes in insurance plans.

There the critics had obvious grounds for their charge. In 1965, drugs used outside hospitals were a modest part of the medical budget and, in any case, Medicare reformers assumed there would be persistent expansions of populations and services covered. Neither development took place according to plan. As pharmaceuticals came to play a larger role in medical care and as the world of private American health financing diverged from the older Blue Cross–Blue Shield model, Medicare did become an outlier in both form and substance as it fell short of the breadth of services covered by many private plans. Medicare beneficiaries were not getting the prescription drug coverage that had become standard for other insured Americans.

Modernization

As of 2003 Medicare could be perceived as unfair in two ways: Medicare beneficiaries had more comprehensive coverage and choice among providers than many insured nonretired persons, but they also had less coverage of increasingly important and expensive pharmaceuticals. Enter the Medicare Modernization Act of 2003, a fantastically complex piece of legislation designed to combat both "unfairnesses" by rolling them into a common call for "modernization."[40]

Medicare beneficiaries would obtain drug coverage under the MMA in a "choice of plan" form that relies on private insurance provision, competition, and consumer choice. Moreover, the statute goes beyond drug coverage to pursue the "modernization" of other Medicare provisions. Through a complex set of incentives and financing arrangements Medicare promotes movement out of traditional Medicare into private plans that look like those available to most other Americans who have health insurance. "Modernization" in this guise also implicitly promises cost containment through competition. Indeed, the statute goes so far as to prohibit the one proven cost-constraint mechanism in Medicare's arsenal, the use of its market power to bargain for lower prices—a technique that apparently has too close an ideological relationship to government price setting or regulation.

This description oversimplifies matters, and there are indeed many devils in the MMA's details. But this discussion is about social insurance fundamentals. Hence we want to emphasize here only the disjunction between the basic ideas of risk pooling and shared sacrifice that animate social insurance and the directions that "reforms" like the MMA suggest for the future of Medicare.

The basic idea is just this: the dynamic promoted by the MMA is the dynamic of risk segmentation, not risk pooling. "Plans" must compete on price and coverage, which in the health insurance industry means competing for healthy beneficiaries. As these healthy beneficiaries are siphoned off into private plans, the pool of insured persons remaining in the traditional program will become riskier and riskier, which translates into more and more expensive. And, of course, the funds that are subtracted from the traditional program to pay for participation in the privatized medicine market will be unavailable to support the traditional program. Traditional Medicare will, therefore, look more and more expensive—and financially troubled—not because of any increased costs, but because high risks have now been separated from low risks.

A number of responses can be imagined to deal with this worsening fiscal picture in the traditional program: (1) moving everyone into private plans, with subsidies for lower-income and unhealthy beneficiaries who cannot afford the premiums; (2) increasing subsidies to the traditional Medicare program through general taxation; (3) raising premiums or lowering subsidies for more well-to-do participants in Part B of the program. Other scenarios are obviously available as well.

Note, however, that all of these approaches undermine the basic social contract that has made social insurance both politically popular and reasonably stable. Now participants will see themselves not as being in a common pool and sharing common risks, but as being in separate plans they have "chosen." Some will see themselves as insured through their contributions to the system, while others are subsidized recipients of governmental largesse. How that vision will play itself out in Americans' continued willingness to provide generous coverage to the nation's least healthy citizens remains to be seen. But in our view it is a dangerous experiment that threatens the socially valuable "us-us" politics that has characterized our major social insurance programs, which are like little else in contemporary American public life.

The Medicare Modernization Act was in many respects legislation by stealth. In this statute and elsewhere, "modernization" has become a code word that masks ideological hostility to the social insurance structure with which Social Security and Medicare began. It holds out the hope—for who can be against modernizing?—that truly modern systems of social provision will be both more affordable and fairer than "relics" of our New Deal and Great Society past that have outlived their usefulness. And in our current political context, for many being "modern" means understanding the power of individual choice, market competition, and personal responsibility to remake social policy to fit the demands of the twenty-first century.

ENTER THE AFFORDABLE CARE ACT

The Affordable Care Act in many ways carries forward the MMA approach to modernizing. The ACA does not do a great deal to change the structure of Medicare itself. It plugs the so-called donut hole in pharmaceutical coverage that was created, for arcane budgetary reasons, by the MMA. It also launches Medicare into a series of experiments that attempt to demonstrate the power of "evidence-based medicine" to reduce medical care costs. The prospects for these experiments in cost containment are highly uncertain. What is certain is that these provisions have given opponents of government-provided health insurance a new argument. Experiments to allocate care on the basis of proven results have been portrayed as the creation of "death panels" that will decide who is to live and who is to die based on the willingness of Medicare to pay for their health services. There are, of course, no death panels, but the belief that there are has turned out to be a deathless zombie that haunts discussions of the Affordable Care Act and delegitimizes the act with a substantial portion of the public.

We say that the ACA carries forward the approach of the MMA, however, largely because of roads not taken. Rather than broadening the population served by Medicare, the ACA attempts to cover uninsured Americans by subsidizing private insurance, mandating its purchase, and creating exchanges where uninsured Americans can presumably become informed shoppers for health insurance coverage. This is in many ways a market model on steroids, the steroids being federal government subsidies and state government facilitation of insurance marketing through the establishment of the health insurance exchanges. The political compromises here are obvious. As we suggested earlier, mindful of the Clinton health care debacle, engineered largely by private health insurance companies, the Obama administration bought the support of the private insurance industry by providing it with a new group of customers both mandated and subsidized to purchase insurance. Fragmentation of the insurance market combined with a continuing prohibition on Medicare using its bargaining power effectively does nothing for cost containment with respect to medical care inflation. And no public program has been created to compete with private health insurance. The so-called public option suggested during development of the ACA ended up on the cutting-room floor.[41]

The Affordable Care Act not only fails to extend the common pool features of Medicare, but its subsidy provisions also violate a much-valued characteristic of social insurance programs: the avoidance of means tests to obtain benefits. Means testing is a necessary element of the ACA's subsidy provisions, which will, it is hoped, allow lower-income Americans to purchase some form of health insurance through the health insurance exchanges. And potentially the largest increase of health insurance coverage in the ACA will result not from the increased availability of private insurance, but rather from the act's expansions in Medicaid, the health insurance program for the aged, disabled, and poor—another means-tested program.[42]

It is hard to argue, and we will not, with the motivation of the ACA's sponsors and supporters. Broadening health insurance coverage to include more than 50 million uninsured Americans is a worthy goal—as is any attempt to get a handle on cost inflation in health care expenses in the United States. But we believe that the idea that these goals are best pursued through market-mimicking and means-tested social provision is profoundly misguided. Fragmented risk pools will not promote either perceptions of fairness or us-us politics in the provision of health insurance. And patient choice and competition among insurers has no demonstrated record of cost control in medical care either in the United States or elsewhere in the developed world. The MMA and the ACA modernize health insurance in the United States by moving further toward the health insurance models that have long been available in private markets. Both statutes seem to imagine that health care economics works like the market for breakfast cereals and that individual choice in risk bearing is the solution to concerns about both quality and efficiency. We know of no evidence that could sustain these beliefs.[43]

Epilogue

REMEMBER WHAT HAS GONE BEFORE. Chapter 1's stories of human disaster remind us of what we prefer to forget: every life faces multiple threats to economic security. The Rhode Island nightclub fire should remind anyone not only of the danger of accidental death, but also of the costs of accidents like fires and the income lost to those injured by such unexpected events. Enron's collapse not only put its former chief executive in jail but also, more consequentially, devastated the retirement savings of many of the company's workers. The cost of autism provides but another introductory example of how unexpected, unwelcome, and devastating events can threaten—or indeed unravel—a family's economic security.

Those stories further illustrate that such threats span the whole of the life cycle of each individual and, while individually incurred, are common to us all. Chapter 2 shifts from stories to data to provide a macro picture of just how serious these threats are by examining their occurrence in the population as a whole. What to do about them has engaged policy makers, analysts, and the public at large in continuous debates among competing visions of the role of collective provision of assistance to those for whom these six threats have been realized. The competing visions portrayed in Chapter 3 inhabit the long history of policy innovation, revision, and reform described in Chapter 4's thumbnail sketch of the singular American version of social insurance. The whole of Part I, then, is meant to identify the six most prominent threats to economic security and to introduce the ideas that are central to the development of the threat-cushioning role of American social insurance.

Part II's six chapters then shift to more granular description and analysis of American protections against the six economic threats identified in Part I. These chapters are largely descriptive portraits, with few calls to action where protections seem anemic or complaints about excessive spending. No description can hope to be free of the authors' beliefs and commitments, but our intent in these chapters is to inform, not to argue.

Part III—the discussion of how to think wisely about income security programs and their reform—shifts from description to policy evaluation. Our aim here is first to acknowledge that "everyone thinks about public policy on the basis of some political preconceptions," and that means, as two of us wrote more than two decades ago in *America's Misunderstood Welfare State,* the critical observer needs to examine all social welfare "talk" for its ideological perspectives.[1] That premise shapes the chapters evaluating both the troubled state of America's unemployment insurance system and contemporary calls for substantial reforms in the rules of American medical care and Social Security's retirement policies. For example, Chapter 11's portrait of our long-troubled program of state-based unemployment insurance ends up as a call for reform. Chapter 12's review of pro-market ideas for American medical care and Social Security reform concentrates on which reform ideas rest on bogus arguments and which hold out the prospect for defensible adjustment in our medical and retirement programs.

In both chapters we acknowledge our social insurance commitments without presuming that this is all that need be said. Chapter 11 makes clear that programmatic complexity is often the result of inevitable compromises among differing visions of social welfare provision. Means-testing is sometimes essential, as is in-kind provision and local administration. But there are better and worse designs for programs having these features. Chapter 12 does not for a moment deny the fiscal challenges that face Social Security or Medicare. Its call is for realism about the extent and location of the fiscal challenges and clearheadedness about the implications of reform proposals.

Over time, the facts of American life and the details of policy arguments will change. The details of proposals and the complexity of the underlying social realities, combined with the predictably inflated rhetoric of champions and opponents, will challenge both policy makers and ordinary citizens as they attempt to make sense of this or that policy debate. Our hope is that the readers of this book will be better prepared to sift the wheat from the chaff—to see how particular proposals (always described as reforms) do or do not advance a reasonable response to our common threats to family income security. We do not presume that readers will share fully our view that protecting social insurance and ensuring equality of opportunity are the crucial criteria by which any change should be evaluated and simultaneously the values about which Americans most often agree—at least in the abstract. But we would be delighted if, for example, when thinking about future claims made for market-like reforms to social programs, readers would recall the philosophical, historical, and comparative evidence this book brings together. Social insurance is without a doubt a crucial support for market economies. Making social insurance programs more "market-like" is seldom a reform that supports family economic security or, in the long run, the market itself.

Throughout this book we have viewed "universal" social insurance through the lens of a peculiarly American approach to public provision. For Americans, "universal" has generally meant all "workers" or "contributors," not all citizens or residents. We should not leave this discussion, therefore, without underscoring the profoundly traditional, indeed conservative, and work-oriented vision that American universalism embraces. It says not that you are entitled because you are a part of the nation, although that is surely a plausible vision of universality, but that you are entitled because of your contribution to the nation. Funding is linked to earnings, and entitlement is defined largely by years of work. Hence for Americans, universalistic entitlement has always been a concept tied to, supported by and supporting, a market economy. That the protection of social insurance—and the demand for its expansion—should be thought to be the distinctive position of "liberals" is, to say the least, ironic. That the reform of social insurance should be thought to be best accomplished by moving in the direction of market-like devices that shift risks onto individuals and families already buffeted by the staggering economic uncertainties of a rapidly globalizing economy is, in our view, a serious mistake. "Modernization" in this form misunderstands what social insurance is about.

Notes

Chapter 1

1. Tom Mooney, "The Station Nightclub Disaster—How the Fund Has Helped," *Providence Journal-Bulletin,* May 13, 2003, A-01.

2. Michael Mello, "For Many, Time Hasn't Healed Emotional Scars from Deadly Nightclub Fire," *The Day,* November 30, 2003, D8.

3. Abby Goodnough, "5 Years after a Nightclub Fire, Survivors Struggle to Remake Their Lives," *New York Times,* February 17, 2008, A18.

4. Associated Press, "The Station Nightclub Disaster—Last Fire Survivor Leaves Hospital," *Providence Journal-Bulletin,* July 24, 2003, B-03.

5. Rick Massimo, "Station Family Fund Is Doing What It Can for Fire Survivors," *Providence Journal,* February 20, 2008, E-06.

6. National Center on Birth Defects and Development Disabilities, Division of Birth Defects and Development Disabilities, *Community Report from the Autism and Development Disability Monitoring (ADDM) Network* (Atlanta: Centers for Disease Control and Prevention, 2012), 6, http://www.cdc.gov/ncbddd/autism/documents/ADDM-2012-Community-Report .pdf.

7. Amy Lennard Goehner, "A Generation of Autism, Coming of Age," *New York Times,* April 13, 2011, http://www.nytimes.com/ref/health/healthguide/esn-autism-reporters .html.

8. See Michael L. Ganz, "The Costs of Autism," in *Understanding Autism: From Basic Neuroscience to Treatment,* ed. Steven O. Molden and John L. R. Rubenstein (Boca Raton, FL: CRC Press, 2006).

9. Milt Freudenheim, "Battling Insurers over Autism Treatment; Most Resist Big Payments, Challenging Therapists and Disorder's Nature," *New York Times,* December 21, 2004, C1.

10. Julie Appleby, "Who's Uninsured in 2007? It's More than Just the Poor," *USA Today,* March 14, 2007.

11. "Fortune 500, 2001," CNNMoney.com, accessed October 18, 2012, http://money.cnn. com/magazines/fortune/fortune500_archive/full/2001.

12. Kurt Eichenwald and Diana B. Henriques, "Enron Buffed Image to a Shine Even as It Rotted from Within," *New York Times,* February 10, 2002.

13. Quoted in "The Energetic Messiah," *Economist,* June 1, 2000.

14. Brian O'Reilly, "The Power Merchant [ENRON, No. 18] Once a Dull-as-Methane Utility, Enron Has Grown Rich Making Markets Where Markets Were Never Made Before," *Fortune,* April 17, 2000.

15. Eichenwald and Henriques, "Enron Buffed Image."

16. Statement of Jan Fleetham, former Enron employee, in "Protecting the Pensions of Working Americans: Lessons from the Enron Debacle," hearing before the Senate Committee on Health, Education, Labor, and Pensions, 107th Congress (2002), 64–65.

17. Ibid., 65.

18. Interview on *Anderson Cooper 360 Degrees,* CNN, May 25, 2006.

19. David U. Himmelstein, Deborah Thorne, Elizabeth Warren, and Steffie Woolhandler, "Medical Bankruptcy in the United States, 2007: Results of a National Study," *American Journal of Medicine* 122, no. 8 (2009): 742, doi: 10.1016/j.amjmed.2009.04.012.

20. See Center on Budget and Policy Priorities, "Policy Basics: Where Do Our Federal Tax Dollars Go?," August 13, 2012, http://www.cbpp.org/cms/index.cfm?fa=view&id=1258.

Chapter 2

1. U.S. Census Bureau, *Current Population Survey, Annual Social and Economic Supplements* (Washington, DC: Government Printing Office, 2012), Table F-2.

2. Ibid., Table F-6.

3. Elizabeth Warren and Amelia Warren Tyagi, *The Two-Income Trap: Why Middle-Class Mothers and Fathers Are Going Broke* (New York: Basic Books, 2003).

4. See "Changes in U.S. Family Finances from 2007 to 2010: Evidence from the Survey of Consumer Finances," *Federal Reserve Bulletin* 98 (June 2012): 4.

5. Ibid., 30.

6. Ibid., 47–49.

7. Ibid., 63.

8. U.S. Census Bureau, *Statistical Abstract of the United States: 2012* (Washington, DC: Government Printing Office, 2012), 469, Table 721.

9. Ibid., 72, Table 94.

10. U.S. Department of the Treasury, *Income Mobility in the U.S. from 1996 to 2005* (Washington, DC: Government Printing Office, 2008), 7.

11. One might argue that ten years is not a long enough period to allow us to draw any significant conclusions, but research that has examined longer periods suggests similar conclusions. According to a study by the Pew Charitable Trusts, 30% of children from the poorest fifth of families, as compared to 71% from the richest fifth, will achieve incomes in the top three quintiles as adults. See Pew Charitable Trusts Economic Mobility Project, *Pursuing the American Dream: Economic Mobility across Generations* (Washington, DC: Pew Charitable Trusts, 2012), 6.

12. U.S. Census Bureau, *Educational Attainment in the United States: 2009* (Washington, DC: Government Printing Office, 2012), 13, Table 3.

13. Annie E. Casey Foundation, Kids Count Data Center, "Data across States: Infant Mortality—2009," August 2012, http://datacenter.kidscount.org/data/acrossstates/Rankings.aspx?ind=6051.

14. Centers for Disease Control and Prevention, "Deaths and Mortality," last revised March 29, 2012, http://www.cdc.gov/nchs/fastats/deaths.htm.

15. Kenneth D. Kochanek, Jiaquan Xu, Sherry L. Murphy, Arialdi M. Miniño, and Hsiang-Ching Kung, "Deaths: Final Data for 2009," *National Vital Statistics Report* 60, no. 3 (December 29, 2011): 88–92.

16. U.S. Census Bureau, *2010 Census—People and Households* (Washington, DC: Government Printing Office, 2010), Table 1.

17. See U.S. Census Bureau, *Statistical Abstract of the United States—2012 Update* (Washington, DC: Government Printing Office, 2012), Table 699.

18. National Cancer Institute, "Costs of Cancer Care," in "Cancer Trends Progress Report—2007 Update," last revised November 16, 2007, http://progressreport.cancer.gov/2007/doc_detail.asp?pid=1&did=2007&chid=75&coid=726&mid. For a typical anecdote, see also Katharine Stoel Gammon, "Women Struggle with Breast Cancer Expenses," ABCNews.com, October 16, 2007, http://abcnews.go.com/Health/OnCallPlus/story?id=3736060&page=1#.UGhK7qTyb3o.

19. American Heart Association, "Heart Disease and Stroke Statistics—2012 Update at a Glance," *Circulation* 189 (2012).

20. American Heart Association, "Heart Disease and Stroke Statistics—2012 Update," *Circulation* 125 (2012): e-3; American Heart Association, "Heart Disease and Stroke Statistics—2011 Update," *Circulation* 123 (2011): Table 3-1.

21. U.S. Bureau of Labor Statistics, "Labor Force Statistics from the Current Population, Household Data Annual Averages," accessed October 10, 2012, http://www.bls.gov/cps/#tables.

22. See Dan Beucke, "June Jobs: Five Things You Need to Know," *Bloomberg Businessweek,* July 6, 2012, http://www.businessweek.com/articles/2012-07-06/june-jobs-five-things-you-need-to-know.

23. See Dylan Matthews, "The Jobs Report in Five—Nay, Six!—Charts," *Washington Post,* September 7, 2012, http://www.washingtonpost.com/blogs/ezra-klein/wp/2012/09/07/the-jobs-report-in-five-charts-2.

24. U.S. Bureau of Labor Statistics, "Labor Force Statistics from the Current Population Survey, Table A-12," last revised February 5, 2010, http://www.bls.gov/cps/cpsatabs.htm.

25. See U.S. Bureau of Labor Statistics, "Changes to Data Collected on Unemployment Duration," last revised July 8, 2011, http://www.bls.gov/cps/duration.htm.

26. See Michael A. Fletcher, "Extended Jobless Benefits Cut in Eight States," *Washington Post,* May 11, 2012, http://www.washingtonpost.com/business/economy/extended-jobless-benefits-cut-in-eight-states/2012/05/10/gIQAX8X4GU_story.html.

27. U.S. Bureau of Labor Statistics, "Labor Force Statistics from the Current Population Survey, Table A-12," accessed October 1, 2012, http://www.bls.gov/cps/cpsatabs.htm.

28. William Erickson, Sarah von Schrader, and Camille Lee, *2010 Disability Status Report, United States* (Ithaca, NY: Cornell University, 2012), 9.

29. Social Security Administration, "Fact Sheet," March 18, 2011.

30. Society of Actuaries, *2011 Risks and Process of Retirement Survey Report, Key Findings and Issues: Longevity* (Schaumburg, IL: Society of Actuaries, 2011), 5.

31. Jack VanDerhei and Craig Copeland, *The EBRI Retirement Readiness Rating: Retirement Income Preparation and Future Prospects,* Issue Brief 344 (Washington, DC: Employee Benefit Research Institute, 2010), 6.

32. Ibid., 12–13.

33. See ibid., 15–17.

34. See Thomas Day, "Guide to Long Term Care Planning: About Nursing Homes," National Care Planning Council, accessed October 1, 2012, http://www.longtermcarelink.net/eldercare/nursing_home.htm.

Chapter 3

1. For a history of the early poor law, see Paul A. Fideler, *Social Welfare in Pre-industrial England: The Old Poor Law Tradition* (New York: Palgrave Macmillan, 2006). The later poor law is discussed in David R. Green, *Pauper Capital: London and the Poor Law, 1790–1870* (Burlington, VT: Ashgate, 2010). For a brief discussion of the poor law in the United States, see Gerald L. Neuman, "The Lost Century of American Immigration Law (1776–1875)," *Columbia Law Review* 93, no. 8 (1993): 1833, 1846–59.

2. See Charles Murray, *Losing Ground: American Social Policy, 1950–1980* (New York: Basic Books, 1984). 24% is the percentage of respondents who chose "too much welfare" as the main cause for the persistence of poverty; Charles M. Blow, "A Town Without Pity," *New York Times,* August 9, 2013.

3. For a description of the 1996 reform and a preliminary analysis of the impact of the legislation, see Greg J. Duncan and Gretchen Caspary, "Welfare Dynamics and the 1996 Welfare Reform," *Notre Dame Journal of Law, Ethics, and Public Policy* 11 (1997): 605–32.

4. An example of a relevant constitutional protection is the "one person, one vote" principle required by the U.S. Supreme Court in *Baker v. Carr,* 369 U.S. 186 (1962). (Previously, states could draw legislative districts that differed—sometimes widely—by size.) Although that principle remains widely debated among scholars, it surely promotes the egalitarian principle that all persons' votes should be counted equally. An example of an egalitarian governmental program is Head Start, a controversial federal program that provides additional educational services for low-income children.

5. Even during the Great Recession, the American public strongly supported Social Security and Medicare and opposed cuts to those programs. See Harris Interactive, *Cutting Government Spending May Be Popular but Majorities of the Public Oppose Cuts in Many Big Ticket Items in the Budget,* (New York: Harris Interactive, March 1, 2012), http://www.harrisinteractive.com/vault/Harris%20Poll%2024%20-Federal%20spending_3.1.12.pdf; Pew Research Center, *GOP Divided over Benefit Reductions: Public Wants Change in Entitlements, Not Changes in Benefits* (Washington,

DC: Pew Research Center, July 7, 2011), http://www.people-press.org/files/legacy-pdf/7-7-11%20 Entitlements%20Release.pdf. In each of these polls, strong majorities of Americans opposed to cuts to Social Security and government health care programs such as Medicare.

6. In 2003, before the current controversy over the Affordable Care Act, a *Washington Post*–ABC News public opinion poll found that 62% of Americans preferred a universal health care system to the then-current ad hoc insurance system. See Washington Post-ABC News Poll, "Health Care," October 20, 2003, question 47, http://www.washingtonpost.com/wp-srv/politics/ polls/vault/stories/data102003.html. The issue is a partisan one—during the 2008 election campaign, with health care a critical issue, 79% of Democrats but only 44% of Republicans favored a universal health care system based on an individual mandate of the sort eventually adopted by the Affordable Care Act. See Robert J. Blendon, Drew E. Altman, Claudia Deane, John M. Benson, Mollyann Brodie, and Tami Buhr, "Health Care in the 2008 Presidential Primaries," *New England Journal of Medicine* 358 (2008): 417.

7. Federal expenditures for veterans' medical care (including research funding) totaled $48 billion in 2009. Congressional Budget Office, *Potential Costs of Veterans' Health Care* (Washington, DC: Congressional Budget Office, October 2010), viii. According to the Kaiser Family Foundation, state expenditures on health care totaled more than $2 trillion in 2009. See Kaiser Family Foundation, "State Health Facts: Health Care Expenditures by State of Residence (in millions)," 2009, http:// www.statehealthfacts.org/comparemaptable.jsp?ind=592&cat=5. The states spent more than $11 billion funding workers' compensation liabilities in 2004. See Ishita Sengupta and Virginia Reno, "Recent Trends in Workers' Compensation," *Social Security Bulletin* 67 (2007): 17.

8. See Jeffrey L. Barnett and Phillip M. Vidal, *State and Local Government Finances Summary: 2010* (Washington, DC: U.S. Census Bureau, September 2012), 4, Figure 3, http:// www2.census.gov/govs/estimate/summary_report.pdf.

9. See U.S. Census Bureau, "Federal Budget Outlays by Detailed Function: 1990 to 2011," Table 473 in *Statistical Abstract of the United States: 2012* (Washington, DC: Government Printing Office, 2012), http://www.census.gov/compendia/statab/2012/tables/12s0473.pdf.

10. U.S. Congress, Joint Committee on Taxation, *Estimates of Federal Tax Expenditures for Fiscal Years 2011–2015,* prepared for the House Committee on Ways and Means and the Senate Committee on Finance, January 17, 2012, https://www.jct.gov/publications.html?-func=startdown&id=4385.

Chapter 4

1. Franklin Delano Roosevelt, "Inaugural Address," March 4, 1933.

2. Franklin Delano Roosevelt, "Message to the Congress on the Objectives and Accomplishments of the Administration," June 8, 1934.

3. Ibid.

4. Ibid.

5. Ibid.

6. Charles R. Henderson, "State Must Compel Insurance," *Chicago Daily Tribune,* October 28, 1906.

7. Ibid.

8. Theodore Roosevelt, "Speech before the Convention of the National Progressive Party," August 6, 1912.

9. Quoted in "Experts to Study Social Insurance," *New York Times,* December 19, 1915.

10. Ibid.

11. Franklin D. Roosevelt, "Fireside Chat 5: On Addressing the Critics," June 28, 1934.

12. Committee on Economic Security, *Social Security in America: The Factual Background of the Social Security Act as Summarized from Staff Reports to the Committee on Economic Security* (Washington, DC: Social Security Board, 1937), 515.

13. For the following quotations, see Committee on Economic Security, *Report of the Committee on Economic Security* (unpublished report, January 15, 1935), http://www.ssa.gov/ history/reports/ces5.html.

14. Ibid. On unemployment, the Committee on Economic Security reported: "The unprecedented extent and duration of unemployment in the United States since 1930 has left no one who is dependent upon a wage or salary untouched by the dread of loss of work. Unemployment relief distributed as a form of public charity, though necessary to prevent starvation, is not a solution of the problem. It is expensive to distribute and demoralizing to both donor and recipient. *A device is needed which will assure those who are involuntarily unemployed a small steady income for a limited period.*" Committee on Economic Security, *Social Security in America, Part 1: Unemployment Compensation* (unpublished report, 1935), emphasis added, http://www.ssa.gov/history/reports/ces/cesbookc1.html.

15. See Franklin D. Roosevelt, "Message Transmitting to the Congress a Report of the Social Security Board Recommending Certain Improvements in the Law," January 16, 1939, http://www.ssa.gov/history/fdrstmts.html#1939.

16. See "The President's Security Plan," *Hartford Courant*, January 18, 1935; "Bills Backed by President under Fire," *Washington Post*, February 4, 1935; "Votes to Separate FERA and AGE Fund, Ways and Means Committee Would Give Handling of Fund to Social Insurance Board," *New York Times*, February 15, 1935; "Pool Plan Is Urged on Job Insurance," *New York Times*, March 3, 1935.

17. Carmen D. Solomon, *Major Decisions in the House and Senate Chambers on Social Security: 1936‒1985* (Washington, DC: Congressional Research Service, 1986), 9.

18. Ibid., 11.

19. "Social Security Bill Voted; Will Benefit 30,000,000," *New York Times*, August 10, 1935.

20. Franklin D. Roosevelt, "1938 Advisory Council Report—President's Letter of Transmittal to Congress," http://www.ssa.gov/history/reports/38advisepres.html.

21. Ibid.

22. According to a *New York Times* report, "One small amendment to the proposal was passed, an increase from $15 to $20 per month in the maximum amount of federal matching funds for states to help the blind." "House Passes Bill to Widen Security," *New York Times*, June 11, 1939.

23. "Increased Pensions for the Aged," *Washington Post*, August 6, 1939.

24. "Amendments Signed by President," *Washington Post*, August 13, 1939.

25. "Seeks to Put All Social Insurance in a Federal Pool," *New York Times*, October 5, 1941.

26. Harry S. Truman, "Special Message to the Congress Recommending a Comprehensive Health Program," November 19, 1945, http://www.trumanlibrary.org/publicpapers/index.php?pid=483.

27. Ibid.

28. Quoted in "Fishbein Assails New Health Plan, Truman's National Program Condemned as 'Socialized Medicine' at Its Worst," *New York Times*, November 27, 1945.

29. See Solomon, *Major Decisions in the House and Senate*, 34.

30. Dwight D. Eisenhower, "Special Message to the Congress on Old Age and Survivors Insurance and of Federal Grants-in-Aid for Public Assistance Programs," January 14, 1954, http://www.ssa.gov/history/ikestmts.html#pubasst.

31. "Backing Given to Social Aid," *Baltimore Sun*, May 23, 1954. Arthur Larson served as undersecretary of labor, head of the United States Information Agency, and special assistant to the president during the Eisenhower administration.

32. Quoted in ibid.

33. Solomon, *Major Decisions in the House and Senate*, 36–37.

34. Carmen DeNavas-Walt, Bernadette D. Proctor, and Jessica C. Smith, *Income, Poverty, and Health Insurance Coverage in the United States: 2011* (Washington, DC: Government Printing Office, 2012), 66.

35. Ibid., 71–73.

36. Lyndon B. Johnson, "Remarks with President Truman at the Signing in Independence of the Medicare Bill," July 30, 1965, http://www.lbjlib.utexas.edu/johnson/archives.hom/speeches.hom/650730.asp.

37. Ibid.

38. Theodore A. Marmor, *The Politics of Medicare*, 2nd ed. (Hawthorne, NY: Aldine de Gruyter, 2000), 10–17.

39. Ibid., 17–23.

40. See "The Average Cost of Nursing Home Care Moves Upward in 2012," Elder Law Answers, last revised November 9, 2012, http://www.elderlawanswers.com/the-average-cost-of-nursing-home-care-moves-upward-in-2012-10021.

41. See *National Federation of Independent Business v. Sebelius,* 132 S. Ct. 603 (2011).

42. Scott Clement, "Six Charts to Explain Health-Care Polling," *Washington Post,* June 28, 2012, http://www.washingtonpost.com/blogs/the-fix/post/six-charts-to-explain-health-care-pol ling/2012/06/28/gJQAlBrn8V_blog.html.

43. Richard M. Nixon, "Statement on Signing the Social Security Amendments of 1972," October 30, 1972, http://www.ssa.gov/history/nixstmts.html#1972.

44. Ronald Reagan, "Remarks on Signing the Social Security Amendments of 1983," April 20, 1983, http://www.ssa.gov/history/reaganstmts.html#1983.

45. George H. W. Bush, "Address before a Joint Session of Congress on the State of the Union," January 31, 1991, http://www.ssa.gov/history/bushstmts.html.

46. George W. Bush, "Statement on Signing the Medicare Prescription Drug and Modernization Act of 2003," December 8, 2003.

47. See, for example, Michael Tanner, *Still a Better Deal: Private Investment vs. Social Security,* Policy Analysis No. 692 (Washington, DC: Cato Institute, February 13, 2012), http://www.cato.org/sites/cato.org/files/pubs/pdf/PA692.pdf.

Part Notes

1. See Michael J. Graetz and Jerry L. Mashaw, *True Security: Rethinking American Social Insurance* (New Haven, CT: Yale University Press, 1999).

Chapter 5

1. Carmen DeNavas-Walt, Bernadette D. Proctor, and Jessica C. Smith, *Income, Poverty, and Health Insurance Coverage in the United States: 2011* (Washington, DC: Government Printing Office, 2012), 14.

2. Katharine Bradbury, *Trends in U.S. Family Income Mobility, 1969–2006,* Working Paper 11-10 (Boston: Federal Reserve Bank of Boston, October 20, 2011), 38–40, http://www.bos.frb.org/economic/wp/wp2011/wp1110.pdf.

3. Robert Rector and Rachel Sheffield, *Understanding Poverty in the United States: Surprising Facts about America's Poor,* Executive Summary Backgrounder No. 2607 (Washington, DC: Heritage Foundation, September 13, 2011), 1, http://thf_media.s3.amazonaws.com/2011/pdf/bg2607.pdf. The authors go much further, arguing that "real material hardship . . . is limited in scope and severity." To support their case, they present a wide range of data on the lives of the American poor—the absence of malnutrition and stunting, high average size of living space, and wide ownership of modern amenities. In doing so, they tend to gloss over the issue of quality: a ten-year-old desktop computer is not an iPad, an old jalopy is not a new car, and a living space in a poor inner-city neighborhood is much different in character from a suburban home of the same size. They ignore other data we present on the consequences of birth into a poor family and vastly overstate their argument.

4. Julia B. Isaacs, Tracy Vericker, Jennifer Macomber, and Adam Kent, *Kids' Share: An Analysis of Federal Expenditures on Children through 2008* (Washington, DC: Urban Institute and Brookings Institution, 2009), 16, http://www.brookings.edu/~/media/research/files/reports/2009/12/09%20kids%20share%20isaacs/1209_kids_share_isaacs.pdf.

5. Connie F. Citro and Robert T. Michael, *Measuring Poverty: A New Approach* (Washington, DC: National Academy Press, 1995), 3–7.

6. Kathleen Short, *The Research Supplemental Poverty Measure: 2010,* Current Population Reports P60-241 (Washington, DC: U.S. Census Bureau, November 2011), http://www.census.gov/prod/2011pubs/p60-241.pdf.

7. Ibid., 10, Figure 4.

8. U.S. Census Bureau, "Income, Poverty and Health Insurance in the United States: 2011—Tables & Figures," Current Population Survey: 2012, Table 5, accessed November 8, 2012, http://www.census.gov/hhes/www/poverty/data/incpovhlth/2011/tables.html.

9. U.S. Department of Health and Human Services, "Indicators of Welfare Dependence: Annual Report to Congress, 2003," Appendix A, Table TANF 1, accessed November 8, 2012, http://aspe.hhs.gov/HSP/indicators03/index.htm.

10. Ibid., Appendix A, Table TANF 6.

11. Ibid., Appendix A, Tables TANF 8 and 9.

12. Center on Budget and Policy Priorities, *Policy Basics: An Introduction to TANF* (Washington, DC: Center on Budget and Policy Priorities, July 22, 2010), 1, http://www.cbpp.org/files/7-22-10tanf2.pdf.

13. Ibid., 3.

14. Liz Schott, LaDonna Pavetti, and Ife Finch, *How States Have Spent Federal and State Funds under the TANF Block Grant* (Washington, DC: Center on Budget and Policy Priorities, August 7, 2012), 3, http://www.cbpp.org/files/8-7-12tanf.pdf.

15. Pamela J. Loprest, *How Has the TANF Caseload Changed over Time?*, Brief 08 (Washington, DC: Urban Institute, March 2012), 2, http://www.acf.hhs.gov/sites/default/files/opre/change_time_1.pdf.

16. U.S. Department of Health and Human Services, Administration for Children and Families, Office of Family Assistance, *Temporary Assistance for Needy Families Program: Ninth Report to Congress* (Washington, DC: Government Printing Office, 2012), 75, http://www.acf.hhs.gov/sites/default/files/ofa/9th_report_to_congress_3_26_12.pdf.

17. Center on Budget and Policy Priorities, *Chart Book: TANF at 16* (Washington, DC: Center on Budget and Policy Priorities, August 22, 2012), 3, http://www.cbpp.org/files/8-22-12tanf.pdf.

18. U.S. Department of Health and Human Services, Administration for Children and Families, Office of Family Assistance, *Temporary Assistance for Needy Families Program: Eighth Annual Report to Congress* (Washington, DC: Government Printing Office, 2009), v, http://archive.acf.hhs.gov/programs/ofa/data-reports/annualreport8/TANF_8th_Report_111908.pdf.

19. Ibid., vii.

20. Ibid.

21. Ibid., x.

22. U.S. Department of Health and Human Services, Office of the Assistant Secretary for Planning and Evaluation, *Information on Poverty and Income Statistics: A Summary of 2011 Current Population Survey Data,* ASPE Issue Brief (Washington, DC: U.S. Department of Health and Human Services, September 13, 2011), 4, http://aspe.hhs.gov/poverty/11/ib.pdf.

23. U.S. Department of Health and Human Services, *Ninth Report to Congress,* VIII-63.

24. Peter Edelman and Barbara Ehrenreich, "Why Welfare Reform Has Failed," *Washington Post,* December 6, 2009.

25. U.S. Department of the Treasury, *Agency Financial Report: Fiscal Year 2011* (Washington, DC: Government Printing Office, November 15, 2011), 33, http://www.treasury.gov/about/budget-performance/annual-performance-plan/Documents/FY%202011%20AFR-Final%20Version.pdf. Department auditors argue that $14–$17 billion of the total are overclaims. Ibid.

26. Jimmy Charite, Indivar Dutta-Gupta, and Chuck Marr, *Studies Show Earned Income Tax Credit Encourages Work and Success in School and Reduces Poverty* (Washington, DC: Center on Budget and Policy Priorities, June 26, 2012), 1, http://www.cbpp.org/files/6-26-12tax.pdf.

27. Ibid.

28. Tax Policy Center, Urban Institute and Brookings Institution, *The Tax Policy Briefing Book: A Citizens' Guide for the 2012 Election and Beyond* (Washington, DC: Tax Policy Center, 2012), II-1-4, http://www.taxpolicycenter.org/briefing-book/TPC_briefingbook_full.pdf.

29. Center on Budget and Policy Priorities, *Policy Basics: The Child Tax Credit* (Washington, DC: Center on Budget and Policy Priorities, 2012), 1–2, http://www.cbpp.org/files/policybasics-ctc.pdf.

30. Elaine Maag, "Who Benefits from the Dependent Exemption?," *Tax Notes* (Tax Policy Center, Urban Institute and Brookings Institution), December 20, 2010, 1, http://www .taxpolicycenter.org/UploadedPDF/1001478-Tax-Facts-Dependent-Exemption-Maag.pdf.

31. These rates are for a married couple filing jointly. Tax Rate Schedule Y-2, Internal Revenue Code section 1(d) (2013).

32. Trip Gabriel, "Gingrich Campaign Defends Remarks on Food Stamps," *New York Times,* January 6, 2012.

33. Kathleen FitzGerald, Emily Holcombe, Molly Dahl, and Jonathan Schwabish, "An Overview of the Supplemental Nutrition Assistance Program," Congressional Budget Office, April 19, 2012, http://www.cbo.gov/publication/43175.

34. U.S. Bureau of Labor Statistics, "Employment, Hours, and Earnings from the Current Employment Statistics Survey (National): 2008–2009," accessed November 14, 2012, http://data. bls.gov/pdq/SurveyOutputServlet.

35. U.S. Department of Agriculture, Economic Research Service, *The 2002 Farm Bill: Provisions and Economic Implications* (Washington, DC: Government Printing Office, April 2002), 3, http://www.ers.usda.gov/media/264043/ap022_4_.pdf.

36. U.S. Department of Agriculture, Food and Nutrition Service, Office of Research and Analysis, *Building a Healthy America: A Profile of the Supplemental Nutrition Assistance Program* (Alexandria, VA: U.S. Department of Agriculture, April 2012), 13, http://www.fns .usda.gov/ora/MENU/Published/snap/FILES/Other/BuildingHealthyAmerica.pdf.

37. President Obama certainly bears responsibility for the 13.6% SNAP benefit increase included in the American Recovery and Reinvestment Act of 2009. This likely explains $9 billion of the FY 2011 $72 billion cost, or a quarter of the increase from FY 2007. President Bush, for his part, did veto the Farm Bill of 2008. The Democratic Congress overrode him. That bill loosened some eligibility requirements and increased the minimum benefit.

38. U.S. Department of Agriculture, *Building a Healthy America,* 2.

39. Ibid., 25.

40. Ibid., 8.

41. U.S. Department of Agriculture, Food and Nutrition Service, "WIC Program Participation and Costs (Data as of November 9, 2012)," accessed November 14, 2012, http://www.fns.usda .gov/pd/wisummary.htm.

42. U.S. Department of Agriculture, Food and Nutrition Service, "Women, Infants, and Children: Frequently Asked Questions about WIC," last revised July 13, 2012, http://www.fns .usda.gov/wic/faqs/faq.htm.

43. Ibid.

44. U.S. Department of Agriculture, "WIC Program Participation and Costs."

45. Marianne Bitler, Janet Curie, and John Karl Scholz, "WIC Eligibility and Participation," *Journal of Human Resources* 38, supplement (2003): 1139–79.

46. U.S. Department of Agriculture, Food and Nutrition Service, "The School Breakfast Program," last revised August 2012, http://www.fns.usda.gov/cnd/Breakfast/AboutBFast/ SBPFactSheet.pdf; U.S. Department of Agriculture, Food and Nutrition Service, "National School Lunch Program," last revised August 2012, http://www.fns.usda.gov/cnd/Lunch/AboutLunch/ NSLPFactSheet.pdf.

47. Ibid.

48. Ibid.

49. For information on states' particular standards for Medicaid and CHIP eligibility, see Kaiser Commission on Medicaid and the Uninsured, *Where Are States Today? Medicaid and CHIP Eligibility Levels for Children and Non-disabled Adults* (Washington, DC: Kaiser Family Foundation, March 2013), http://www.kff.org/medicaid/upload/7993-03.pdf. One would be forgiven for believing that CHIP is financed entirely by the federal government. The Affordable Care Act of 2010 maintains the CHIP eligibility standards in place through 2019. In 2015, the enhanced CHIP federal matching rate will be increased by 23 percentage points, bringing the average federal matching rate for CHIP to 93%. Centers for Medicare and Medicaid Services,

"Children's Health Insurance Program Financing," accessed November 14, 2012, http://www.medicaid.gov/Medicaid-CHIP-Program-Information/By-Topics/Financing-and-Reimbursement/Childrens-Health-Insurance-Program-Financing.html.

50. DeNavas-Walt et al., *Income, Poverty, and Health Insurance Coverage*, 70.

51. Michael E. Martinez and Robin A. Cohen, *Health Insurance Coverage: Early Release of Estimates from the National Health Interview Survey, January–September 2011* (Hyattsville, MD: National Center for Health Statistics, March 2012), http://www.cdc.gov/nchs/data/nhis/earlyrelease/Insur201203.pdf.

52. DeNavas-Walt et al., *Income, Poverty, and Health Insurance Coverage*, 70.

53. Estes et al., *Health Policy: Crisis and Reform*, 6th ed. (Burlington, MA: Jones & Bartlett, 2012), 631.

54. Analysis of the Urban Institute Health Policy Center's ACS Medicaid/CHIP Eligibility Simulation Model based on data from the Integrated Public Use Microdata Series, as reported in Genevieve M. Kenney, Victoria Lynch, Jennifer Haley, Michael Huntress, Dean Resnick, and Christine Coyer, *Gains for Children: Increased Participation in Medicaid and CHIP in 2009* (Washington, DC: Urban Institute, August 2011), 19, http://www.urban.org/UploadedPDF/412379-Gains-for-Children.pdf.

55. Kaiser Family Foundation, "Medicaid Payments per Enrollee, FY 2009," accessed November 15, 2012, http://www.statehealthfacts.org/comparemaptable.jsp?ind=183&cat=4.

56. Karen E. Lynch, *The Child Care and Development Block Grant: Background and Funding*, CRS Report RL30785 (Washington, DC: Congressional Research Service, January 28, 2010), 1, http://www.policyarchive.org/handle/10207/bitstreams/19845.pdf.

57. National Child Care Information and Technical Assistance Center, *Child Care and Development Fund: Report of State and Territory Plans FY 2010–2011* (Washington, DC: U.S. Department of Health and Human Services, 2011), 27, http://occ-archive.org/files/resources/sp1011full-report.pdf.

58. U.S. Department of Health and Human Services, Office of Child Care, "Table 1, 2010 CCDF Data Tables (Preliminary Estimates)," last revised December 1, 2011, http://www.acf.hhs.gov/programs/occ/resource/ccdf-data-10acf800-preliminary.

59. Administration for Children and Families, "Child Care and Development Fund Fact Sheet," November 2009, http://www.acf.hhs.gov/programs/ccb/ccdf/factsheet.htm.

60. U.S. Department of Health and Human Services, Administration for Children and Families, *Fiscal Year 2012: Justification of Estimates for Appropriations Committees* (Washington, DC: Government Printing Office, 2012), 55, http://www.acf.hhs.gov/sites/default/files/olab/2012_all.pdf.

61. Census Bureau data suggest that about 5 million children under 5 years of age are living in families with incomes below the FPL. The program subsidizes only 1.7 million children monthly.

62. Office of Head Start, "Head Start Services," accessed November 15, 2012, http://www.acf.hhs.gov/programs/ohs/about/head-start.

63. U.S. Department of Health and Human Services, Administration for Children and Families, Office of Head Start, *Biennial Report to Congress: The Status of Children in Head Start Programs* (Arlington, VA: Head Start Resource Center, 2007), 132–33.

64. Ibid., 5–7.

65. Michael L. Anderson, "Multiple Inference and Gender Differences in the Effects of Early Intervention: A Reevaluation of the Abecedarian, Perry Preschool, and Early Training Projects," *Journal of the American Statistical Association* 103 (2008): 1481–95; Janet Currie. "Early Childhood Education Programs," *Journal of Economic Perspectives* 15, no. 2 (2001): 213–38, cited in David Deming, "Early Childhood Intervention and Life-Cycle Skill Development: Evidence from Head Start," *American Economic Journal: Applied Economics* 1, no. 3 (2009): 111–34.

66. See Deming, "Early Childhood Intervention," 130. At least one significant study with short-term results to the contrary exists and has found its way into the popular press. In 2011, *Time* magazine ran an article stating: "There is indisputable evidence about the program's effectiveness, provided by the Department of Health and Human Services: Head Start simply does not work"

(Joe Klein, "Time to Ax Public Programs That Don't Yield Results," *Time,* July 7, 2011). This conclusion, like the more positive results reported in the text, remains highly controversial. In fact most studies find positive results, but often measure different outcomes, using different methodologies and different time frames. For a review of the literature see Chloe Gibbs et al., *Does Head Start Do Any Lasting Good?*, No. w17452, National Bureau of Economic Research, 2011, forthcoming in *The War on Poverty: A 50-Year Retrospective* (Martha Bailey and Sheldon Danziger, eds.).

67. See Child Trends DataBank, "Percentage of Children Ages Three to Four Currently Attending a Head Start Program, 1991–2005," accessed May 30, 2013, http://www.childtrendsdatabank.org/sites/default/files/97_Tab01.pdf.

68. Statement of Gregory D. Kutz, managing director, Forensic Audits and Special Investigations, U.S. Government Accountability Office, "Head Start—Undercover Testing Finds Fraud and Abuse at Selected Head Start Centers," testimony before the House Committee on Education and Labor (2010), 11–12, http://www.gao.gov/assets/130/124660.pdf.

69. National Center for Education Statistics, Institute of Education Sciences, "Fast Facts," accessed November 15, 2012, http://nces.ed.gov/fastfacts.

70. U.S. Department of Education, "The Federal Role in Education," accessed November 15, 2012, http://www2.ed.gov/about/overview/fed/role.html.

71. Mark Dixon, *Public Education Finances: 2010,* U.S. Census Bureau Publication G10-ASPEF (Washington, DC: Government Printing Office, 2012), 8, Table 8.

72. U.S. Department of Education, National Center for Homeless Education, *Education for Homeless Children and Youth Program: Data Collection Summary* (Washington, DC: National Center for Homeless Education, June 2011), 4, http://center.serve.org/nche/downloads/data_comp_0708-0910.pdf.

73. U.S. Department of Housing and Urban Development, Office of Community Planning and Development, *The 2010 Annual Homeless Assessment Report to Congress* (Washington, DC: Department of Housing and Urban Development, 2011), 5–10.

74. U.S. Department of Housing and Urban Development, "An Overview of the HUD Budget: How HUD Funding Furthers Our Mission," accessed November 15, 2012, http://portal.hud.gov/hudportal/documents/huddoc?id=2012BudgetOverview032011.pdf.

75. See U.S. Department of Housing and Urban Development, *Fiscal Year 2013 Program and Budget Initiatives: Affordable Housing Rental Assistance,* 43–44, accessed November 18, 2012, http://portal.hud.gov/hudportal/documents/huddoc?id=CombBudget2013.pdf (calculations by the authors).

76. U.S. Department of Housing and Urban Development, "Overview of the HUD Budget."

77. Ibid.

78. U.S. Department of Housing and Urban Development, "Housing Choice Vouchers Fact Sheet," accessed November 18, 2012, http://portal.hud.gov/hudportal/HUD?src=/program_offices/public_indian_housing/programs/hcv/about/fact_sheet.

79. See U.S. Department of Housing and Urban Development, *Fiscal Year 2013 Program and Budget Initiatives,* 43 (calculations by the authors).

80. See ibid., 44.

81. Yonah Freemark and Lawrence J. Vale, "Illogical Housing Aid," *New York Times,* October 30, 2012.

82. See Arloc Sherman, "Poverty and Financial Distress Would Have Been Substantially Worse in 2010 without Government Action, New Census Data Show," Center for Budget and Policy Priorities, November 7, 2011, http://www.cbpp.org/cms/?fa=view&id=3610.

83. DeNavas-Walt et al., *Income, Poverty, and Health Insurance Coverage,* 14, Table 3.

84. Jason DeParle, "Harder for Americans to Rise from Lower Rungs," *New York Times,* January 4, 2012.

Chapter 6

1. Geoff Earle, "Swing Conservative: The Perilous Bipartisanship of Lindsey Graham," *Washington Monthly,* April 2005, http://www.washingtonmonthly.com/features/2005/0504.earle.html.

2. Lloyd Grove, "Lindsey Graham, a Twang of Moderation," *Washington Post,* October 7, 1998, D01.

3. Earle, "Swing Conservative."

4. Ibid.

5. Susan Page, "Six Men Who'll Shape the Future," *USA Today,* March 10, 2005, http://usatoday30.usatoday.com/news/washington/2005-03-09-social-security-six_x.htm.

6. Earle, "Swing Conservative."

7. Charles Babington and Jim VandeHei, "Republicans Float Ideas for Social Security," *Washington Post,* March 6, 2005, A06.

8. See, for example, Thomas E. Nugent, "Graham Crackers," *National Review,* January 4, 2005, http://www.nationalreview.com/articles/213288/graham-crackers-social-security/thomas-e-nugent.

9. Page, "Six Men Who'll Shape the Future."

10. Earle, "Swing Conservative."

11. American Council of Life Insurers, *2011 Life Insurers Fact Book* (Washington, DC: American Council of Life Insurers, 2011), 35, 61.

12. Ibid., 73.

13. Ibid.

14. Employee Benefit Research Institute, *Tax Expenditures and Employee Benefits: Estimates from the FY 2011 Budget,* Facts from EBRI, March 2010, 2, http://www.ebri.org/pdf/publications/facts/FS-209_Mar10_Bens-Rev-Loss.pdf. Employees do pay a tax on employer premium payments for benefit value in excess of $50,000.

15. U.S. Bureau of Labor Statistics, National Compensation Survey, March 2012, Table 16, "Life Insurance Benefits—Access, Participation, and Take-Up Rates."

16. See ibid., Table 19, "Life Insurance Plans—Fixed Multiple of Annual Earnings Benefit Formulas, Civilian Workers."

17. Ibid., Table 16.

18. Ibid.

19. Insurance Information Institute, *The Insurance Fact Book 2012* (New York: Insurance Information Institute, 2012), 25.

20. U.S. Department of Labor, National Compensation Survey, March 2012, Table 20, "Life Insurance Plans—Maximum Benefit Amount, Civilian Workers."

21. American Council of Life Insurers, *2011 Life Insurers Fact Book,* 66.

22. See ibid., 64.

23. LIMRA LL Global, "Ownership of Individual Life Insurance Falls to 50-Year Low, LIMRA Reports," news release, August 30, 2010, http://www.limra.com/Posts/PR/News_Releases/Ownership_of_Individual_Life_Insurance_Falls_to_50-Year_Low,_LIMRA_Reports.aspx. The figures in this paragraph come from a regular survey conducted by an industry association called LIMRA, which describes itself as "a worldwide association of insurance and financial services companies, established to help its members improve their marketing and distribution effectiveness." LIMRA LL Global, "Facts about LIMRA," accessed November 20, 2012, http://www.limra.com/PDFs/NewsCenter/Materials/factsabout.pdf. Reporters quote LIMRA data in reputable business publications, so we will assume that whatever tendency an industry group might have to present a distorted picture of private data is held in check by the group's concern for reputation.

24. Leslie Scism, "More Go without Life Insurance," *Wall Street Journal,* August 29, 2010, http://online.wsj.com/article/SB10001424052748704342504575459232913104238.html.

25. U.S. Social Security Administration, "Social Security Survivors Benefits: Protection You and Your Family Can Count On," last revised April 2, 2012, http://www.ssa.gov/survivorplan/index.htm.

26. U.S. Social Security Administration, *Social Security: Understanding the Benefits* (Washington, DC: Government Printing Office, 2012), 21, http://www.ssa.gov/pubs/10024.pdf.

27. Ibid., 12.

28. U.S. Social Security Administration, "Monthly Statistical Snapshot, October 2012," Table 2, http://www.ssa.gov/policy/docs/quickfacts/stat_snapshot.

29. Ibid.

30. U.S. Social Security Administration, *Annual Statistical Supplement to the Social Security Bulletin, 2011* (Washington, DC: Government Printing Office, 2011), Table 4.A5, "Total Annual Benefits Paid from OASI Trust Fund, by Type of Benefit, Selected Years 1937–2010," http://www.ssa.gov/policy/docs/statcomps/supplement/2011/4a.pdf.

31. American Council of Life Insurers, *2011 Life Insurers Fact Book,* 47.

32. National Academy of Social Insurance, *Fact Sheet: Social Security Pays Benefits in the Wake of September 11th Attacks,* 1, accessed November 20, 2012, http://www.nasi.org/sites/default/files/research/Survivor_Fact_Sheet_SS_3_11_02.pdf.

33. Ibid.

34. The data represented in Figure 6.5 are also consistent across time. The U.S. level of 0.7% of GDP spent on survivor benefits has not changed since 2003. See American Council of Life Insurers, *2011 Life Insurers Fact Book,* Table 4.5.

35. National Funeral Directors Association, "Funeral Service Facts," accessed November 20, 2012, http://nfda.org/media-center/statistics.html#fsfacts.

Chapter 7

1. This vignette is a factual account gleaned from interviews. We have changed the name of the ill woman and refrained from using the company name because of an impending legal action. Available polling data demonstrate that Robina's struggles are not unusual for a cancer patient. See Kaiser Family Foundation, "USA Today/Kaiser/Harvard Survey Highlights Problems in the Health Care System through the Experiences of People with Cancer," November 17, 2006, http://kff.org/other/poll-finding/usa-todaykaiserharvard-survey-highlights-problems-in-the.

2. Barack Obama, "Remarks by the President on the Affordable Care Act and the New Patients' Bill of Rights," Office of the Press Secretary, White House, June 22, 2010, http://www.whitehouse.gov/the-press-office/remarks-president-affordable-care-act-and-new-patients-bill-rights.

3. Statement of Douglas W. Elmendorf, director, Congressional Budget Office, "Analysis of the Major Health Care Legislation Enacted in March 2010," before the Subcommittee on Health Committee on Energy and Commerce, U.S. House of Representatives (March 30, 2011), 2.

4. David U. Himmelstein, Deborah Thorne, Elizabeth Warren, and Steffie Woolhandler, "Medical Bankruptcy in the United States, 2007: Results of a National Study," *American Journal of Medicine* 122, no. 8 (2009): 741–46, doi: 10.1016/j.amjmed.2009.04.012.

5. Theodore R. Marmor and Jonathan Oberlander, "Health Reform: The Fateful Moment," *New York Review of Books,* August 13, 2009.

6. The historic "health care case" is *National Federation of Independent Business v. Sebelius,* 132 S. Ct. 2566 (2012).

7. Congressional Budget Office, "Lessons from Medicare's Demonstration Projects on Disease Management, Care Coordination, and Value-Based Payment," Issue Brief, January 18, 2012.

8. U.S. National Highway Traffic Safety Administration, *Traffic Safety Facts,* as cited in U.S. Census Bureau, *Statistical Abstract of the United States, 2011–12* (Washington, DC: Government Printing Office, 2012), Table 1106.

9. Berhanu Alemayehu and Kenneth E. Warner, "The Lifetime Distribution of Healthcare Costs," *Health Services Research* 39, no. 3 (2004): 627–42. We adjust to current dollars the researchers' calculation of $316,000 in year 2000 dollars.

10. Himmelstein et al., "Medical Bankruptcy in the United States."

11. Institute of Medicine of the National Academies, *Insuring America's Health: Principles and Recommendations* (Washington, DC: National Academies Press, 2004), 22.

12. Approximately 64% of the population had employment-based health insurance in 1999; the number had dropped to 55.1% by 2011. U.S. Census Bureau, Current Population Survey, Annual Social and Economic Supplements, 2011, "Health Insurance Historical Tables," Table HIB-1, http://www.census.gov/hhes/www/hlthins/data/historical/HIB_tables.html.

13. U.S. Congress, Joint Committee on Taxation, *Estimates of Federal Tax Expenditures for Fiscal Years 2010–2014,* prepared for the House Committee on Ways and Means and the Senate Committee on Finance, December 15, 2010, 47.

14. David I. Auerbach and Arthur L. Kellermann, "A Decade of Health Care Cost Growth Has Wiped Out Real Income Gains for an Average US Family," *Health Affairs* 30, no. 9 (2011): 1630–36.

15. Kaiser Family Foundation and Health Research & Educational Trust, *Employer Health Benefits: 2012 Annual Survey* (Menlo Park, CA: Kaiser Family Foundation, 2012), 50, Exhibit 3.1.

16. Ibid., 171, Exhibit 11.1. See also KPMG Survey of Employer-Sponsored Health Benefits, 1991, 1993, 1995, 1998 (information at Kaiser Family Foundation, Employer Health Benefits Annual Survey Archives, http://kff.org/health-costs/report/employer-health-benefits-annual-survey-archives).

17. Kaiser Family Foundation and Health Research & Educational Trust, *Employer Health Benefits: 2012 Annual Survey,* 80, Exhibit 6.7; see also 75, Exhibit 6.7.

18. Ibid., 110, Exhibit 7.6.

19. Himmelstein et al., "Medical Bankruptcy in the United States," 743, Table 2.

20. David Dranove and Michael L. Millenson, "Medical Bankruptcy: Myth Versus Fact," *Health Affairs* 25, no. 2 (2006): W74–W83 (published online), doi: 10.1377/hlthaff.25.w74.

21. One of our coauthors can report that his wife was denied individual coverage in 2006 for the stated reason that "two visits to a medical specialist in the prior six month period" constituted a statistical predictor of ill health.

22. For a description of New Jersey's struggles to regulate health care premiums without imposing a mandate, see Jonathan Cohn, "The New Jersey Experience: Do Insurance Reforms Unravel without an Individual Mandate?," *Kaiser Health News,* March 2012, http://www.kaiser-healthnews.org/stories/ 2012/march/21/nj-ind-mandate-case-study.aspx. See also "Junk Health Insurance: Stingy Plans May be Worse than None at All," *Consumer Reports,* March 2012.

23. This is but the briefest review of Medicare's financing. In practice, Medicare recipients are still responsible for considerable out-of-pocket costs: a deductible amounting to the cost of one day of hospital care in Part A, both deductibles and coinsurance in Part B, and quite complicated cost sharing in the drug program, Part D. This helps to explain why some 75% of those participating in Medicare buy supplementary coverage, itself evidence that Americans want to avoid payments at the point of receiving care.

24. See, for instance, the testimony of Mark E. Miller, Ph.D., executive director, Medicare Payment Advisory Commission, before the Committee on the Budget, U.S. House of Representatives, June 28, 2007. Surprisingly, despite ACA provisions intended to eliminate the gap in cost, private plans continue to cost Medicare more than the traditional program. See Medicare Payment Advisory Commission, *Report to the Congress: Medicare Payment Policy* (Washington, DC: MedPAC, March 2013), 287–89, http://www.medpac.gov/documents/Mar13_EntireReport.pdf.

25. See statement of Peter R. Orszag, director, Congressional Budget Office, "The Overuse, Underuse, and Misuse of Health Care," before the Committee on Finance, U.S. Senate (July 17, 2008), 3–6. See also Agency for Healthcare Research and Quality, *Fact Sheet: Improving Health Care Quality,* AHRQ Publication No. 02-P032 (Rockville, MD: Agency for Healthcare Research and Quality, September 2002), http://www.ahrq.gov/news/qualfact.pdf. For manipulable data on regional variation in the provision of health care, see "The Dartmouth Atlas of Health Care," http://www.dartmouthatlas.org.

26. Boards of Trustees, Federal Hospital Insurance and Federal Supplementary Medical Insurance Trust Funds, *The 2010 Annual Report of the Boards of Trustees of the Federal Hospital Insurance and Federal Supplementary Medical Insurance Trust Funds* (Washington, DC: Boards of Trustees, August 5, 2010), 78, http://www.cms.gov/Research-Statistics-Data-and-Systems/Statistics-Trends-and-Reports/ReportsTrustFunds/Downloads/TR2010.pdf.

27. As of mid-2013, thirteen governors were on record as saying their states will not participate in the Medicaid expansion, and six others were leaning against doing so. See Advisory Board Company, Daily Briefing, "Where Each State Stands on ACA's Medicaid Expansion," accessed June 4, 2013, http://www.advisory.com/Daily-Briefing/2012/11/09/MedicaidMap#lightbox/1.

28. Julie Appleby and Christopher Weaver, "After Much Scrutiny, HHS Releases Health Insurance Exchange Rules," *Kaiser Health News,* July 11, 2011, http://www.kaiserhealthnews.org/stories/2011/july/11/health-insurance-exchange-regulations-released.aspx.

29. See Theodore Marmor and Jonathan Oberlander, "From HMOs to ACOs: The Quest for the Holy Grail in U.S. Health Policy," *Journal of General Internal Medicine* 27, no. 9 (2012): 1215–18.

30. See, for instance, Ronald A. Paulus, Karen Davis, and Glenn D. Steele, "Continuous Innovation in Health Care: Implications of the Geisinger Experience," *Health Affairs* 27, no. 5 (2008): 1235–45.

31. Theodore Marmor, Jonathan Oberlander, and Joseph White, "Medicare and the Federal Budget: Misdiagnosed Problems, Inadequate Solutions," *Journal of Policy Analysis and Management* 30, no. 4 (2011): 928–34, doi: 10.1002/pam.20606; Theodore R. Marmor, Jonathan Oberlander, and Joseph White, "The Obama Administration's Options for Health Care Cost Control: Hope vs. Reality," *Annals of Internal Medicine* 150 (2009): 485–89.

32. RAND Corporation, *The Health Insurance Experiment: A Classic RAND Study Speaks to the Current Health Care Reform Debate,* Health Research Highlights (Santa Monica, CA: RAND Corporation, 2006), http://www.rand.org/content/dam/rand/pubs/research_briefs/2006/RAND_RB9174.pdf.

33. In fact, they did more than ignore international experience. Paying attention to what might be learned turned out to be a disqualifier for government service. In 2010–2011, Republicans in the U.S. Senate refused to allow a confirmation vote on President Obama's choice to implement reform, Dr. Donald Berwick. According to the *New York Times,* "Republicans caricatured Dr. Berwick as an advocate of health care rationing because of comments he had made before coming to Washington. He had, for example, lavishly praised the British health care system." Robert Pear, "Obama's Pick to Head Medicare and Medicaid Resigns Post," *New York Times,* November 23, 2011.

34. Karen Davis, Cathy Schoen, Stephen C. Schoenbaum, Michelle M. Doty, Alyssa L. Holmgren, Jennifer L. Kriss, and Katherine K. Shea, *Mirror Mirror on the Wall: An International Update on the Comparative Performance of American Health Care* (New York: Commonwealth Fund, May 2007), 5, Figure 2, http://www.commonwealthfund.org/usr_doc/1027_Davis_mirror_mirror_international_update_final.pdf. See also Theodore R. Marmor, Richard Freeman, and Kieke G. H. Okma, eds., *Comparative Studies and the Politics of Modern Medical Care* (New Haven, CT: Yale University Press, 2009).

35. In 2008, Americans averaged 3.9 physician consultations annually, compared to 5.5 in Canada and 5.9 in the United Kingdom. In 2009, the average length of hospitalization for an acute illness was 5.4 days in the United States, compared to 6.8 in the United Kingdom and 7.7 in Canada. See Organisation for Economic Co-operation and Development, OECD.StatExtracts, iLibrary, "Health Status," 2012, http://stats.oecd.org/index.aspx?DataSetCode=HEALTH_STAT.

36. Everyone, it seems, includes Americans. When one of our wives developed an infection while in Italy, we visited a clinic, where she saw a doctor without wait and received a prescription that we filled at the on-site pharmacy. When offered a credit card for payment, the doctor looked puzzled. We, no doubt, had similar looks on our faces when the doctor waved us away. Such are the lessons we learn about cultural differences when traveling.

37. For a comparison of American doctors' salaries with those of their international counterparts (and a criticism of higher wages in America), see Miriam J. Laugesen and Sherry A. Glied, "Higher Fees Paid to US Physicians Drive Higher Spending for Physician Services Compared to Other Countries," *Health Affairs* 30, no. 9 (2011): 1647–56, doi 10.1377.

38. Roundtable on Evidence-Based Medicine, Institute of Medicine, "Excess Administrative Costs," in *The Healthcare Imperative: Lowering Costs and Improving Outcomes—Workshop Series Summary,* ed. Pierre L. Yong, Robert S. Saunders, and LeighAnne Olsen (Washington, DC: National Academies Press, 2010). The Center for American Progress reports an even higher estimate—$361 billion spent annually on administrative costs—and characterizes at least half of those costs as unnecessary or excessive. See Elizabeth Wikler, Peter Basch, and David Cutler, *Paper Cuts: Reducing Health Care Administrative Costs* (Washington, DC: Center for American Progress, June 2012), 1–3, http://www.americanprogress.org/wp-content/uploads/issues/2012/06/pdf/paper-cuts_final.pdf.

Chapter 8

1. GDP percentage change based on chained 2005 dollars. Data from U.S. Bureau of Economic Analysis, "Percent Change from Preceding Period (Excel)," in "National Economic Accounts, Gross Domestic Product," May 30, 2013, http://www.bea.gov/national/index.htm#gdp.

2. Brian Moynihan, written testimony for the Financial Crisis Inquiry Commission, in "First Public Hearing of the Financial Crisis Inquiry Commission," day 1, session 1, financial institution representatives, January 13, 2010, 20, http://groups.haas.berkeley.edu/realestate/research/rosen/FCIC_Public_Hearing_2010-0113-Transcript.pdf.

3. Data from U.S. Bureau of Labor Statistics database, accessed June 13, 2013, http://data.bls.gov/cgi-bin/surveymost.

4. Financial Crisis Inquiry Commission, *Financial Crisis Inquiry Commission Report* (Washington, DC: FCIC, November 10, 2010), 391, http://fcic-static.law.stanford.edu/cdn_media/fcic-reports/fcic_final_report_chapter21.pdf.

5. U.S. Department of Labor, Employment and Training Administration, "UI Program Outlay," http://www.doleta.gov/unemploy/chartbook.cfm.

6. Hannah Shaw and Chad Stone, *Key Things to Know about Unemployment Insurance* (Washington, DC: Center on Budget and Policy Priorities, December 20, 2011), 1, http://www.cbpp.org/files/12-16-11ui.pdf.

7. "How Will the $787 Billion Stimulus Package Affect You?," *USA Today,* February 17, 2009.

8. U.S. Government Accountability Office, *Unemployment Insurance: Economic Circumstances of Individuals Who Exhausted Benefits,* GAO-12-408, Report to the Chairman, Committee on Finance, U.S. Senate (Washington, DC: Government Accountability Office, February 2012), http://www.gao.gov/assets/590/588680.pdf.

9. For a discussion of the exclusion of certain workers from the UI pool, see Gillian Lester, "Unemployment Insurance and Wealth Redistribution," *UCLA Law Review* 49, no. 1 (2001): 334–58, 365–69.

10. Congressional Budget Office, "Unemployment Insurance Benefits and Family Income of the Unemployed," November 17, 2010, http://www.cbo.gov/publication/25115.

11. For a more detailed description of the survey methodology, see U.S. Bureau of Labor Statistics, "Where Do the Statistics Come From?," in "Labor Force Statistics from the Current Population Survey," http://www.bls.gov/cps/cps_htgm.htm#where.

12. For a conservative take on this phenomenon—at least during a Democratic administration—see Aparna Mathur and Matthew H. Jensen, "Why the Real Unemployment Rate Is 15.6%," American Enterprise Institute, January 6, 2012, http://www.aei.org/press/economics/why-the-real-unemployment-rate-is-156.

13. There is a residual federal unemployment insurance tax, a 0.8% levy on the first $7,000 of each employee's wages. This $56 per covered worker pays for state administrative costs and helps build up the Extended Benefits program reserve. The federal government share of total UI funding was 17% in prerecession 2006.

14. State "minimum and maximum rate" and "wages subject to tax" data are from U.S. Department of Labor, Employment and Training Administration, Office of Unemployment Insurance, *Significant Provisions of State Unemployment Insurance Laws, Effective January 2012* (Washington, DC: U.S. Department of Labor, January 2012), http://www.ows.doleta.gov/unemploy/content/sigpros/2010-2019/January2012.pdf.

15. U.S. Department of Labor, Employment and Training Administration, "Unemployment Insurance Chartbook," Section B.8, http://www.doleta.gov/unemploy/chartbook.cfm.

16. U.S. Department of Labor, Employment and Training Administration, *Significant Provisions of State Unemployment Insurance Laws*.

17. December 2007 data from U.S. Department of Labor, Employment and Training Administration, "Unemployment Insurance Chartbook."

18. Richard Nixon, "Statement on Signing the Employment Security Amendments of 1970," August 10, 1970. For a history of the balance between state and federal regulation of unemployment benefits, see Joseph E. Hight, "Unemployment Insurance: Changes in the Federal-State Balance," *University of Detroit Journal of Urban Law* 59 (1982): 615–29.

19. For a more detailed description of the EUC program, see Julie Tersigni, "Without Restoring Insolvent Unemployment Trust Funds and Increasing Federal Reserves, the 2007–2009 Recessions May Cause the Depletion of the Unemployment Trust Fund," *Rutgers Journal of Law and Public Policy* 9 (2012): 702, 712–24. Despite its alarmist title, this article recounts the legislative and political history of the federal legislation.

20. U.S. Government Accountability Office, *Unemployment Insurance: Low-Wage and Part-Time Workers Continue to Experience Low Rates of Receipt,* GAO-07-1147 (Washington, DC: Government Printing Office, September 2007), 3, http://www.gao.gov/assets/270/266500.pdf.

21. Testimony of Martin Feldstein, professor of economics, Harvard University, to the Senate Finance Committee (January 24, 2007), http://www.finance.senate.gov/imo/media/doc/012408mftest.pdf. Professor Feldstein continued: "That would lower earnings and total spending. I think food stamps and SSI payments and TANF are therefore a preferred form of increased transfer."

22. Gary Solon, "Labor Supply Effects of Extended Unemployment Benefits," *Journal of Human Resources* 14, no. 2 (1979): 247–55. Solon also sees a way UI might lead to higher employment: since a job search is a requirement of receiving benefits, some who might have dropped out of the workforce, possibly retiring or claiming disability, end up finding new jobs.

23. Robert Barro, "The Folly of Subsidizing Unemployment," *Wall Street Journal,* August 30, 2010.

24. See David R. Howell and Bert M. Azizoglu, "Unemployment Benefits and Work Incentives: The U.S. Labor Market in the Great Recession," Working Paper 257, Political Economy Research Institute, University of Massachusetts, Amherst, May 2011. See also Bhashkar Mazumder, "How Did Unemployment Insurance Extensions Affect the Unemployment Rate in 2008–10?," *Chicago Federal Letter,* April 2011, 285; Rob Valletta and Katherine Kuang, "Extended Unemployment and UI Benefits," *FRBSF Economic Letter,* April 19, 2010; Shigeru Fujita, "Economic Effects of the Unemployment Insurance Benefit," *Business Review* (Federal Reserve Bank of Philadelphia), fourth quarter 2010; Shigeru Fujita, "Effects of Extended Unemployment Insurance Benefits: Evidence from the Monthly CPS," Working Paper 10-35/R, Federal Reserve Bank of Philadelphia, January 2011; Jesse Rothstein, "Unemployment Insurance and Job Search in the Great Recession," Working Paper 17534, National Bureau of Economic Research, October 2011.

25. Alison M. Shelton, *Unemployment Insurance Provisions in the American Recovery and Reinvestment Act of 2009* (Washington, DC: Congressional Research Service, March 4, 2009).

26. *Economic Report of the President* (Washington, DC: Government Printing Office, 2012), 204.

27. Katharine Abraham and Jason Furman, "Reforming Unemployment Insurance to Protect Jobs and Incomes for American Workers," White House, Council of Economic Advisers, June 18, 2012, http://www.whitehouse.gov/blog/2012/06/18/reforming-unemployment-insurance-protect-jobs-and-incomes-american-workers. Twenty-four states already had work-sharing programs before the new incentive was offered. *Economic Report of the President,* 204.

28. Andreas Crimmann, Frank Wießner, and Lutz Bellmann, *The German Work-Sharing Scheme: An Instrument for the Crisis,* Conditions of Work and Employment Series No. 25 (Geneva: International Labour Office, 2010).

29. Shaw and Stone, *Key Things to Know about Unemployment Insurance.*

30. Gray Rohrer, "Gov. Rick Scott Signs Unemployment Compensation Reform into Law," *Sunshine State News,* June 29, 2011, http://www.sunshinestatenews.com/story/gov-rick-scott-signs-unemployment-compensation-reform-law. See also Arthur Delaney, "Rick Scott's Florida Unemployment Reform Shortchanges the Jobless: Formal Complaint," Huffington Post, May 25, 2012, http://www.huffingtonpost.com/2012/05/25/rick-scott-florida-unemployment-reform_n_1545360.html.

Chapter 9

1. Z. Nazarov and C. G. Lee, "Disability Statistics from the Current Population Survey (CPS)," 2012, Cornell University Rehabilitation Research and Training Center on Disability Demographics and Statistics (StatsRRTC), accessed September 12, 2012, http:www.disabilitystatistics.org.

2. Brian Faler, "Federal Disability Insurance Nears Collapse," *Bloomberg Businessweek,* May 31, 2012.

3. Eduardo Porter, "Disability Insurance Causes Pain," *New York Times,* April 24, 2012.

4. U.S. Congress, Joint Committee on Taxation, *Estimates of Federal Tax Expenditures for Fiscal Years 2009–2013,* prepared for the House Committee on Ways and Means and the Senate Committee on Finance, January 11, 2010, 43.

5. See U.S. Bureau of Labor Statistics, National Compensation Survey, March 2011, Table 17, "Insurance Benefits: Access, Participation, and Take-Up Rates, Civilian Workers."

6. Only 2% of disabled workers receive benefits greater than 67% of their previous earnings. See ibid., Table 31, "Long-Term Disability Plans: Fixed Percent of Annual Earnings, Civilian Workers." March 2011.

7. Ibid., Table 26, "Short-Term Disability Plans: Duration of Benefits, Civilian Workers."

8. Council for Disability Awareness, "The 2012 Council for Disability Awareness Long-Term Disability Claims Review," 2012, http://www.disabilitycanhappen.org/research/CDA_LTD_Claims_Survey_2012.asp.

9. Ann Carrns, "Most Workers Lack Disability Insurance, Survey Finds," *New York Times,* May 1, 2012.

10. Ishita Sengupta, Virginia Reno, John F. Burton Jr., and Marjorie Baldwin, *Workers' Compensation: Benefits, Coverage, and Costs, 2010* (Washington, DC: National Academy of Social Insurance, 2012), 3, 7. Separate federal programs cover federal government civilian employees and specific at-risk workers, including coal miners with black lung disease, longshoremen and harbor workers, employees of overseas U.S. government contractors, energy industry workers, and military veterans. This pushes the breadth of federal coverage to about nine in ten American workers.

11. H. Allan Hunt, "Benefit Adequacy in State Workers' Compensation Programs," *Social Security Bulletin* 65, no. 4 (2003/2004): 24–30.

12. David L. Durbin, Dan Corro, and Nurhan Helvacian, "Workers' Compensation Medical Expenditures: Price vs. Quantity," *Journal of Risk and Insurance* 63, no. 1 (1996): 13–33. See also Kenneth W. Schafermeyer, "A Study of the Additional Costs of Dispensing Workers' Compensation Prescriptions," *Research in Social and Administrative Pharmacy* 3, no. 1 (2007): 123–36, which notes the higher average cost of prescriptions procured by workers' compensation patients compared to cash-paying patients.

13. An initial goal of workers' compensation programs was to replace litigation between injured employees and their employers with an easily administrable compensation system. For a brief history, see Price V. Fishback and Shawn Everett Kantor, "The Adoption of Workers' Compensation in the United States, 1900–1930," *Journal of Law and Economics* 41, no. 2 (1998): 305–42.

14. Sengupta et al., *Workers' Compensation,* 5.

15. Ibid., 41.

16. Ibid., 43.

17. Xuguang (Steve) Guo and John F. Burton Jr., "Workers' Compensation: Recent Developments in Moral Hazard and Benefit Payments," *Industrial and Labor Relations Review* 63, no. 2 (2010): 343.

18. 42 U.S.C. § 424a(a)(5) (2012). See also U.S. Social Security Administration, *Annual Statistical Report on the Social Security Disability Insurance Program, 2011* (Washington, DC: Social Security Administration, July 2012), 80.

19. J. Paul Leigh, Steven Markowitz, Marianne Fahs, and Philip Landrigan, *Costs of Occupational Injuries and Illnesses* (Ann Arbor: University of Michigan Press, 2000), 195–97.

20. Sengupta et al., *Workers' Compensation,* 9.

21. See U.S. Bureau of Labor Statistics data, 2013, http://www.bls.gov/iif/oshwc/cfoi/cfch0010.pdf.

22. Section 223(d)(1) of the Social Security Act, 42 U.S.C. § 423(d)(1)(A).

23. Ibid. The wage ceiling is adjusted annually to account for inflation. The figure for 2012 was $1,010; this was increased slightly, to $1,040, in 2013. For current and historical ceiling information, see U.S. Social Security Administration, "Automatic Determination in Recent Years," http://www.ssa.gov/OACT/COLA/autoAdj.html.

24. See U.S. Social Security Administration, "Part III: Listing of Impairments," in "Disability Evaluation under Social Security (Blue Book—September 2008)," http://www.ssa.gov/disability/professionals/bluebook/listing-impairments.htm.

25. U.S. Social Security Administration, *Annual Statistical Report on the Social Security Disability Insurance Program, 2011.*

26. The average processing time for a hearing before an ALJ was about one year in 2012. See U.S. Social Security Administration, "National Hearings Average Processing Time (FY 2008–FY2012)," http://ssa.gov/appeals/charts/National_Hearing_APT_FY2008-FY2012_4th_Qtr.pdf. Of course, the year an applicant spends awaiting the processing of a claim before the ALJ is tacked onto the time spent pursuing the claim through the state agency in the first instance.

27. U.S. Social Security Administration, *Annual Statistical Report on the Social Security Disability Insurance Program, 2011,* 126, Table 50.

28. U.S. Social Security Administration, "2013 Agency Budget Overview," 2012, 13, http://www.ssa.gov/budget/2013BudgetOverview.pdf.

29. U.S. Social Security Administration, Office of the Inspector General, "Cooperative Disability Investigations (CDI)," accessed November 20, 2012, http://oig.ssa.gov/cooperative-disability-investigations-cdi.

30. U.S. Social Security Administration, *Annual Statistical Report on the Social Security Disability Insurance Program, 2011,* 131, Table 53.

31. Ibid., 21, Table 3.

32. Dan Black, Kermit Daniel, and Seth Sanders, "The Impact of Economic Conditions on Participation in Disability Programs: Evidence from the Coal Boom and Bust," *American Economic Review* 92, no. 1 (2002): 27–50. See also David H. Autor and Mark G. Duggan, "The Rise in the Disability Rolls and the Decline in Unemployment," *Quarterly Journal of Economics* 118, no. 1 (2003): 157–205.

33. See Mark G. Duggan and Scott A. Imberman, "Why Are the Disability Rolls Skyrocketing? The Contribution of Population Characteristics, Economic Conditions, and Program Generosity," in *Health at Older Ages: The Causes and Consequences of Declining Disability among the Elderly,* ed. David M. Cutler and David A. Wise (Chicago: University of Chicago Press, 2009).

34. Ibid., 339.

35. On October 9, 1984, President Reagan signed into law H.R. 3755 (Public Law 98-460), the Social Security Disability Benefits Reform Act of 1984. The president's signing statement noted: "This legislation, which has been formulated with the support of the Administration and passed by unanimous vote in both Houses of Congress, should restore order, uniformity, and consensus in the disability program. It maintains our commitment to treat disabled American citizens fairly and humanely while fulfilling our obligation to the Congress and the American taxpayers to administer the disability program effectively." Ronald Reagan, "Statement on Signing the Social Security Disability Benefits Reform Act of 1984," October 9, 1984, http://www.reagan.utexas.edu/archives/speeches/1984/100984d.htm.

36. U.S. Social Security Administration, *Annual Statistical Report on the Social Security Disability Insurance Program, 2011,* 25, Table 6.

37. Congressional Budget Office, *Policy Options for the Social Security Disability Program* (Washington, DC: Congressional Budget Office, July 2012), 10.

38. U.S. Social Security Administration, *Supplemental Security Income Annual Statistical Report, 2011* (Washington, DC: Social Security Administration, September 2012), 22, Table 5.

39. Medicaid beneficiaries residing in nursing homes do not qualify for SSI cash benefits beyond $30 per month. This subsidy finances "small comfort items not provided by the institution."

40. U.S. Social Security Administration, *Supplemental Security Income Annual Statistical Report, 2011,* Table 15.

41. Ibid., 153, Table 77.

42. Ibid., 137, Table 69.

43. Center on Budget and Policy Priorities, "Policy Basics: Introduction to Supplemental Security Income," January 13, 2011, http://www.cbpp.org/cms/?fa=view&id=3370.

44. Information in this section is adapted from U.S. Social Security Administration, Office of Retirement and Disability Policy, "Annual Statistical Supplement, 2012," accessed November 21, 2012, http://www.ssa.gov/policy/docs/statcomps/supplement/2012/tempdisability.html.

45. Authors' calculations from Organisation for Economic Co-operation and Development, Social Expenditure Database (SOCX), Aggregated Data, http://www.oecd.org/els/social/expenditure.

46. See Richard V. Burkhauser and Mary C. Daly, *The Declining Work and Welfare of People with Disabilities: What Went Wrong and a Strategy for Change* (Washington, DC: American Enterprise Institute Press, 2011).

47. Organisation for Economic Co-operation and Development, Directorate for Employment, Labour and Social Affairs, *Sickness, Disability and Work: Keeping on Track in the Economic Downturn,* background paper (Paris: OECD, 2009), 40, Table A2.11.

48. The supercommittee failed to agree on the plan of its cochairs, Democrat Erskine Bowles and Republican Alan Simpson. See the draft document *Co-chairs' Proposal,* November 2010, http://www.fiscalcommission.gov/sites/fiscalcommission.gov/files/documents/CoChair_Draft.pdf.

Chapter 10

1. See Carmen DeNavas-Walt, Bernadette D. Proctor, and Jessica C. Smith, *Income, Poverty, and Health Insurance Coverage in the United States: 2011* (Washington, DC: Government Printing Office, 2012), 15.

2. See U.S. Social Security Administration, "Historical Background and Development of Social Security," accessed November 20, 2012, http://www.ssa.gov/history/briefhistory3.html. The Civil War pension program provided benefits for disabilities "incurred as a direct consequence of . . . military duty." This program differed from the military pensions that had existed since the American Revolution in that widows and orphans could receive pensions equal to those that would have been paid to their deceased soldier husbands/fathers had the men been disabled instead of killed. In 1890, Congress severed the link with military service and made any Civil War veteran eligible to receive a pension. In 1906, Congress made old age a sufficient qualification for benefits, making the program more similar to the later Social Security program. Ibid.

3. See Patrick W. Seburn, "Evolution of Employer-Provided Defined Benefit Provisions," *Monthly Labor Review* 114 (December 1991): 17–18.

4. Laura B. Shrestha, *Life Expectancy in the United States* (Washington, DC: Congressional Research Service 2006), 3.

5. See Revenue Act of 1921, Public Law 67-98, 42 Stat. 310 (1921), as described in Seburn, "Evolution of Employer-Provided Defined Benefit Provisions," 18.

6. Michael J. Graetz and Jerry L. Mashaw, *True Security: Rethinking American Social Insurance* (New Haven, CT: Yale University Press 1999), 105–6.

7. "Studebaker Shutdown Dims Bright Future," *New York Times,* August 10, 1964.

8. Robert Metz, "Workers Finding Pensions Empty," *New York Times,* August 16, 1964, sec. 3, 1.

9. See John W. Thompson, "Defined Benefit Plans at the Dawn of ERISA," U.S. Bureau of Labor Statistics, March 30, 2005, http://www.bls.gov/opub/cwc/cm20050325ar01p1.htm.

10. Pension Benefit Guaranty Corporation, *2011 PBGC Annual Report* (Washington, DC: PBGC, 2011), iv, http://www.pbgc.gov/documents/2011-annual-report.pdf.

11. Joan Gralla, "U.S. Munis Face $2 Trillion in Unfunded Pension Costs," Reuters, July 2, 2012, http://www.reuters.com/article/2012/07/02/us-usa-municipals-moodys-idUSBRE8611 9220120702.

12. Roger Lowenstein, "The End of Pensions," *New York Times,* October 30, 2005, http://www.nytimes.com/2005/10/30/magazine/30pensions.html?pagewanted=print&_r=0.

13. See Employee Benefit Research Institute, *History of 401(k) Plans: An Update* (Washington, DC: Employee Benefit Research Institute, February 2005), 2, http://www.ebri.org/pdf/publications/facts/0205fact.a.pdf.

14. See Jacob S. Hacker, *The Great Risk Shift* (Oxford: Oxford University Press, 2006).

15. See Zvi Bodie, Alan J. Marcus, and Robert C. Merton, "Defined Benefit versus Defined Contribution Pension Plans: What Are the Real Trade-Offs?," in *Pensions in the U.S. Economy,* ed. Zvi Bodie, John B. Shoven, and David A. Wise (Chicago: University of Chicago Press 1988), 139. It is argued that the PBGC does not need to cover defined-contribution plans because, unlike defined-benefit plans, they are by definition fully funded. Ibid. That fact does not, however, address the risk that the pension fund will perform poorly, as happened in the case of Enron, for example. Ibid., 145.

16. U.S. Congress, Joint Committee on Taxation, *Estimates of Federal Tax Expenditures for Fiscal Years 2009–2013,* prepared for the House Committee on Ways and Means and the Senate Committee on Finance, January 11, 2010, 43.

17. Leonard E. Burman, William G. Gale, Matthew Hall, and Peter R. Orszag, "Distributional Effects of Defined Contribution Plans and Individual Retirement Accounts," *National Tax Journal* 57, no. 3 (2004): 2, 25–26.

18. Investment Company Institute, "Retirement Assets Total $18.5 Trillion in Second Quarter 2012," last revised September 26, 2012, http://www.ici.org/research/stats/retirement/ret_12_q2.

19. Authors' calculations based on U.S. Census Bureau, *Statistical Abstract of the United States: 2012* (Washington, DC: Government Printing Office, 2012), Table 59.

20. Craig Copeland, *Employment-Based Retirement Plan Participation: Geographic Differences and Trends, 2010,* EBRI Issue Brief 363 (Washington, DC: Employment Benefit Research Institute, October 2011), 8–9.

21. IRAs come in a variety of forms—traditional, Roth, SEP, SIMPLE, self-directed—with differing provisions, rules, and benefits. For our purposes, we will collapse the varieties into one catchall category.

22. See U.S. Department of Labor, Employee Benefits Security Administration, "What You Should Know about Your Retirement Plan," accessed November 24, 2012, http://www.dol.gov/ebsa/publications/wyskapr.html#content.

23. See Economic Recovery Tax Act of 1981, Public Law 97-34, 95 Stat. 172 (1981).

24. Internal Revenue Service, "Retirement Topics—IRA Contribution Limits," accessed November 24, 2012, http://www.irs.gov/Retirement-Plans/Plan-Participant,-Employee/Retirement-Topics-IRA-Contribution-Limits.

25. "The Role of IRAs in U.S. Households' Saving for Retirement, 2011," *ICI Research Perspective* 17, no. 8 (November 2011): 3.

26. Investment Company Institute, "Retirement Assets Total $18.5 Trillion." Another $1.6 trillion is held in private retirement annuities. This is the domain of those with significant savings, likely the top 5% of the income-earning population. No tax subsidy exists for the purchase of annuities.

27. "Appendix: Additional Data on IRA Ownership in 2011," *ICI Research Perspective* 17, no. 8A (November 2011): 7, 9.

28. See Joint Committee on Taxation, *Estimates of Federal Tax Expenditures for Fiscal Years 2009–2013,* 43. The tax deduction for traditional IRA contributions was phased out for singles and heads of households with workplace retirement plans who had modified adjusted gross incomes between $58,000 and $68,000 in 2012 ($92,000 to $112,000 for couples). For IRA owners without retirement plans at work, the deduction was phased out if the couple's income was between $173,000 and $183,000.

29. "Appendix: Additional Data on IRA Ownership," 4.

30. Investment Company Institute, *2012 Investment Company Fact Book: A Review of Trends and Activity in the U.S. Investment Company Industry,* 52nd ed. (Washington, DC: ICI, 2012), 108.

31. Ibid.

32. See U.S. Social Security Administration, *Annual Statistical Supplement to the Social Security Bulletin, 2011* (Washington, DC: Government Printing Office, 2011), 1, http://www.ssa.gov/policy/docs/statcomps/supplement.

33. Ibid., Table 2.A3.

34. Ibid., Table 4.A1.

35. Joint Committee on Taxation, *Estimates of Federal Tax Expenditures for Fiscal Years 2009–2013,* 45.

36. U.S. Social Security Administration, *Annual Statistical Supplement,* Table 4.A1.

37. Ibid., Table 5.A1.

38. U.S. Social Security Administration, "Cost-of-Living Adjustment," last revised October 16, 2012, http://www.ssa.gov/cola. In 2011, due to negligent inflations, the cost-of-living adjustment was 0.0%. In 2012, it crept up to 1.7%.

39. U.S. Social Security Administration, *Annual Statistical Supplement,* 2.

40. See notes 54–55 below and the accompanying discussion.

41. U.S. Social Security Administration, "Primary Insurance Amount," last revised October 16, 2012, http://www.ssa.gov/oact/cola/piaformula.html.

42. See U.S. Social Security Administration, *Annual Statistical Supplement,* 1. Mutual fund and insurance product administrative costs are typically in the range of 3% to 15% of revenues. Their smaller pool size, large marketing and sales expenses, and need to generate profits prevent most from achieving anywhere near SSA's efficiency. An exception to this rule is Vanguard's family of index funds, which often but not always have administrative expenses below 1%.

43. U.S. Social Security Administration, *Annual Report of the Supplemental Security Income Program* (Baltimore: Social Security Administration, 2012), 37–38, Table IV.B6.

44. Ibid., 109, Table V.F1.

45. Ibid., 27, Table IV.A2.

46. Ibid., 45, Table IV.C1.

47. U.S. Bureau of Labor Statistics, "The Editor's Desk: Labor Force Participation," Current Population Survey, July 29, 2008, http://www.bls.gov/opub/ted/2008/jul/wk4/art02.htm.

48. "Transamerica Study Reveals the New Retirement: Working," Business Wire, May 17, 2011, http://www.businesswire.com/news/home/20110517006617/en/Transamerica-Study-Reveals-Retirement-Working.

49. U.S. Bureau of Labor Statistics, "Older Workers," Current Population Survey, July 2008, http://www.bls.gov/spotlight/2008/older_workers.

50. Ibid.

51. Paul N. Van de Water and Arloc Sherman, *Social Security Keeps 21 Million Americans Out of Poverty: A State-by-State Analysis* (Washington, DC: Center on Budget and Policy Priorities, October 16, 2012), 1, http://www.cbpp.org/files/10-16-12ss.pdf.

52. U.S. Social Security Administration, *Social Security Programs throughout the World: Asia and the Pacific, 2010* (Washington, DC: Government Printing Office, 2010); U.S. Social Security Administration, *Social Security Programs throughout the World: Europe, 2012* (Washington, DC: Government Printing Office, 2012).

53. Organisation for Economic Co-operation and Development, *Pensions at a Glance 2011: Retirement-Income Systems in OECD and G20 Countries* (Paris: OECD, 2011), 118–29.

54. Board of Trustees, Federal Old-Age and Survivors Insurance and Federal Disability Insurance Trust Funds, *2012 Annual Report of the Board of Trustees of the Federal Old-Age and Survivors Insurance and Federal Disability Insurance Trust Funds* (Washington, DC: Government Printing Office, 2012), 12.

55. Ibid., 3–5, 11.

56. Ibid., 4.

57. Congressional Budget Office, *Social Security Policy Options* (Washington, DC: Congressional Budget Office, July 2010), 18–19, http://www.cbo.gov/publication/21547.

58. Board of Trustees, *Annual Report of the Board,* 4.

59. Congressional Budget Office, *Social Security Policy Options,* 32, 38.

60. Ibid., 31, 37.

61. Ibid., 20–23, 35.

Chapter 11

1. Suzanne Mettler, *Soldiers to Citizens: The G.I. Bill and the Making of the Greatest Generation* (New York: Oxford University Press, 2005).

2. In 2012, the U.S. Treasury lost just over $100 billion annually from the mortgage interest deduction. By way of comparison, the entire operating budget for the Department of Housing and Urban Development, including all tenant-assistance programs, was $43.4 billion in 2012.

3. When tax expenditures promoting social welfare programs are factored in, the United States spends just over 30% of its GDP on "social expenditures," a figure met or matched by only nine other OECD countries. When tax expenditures are included as social spending, the United States dedicates a larger percentage of its GDP to social spending than several countries known for their

generous social safety nets, including Norway, Canada, and Spain. See Organisation for Economic Co-operation and Development, *Social Spending after the Crisis* (Paris: OECD, 2012), 8, Chart 7. For general discussion of the aptly named "hidden welfare state," see Christopher Howard, *The Welfare State Nobody Knows: Debunking Myths about U.S. Social Policy* (Princeton, NJ: Princeton University Press, 2007); Christopher Howard, *The Hidden Welfare State: Tax Expenditures and Social Policy in the United States* (Princeton, NJ: Princeton University Press, 1997).

4. Rudolf Klein and Theodore R. Marmor, "Reflections on Policy Analysis: Putting It Together Again," in *The Oxford Handbook of Political Science,* ed. Robert E. Goodin (New York: Oxford University Press, 2009).

5. The role of southern senators, who were bent on preserving existing racial stratification in the South, is discussed in Ira Katznelson, Kim Geiger, and Daniel Kryder, "Limiting Liberalism: The Southern Veto in Congress, 1933–1950," *Political Science Quarterly* 108, no. 2 (1993): 283–306. See also Marc Linder, "Farm Workers and the Fair Labor Standards Act: Racial Discrimination in the New Deal," *Texas Law Review* 65 (1987): 1353–80.

Chapter 12

1. Critics have persisted in this language of unaffordability for years. See, for example, the claim that "federal entitlement programs, [unless restructured], will in future decades grow so large relative to our national economy that they will be patently unsustainable no matter how they are financed." Peter Peterson and Neil Howe, *On Borrowed Time: On How the Growth in Entitlement Spending Threatens America's Future* (San Francisco: ICS Press, 1988), 43.

2. For the range of commentary, see Peter J. Ferrera and Michael Tanner, *A New Deal for Social Security* (Washington, DC: Cato Institute, 1998); Stuart M. Butler, "Medicare Price Controls: The Wrong Perspective," *Health Affairs* 17, no. 1 (1998): 72–74. For an example of a defense that is less alarmist, see Sam Beard, Jerry L. Mashaw, and Theodore Marmor, "Is There a Social Security Crisis?," *American Prospect* 8, no. 30 (January 1997).

3. The prescription drug benefit, known as Medicare Part D, is discussed in more detail in Chapter 7. The 2003 legislation touched on areas beyond Part D. See Medicare Modernization Act of 2003, Public Law 108-173, 117 Stat. 2066 (2003); and Susan Adler Channick, "The Medicare Prescription Drug, Improvement, and Modernization Act of 2003: Will It Be Good Medicine for U.S. Health Policy?," *Elder Law Journal* 14 (2006): 246–56.

4. See "Social Security Plan Hits Shoals," *Los Angeles Times,* June 27, 2005, A1. For examples of President Bush's rhetoric on the subject, see George W. Bush, "Remarks in a Discussion on Strengthening Social Security in Greece, New York," *Weekly Compilation of Presidential Documents* 41, no. 21 (May 30, 2005); and the *New York Times* transcript, "We Must Pass Reforms That Solve the Problems of Social Security," *New York Times,* February 3, 2005, 22.

5. For different treatments see Michael J. Graetz and Jerry L. Mashaw, *True Security: Rethinking American Social Insurance* (New Haven, CT: Yale University Press, 1999); Nancy Altman, *The Battle for Social Security: From FDR's Vision to Bush's Gamble* (New York: John Wiley, 2005); Timothy Stoltzfus Jost, "Private or Public Approaches to Insuring the Uninsured: Lessons from International Experience with Private Insurance," *New York University Law Review* 76 (May 2001): 419–64.

6. Graetz and Mashaw, *True Security,* 15–66.

7. See, for example, James Tobin, "The Future of Social Security: One Economist's Assessment," in *Social Security: Beyond the Rhetoric of Crisis,* ed. Theodore R. Marmor and Jerry L. Mashaw (Princeton, NJ: Princeton University Press, 1988). See also Theodore R. Marmor, "Coping with a Creeping Crisis: Medicare at Twenty," in Marmor and Mashaw, *Social Security.*

8. The idea that benefits are "earned" through contributions links to a cultural understanding of "entitlement" programs where both beneficiaries and the wider public agree that the benefits are deserved. There is, by contrast, a budgetary conception of entitlement, where recipients are to receive benefits unless changes in legislation justify denial. These two interpretations are different, but in twenty-first-century America, the second is in wider use. See Jackie Calmes, "Misperceptions of Benefits Make Trimming Them Harder," *New York Times,*

April 3, 2013, A3. Calmes cites a historical expert who points out that the "term entitlement first appeared in the 1950s . . . and was in common use in the 1970s," but that use was in the first sense of a culturally acceptable benefit.

9. For illustrations, see Edward D. Berkowitz, *Robert Ball and the Politics of Social Security* (Madison: University of Wisconsin Press, 2003); Theodore R. Marmor, *The Politics of Medicare,* 2nd ed. (New York: Aldine de Gruyter, 2000); Robert M. Ball, "The Original Understanding on Social Security: Implications for Later Developments," in Marmor and Mashaw, *Social Security,* 17–40; Altman, *Battle for Social Security.*

10. For examples of such language, see David Durenberger, "Senator Durenberger's Crusade: Long-Term Care for All Americans," interview by Val J. Halamandaris, *Caring* 18, no. 9 (September 1999): 22–28; Breaux-Thomas National Bipartisan Commission on the Future of Medicare, "Building a Better Medicare for Today and Tomorrow," March 16, 1999, http://thomas.loc.gov/medicare/bbmtt31599.html. For a discussion, see Theodore R. Marmor, "How Not to Think about Medicare Reform," *Journal of Health Politics, Policy, and Law* 26, no. 1 (February 2001): 107–17.

11. Martin Feldstein, "Rethinking Social Insurance," Presidential Address to the American Economic Association, January 8, 2005, http://www.nber.org/feldstein/aeajan8.pdf.

12. Philip J. Harmelink and Janet Furman Speyrer, "Social Security: Rates of Return and the Fairness of Benefits," *Cato Journal* 14, no. 1 (Spring/Summer 1994): 37–55; Martin Feldstein and Andrew Samwick, "Social Security Rules and Marginal Tax Rates," *National Tax Journal* 45, no. 1 (1992): 1–22.

13. Theodore R. Marmor and Gary J. McKissick, "Medicare's Future: Fact, Fiction and Folly," *American Journal of Law & Medicine* 26, nos. 2–3 (2000): 225–53; Adam Negourney and Janet Elder, "Bush Doesn't Share Public's Priorities, New Poll Indicates," *New York Times,* March 3, 2005, A6; Richard Morin and Dale Russakoff, "Social Security Problems Not a Crisis, Most Say," *Washington Post,* February 10, 2005, A01.

14. National Committee to Preserve Social Security and Medicare, "Disability Insurance and Survivors' Benefits," August 2011, http://www.ncpssm.org/Document/ArticleID/740#.UM4V6XP jnvE; Greg Anrig Jr., "Ten Myths about Social Security," Century Foundation, January 25, 2005, 3, http://old.tcf.org/publications/2005/1/pb507.

15. U.S. Social Security Administration, *Management's Discussion and Analysis* (Washington, DC: Government Printing Office, 2005), http://www.ssa.gov/finance/2005/MDA.pdf.

16. Lawrence H. Thompson, "Paying for Retirement: Sharing the Gain," in *In Search of Retirement Security: The Changing Mix of Social Insurance, Employee Benefits, and Individual Responsibility,* ed. Teresa Ghilarducci, Van Doorn Ooms, John L. Palmer, and Catherine Hill (New York: Century Foundation Press, 2005), 115–25.

17. Paul C. Light, *The True Size of Government* (Washington, DC: Brookings Institution, 1999). The Greenspan Commission is discussed in Chapter 9.

18. Peter Passell, "Investing It: Can Retirees' Safety Net be Saved?," *New York Times,* February 18, 1996, sec. 3, 1.

19. For a discussion, see Theodore R. Marmor, Jerry L. Mashaw, and Philip L. Harvey, *America's Misunderstood Welfare State: Persistent Myths, Enduring Realities* (New York: Basic Books, 1990), especially chap. 1.

20. David Langer, "Does the Social Security Crisis Add Up?," *New York Times,* January 16, 2005. See also David Langer, testimony before the Special Committee on Aging, U.S. Senate, June 30, 1998, http://aging.senate.gov/publications/6301998.pdf.

21. U.S. Social Security Administration, "Social Security Board of Trustees: No Change in Projected Year of Trust Fund Reserve Depletion," press release, May 31, 2013, http://www.ssa.gov/pressoffice/pr/trustee13-pr.html. For a discussion of Social Security financing, see Robert M. Ball with Thomas N. Bethell, *Straight Talk about Social Security* (New York: Century Foundation Press, 1998), 2.

22. The Social Security Advisory Board gives projections for such minor adjustments. See Social Security Advisory Board, *Social Security: Why Action Should Be Taken Soon* (Washington, DC: Government Printing Office, December 2010), 37–44, http://www.ssab.gov/Documents/Sooner_Later_2010.pdf.

23. Boards of Trustees, Federal Hospital Insurance and Federal Supplementary Medical Insurance Trust Funds, *The 2012 Annual Report of the Boards of Trustees of the Federal Hospital Insurance and Federal Supplementary Medical Insurance Trust Funds* (Washington, DC: Boards of Trustees, April 23, 2012), 28–34, http://www.cms.gov/Research-Statistics-Data-and-Systems/Statistics-Trends-and-Reports/ReportsTrustFunds/Downloads/TR2012.pdf.

24. For the forecast levels of the Medicare trusts, see ibid. Jonathan Oberlander discusses the political discourse surrounding Medicare in his aptly titled book *The Political Life of Medicare* (Chicago: University of Chicago Press, 2003); see also Marmor, "How Not to Think about Medicare Reform."

25. Cristina Boccuti and Marilyn Moon, "Comparing Medicare and Private Insurers: Growth Rates in Spending over Three Decades," *Health Affairs* 22, no. 2 (2003): 235.

26. See John Holahan and Stacey McMorrow, *Medicare, Medicaid and the Deficit Debate* (Washington, DC: Urban Institute, April 2012), 3, http://www.urban.org/UploadedPDF/412544-Medicare-Medicaid-and-the-Deficit-Debate.pdf; Medicare Payment Advisory Commission, *Health Care Spending and the Medicare Program: A Data Book* (Washington, DC: MedPAC, June 2012), 7, Figure 1-7, http://www.medpac.gov/documents/Jun12DataBookEntireReport.pdf.

27. Theodore R. Marmor, "From the United States," in *Dutch Welfare Reform in an Expanding Europe: The Neighbours' View,* ed. Erik de Gier, Abram de Swaan, and Machteld Ooijens (Amsterdam: Het Spinhuis, 2004); David A. Squires, *Explaining High Health Care Spending in the United States: An International Comparison of Supply, Utilization, Prices, and Quality,* Publication 1595 (New York: Commonwealth Fund, May 2012), http://www.commonwealthfund.org/~/media/Files/Publications/Issue%20Brief/2012/May/1595_Squires_explaining_high_hlt_care_spending_intl_brief.pdf.

28. For some illustrations, see Stuart Butler and David B. Kendall, "Expanding Access and Choice for Health Care Consumers through Tax Reform," *Health Affairs* 18, no. 6 (1999): 45–57; Henry J. Aaron and Robert D. Reischauer, "The Medicare Reform Debate: What Is the Next Step?," *Health Affairs* 14, no. 4 (1995): 8–30.

29. For a description of HSAs, see Jennifer L. Spiegel, "Employee Driven Health Care: Health Savings Accounts, More Harm than Good," *University of Pennsylvania Journal of Labor and Employment Law* 8, no. 1 (2005): 221–26. See generally Medicare Prescription Drug, Improvement, and Modernization Act of 2003, Public Law 108-173.

30. American Academy of Actuaries, *Medical Savings Accounts: Cost Implications and Design Issues* (Washington, DC: American Academy of Actuaries, May 1995), 2–8. See also Marilyn Moon, Len M. Nichols, and Susan Wall, "Winners and Losers under Medical Savings Accounts," *Spectrum* 70, no. 1 (1997): 26–29; Len M. Nichols, Marilyn Moon, and Susan Wall, *Tax-Preferred Medical Savings Accounts and Catastrophic Health Insurance Plans: A Numerical Analysis of Winners and Losers* (Washington, DC: Urban Institute, April 1996), http://www.urban.org/UploadedPDF/winlose.pdf.

31. See Holahan and McMorrow, *Medicare, Medicaid and the Deficit Debate,* 14; "Health Policy Brief: Medicare Advantage Plans," *Health Affairs,* June 15, 2011, 3, http://healthaffairs.org/healthpolicybriefs/brief_pdfs/healthpolicybrief_48.pdf; Brian Biles, Giselle Casillas, Grace Arnold, and Stuart Guterman, *The Impact of Health Reform on the Medicare Advantage Program: Realigning Payment with Performance* (New York: Commonwealth Fund, October 2012), http://www.commonwealthfund.org/~/media/Files/Publications/Issue%20Brief/2012/Oct/1637_Biles_impact_hlt_reform_Medicare_Advantage_rb.pdf.

32. See Theodore Marmor, "Deficits, Medicare, and Cost Control," Hastings Center, Health Care Cost Monitor blog, accessed June 11, 2013, http://healthcarecostmonitor.thehastingscenter.org/theodoremarmor/deficits-medicare-and-cost-control.

33. For discussion of the history of Medicare, see Marmor, *Politics of Medicare.*

34. Ibid., 10.

35. Medicare's Part B—the insurance against physician expenses—was a complete surprise in legislative deliberations of 1965. It was suggested by former opponents of Medicare who realized that the Democratic electoral landslide of 1964 made delay in Medicare's hospital insurance impossible and provided incentives to expand Medicare.

To dissuade further expansion, Democrat Wilbur Mills, chairman of the House Ways and Means Committee, and ranking Republican John Byrnes led a strategy that produced Part B and the Medicaid program, neither of which had been anticipated by the incremental strategists in the Johnson administration. Although the American Medical Association was not part of the detailed bargaining, Congress declined to use a fee schedule, which would have allowed the government to set prices for services provided to Part B recipients. Instead, doctors remained able to charge their "usual and customary" fees so long as the fees were "reasonable," thus they retained tremendous leeway in pricing their services. See ibid., 80–81.

36. Aaron and Reischauer, "Medicare Reform Debate," 20.

37. Ibid., 15.

38. Boccuti and Moon, "Comparing Medicare and Private Insurers," 230–37; Marmor and McKissick, "Medicare's Future."

39. Henry J. Aaron, statement before the House Ways and Means Committee, April 27, 2012, 7–8, http://waysandmeans.house.gov/uploadedfiles/aaron_testimony_final_4-27-2012 .pdf.

40. For a discussion of the political context that produced the MMA, see Jonathan Oberlander, "Through the Looking Glass: The Politics of the Medicare Prescription Drug, Improvement, and Modernization Act," *Journal of Health Politics, Policy, and Law* 32, no. 2 (2007): 187–219; Timothy S. Jost, "The Most Important Health Care Legislation of the Millennium (So Far): The Medicare Modernization Act," *Yale Journal of Health Policy, Law, and Ethics* 5, no. 1 (2005): 437–49; Jacob S. Hacker and Theodore R. Marmor, "Medicare Reform: Fact, Fiction, and Foolishness," *Public Policy and Aging Report* 13 (2004): 20–23; Bruce C. Vladeck, "The Struggle for the Soul of Medicare," *Journal of Law, Medicine, and Ethics* 32, no. 3 (2004): 410–15.

41. Theodore Marmor, Jonathan Oberlander, and Joseph White, "The Obama Administration's Options for Health Care Cost Control: Hope Versus Reality," *Annals of Internal Medicine* 150, no. 7 (2009): 485–89.

42. The Supreme Court's decision in the health care cases, *National Federation of Independent Business v. Sebelius,* 132 S. Ct. 2566 (2012), cast some doubt over the ACA's extension of Medicaid. It is clear that any state wishing to provide its residents the increased access to Medicaid the ACA provides will be able to do so. At the same time, states wishing to resist the expansion of Medicaid—whether for philosophical, political, or budgetary reasons—will be able to do so as a result of the Supreme Court's ruling, an outcome not contemplated by Congress when it enacted the ACA. See ibid., 2601–09.

43. For a cautionary tale about Europe's experience with insurance exchanges, the centerpiece of the ACA, see Ewout van Ginneken and Katherine Swartz, "Implementing Insurance Exchanges—Lessons from Europe," *New England Journal of Medicine* 367, no. 8 (2012): 691–93.

Epilogue

1. Theodore R. Marmor, Jerry L. Mashaw, and Philip Harvey, *America's Misunderstood Welfare State: Persistent Myths, Enduring Realities* (New York: Basic Books, 1990), 237.

Index

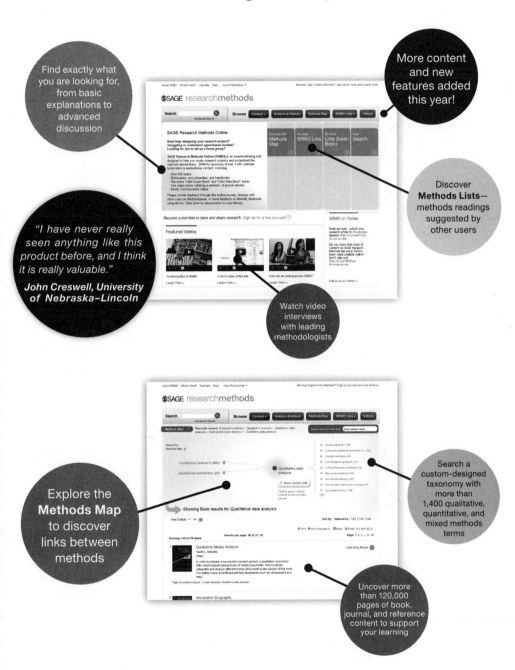

SAGE researchmethods

The essential online tool for researchers from the world's leading methods publisher

Find exactly what you are looking for, from basic explanations to advanced discussion

More content and new features added this year!

"I have never really seen anything like this product before, and I think it is really valuable."

John Creswell, University of Nebraska–Lincoln

Discover **Methods Lists**— methods readings suggested by other users

Watch video interviews with leading methodologists

Explore the **Methods Map** to discover links between methods

Search a custom-designed taxonomy with more than 1,400 qualitative, quantitative, and mixed methods terms

Uncover more than 120,000 pages of book, journal, and reference content to support your learning

Find out more at
www.sageresearchmethods.com